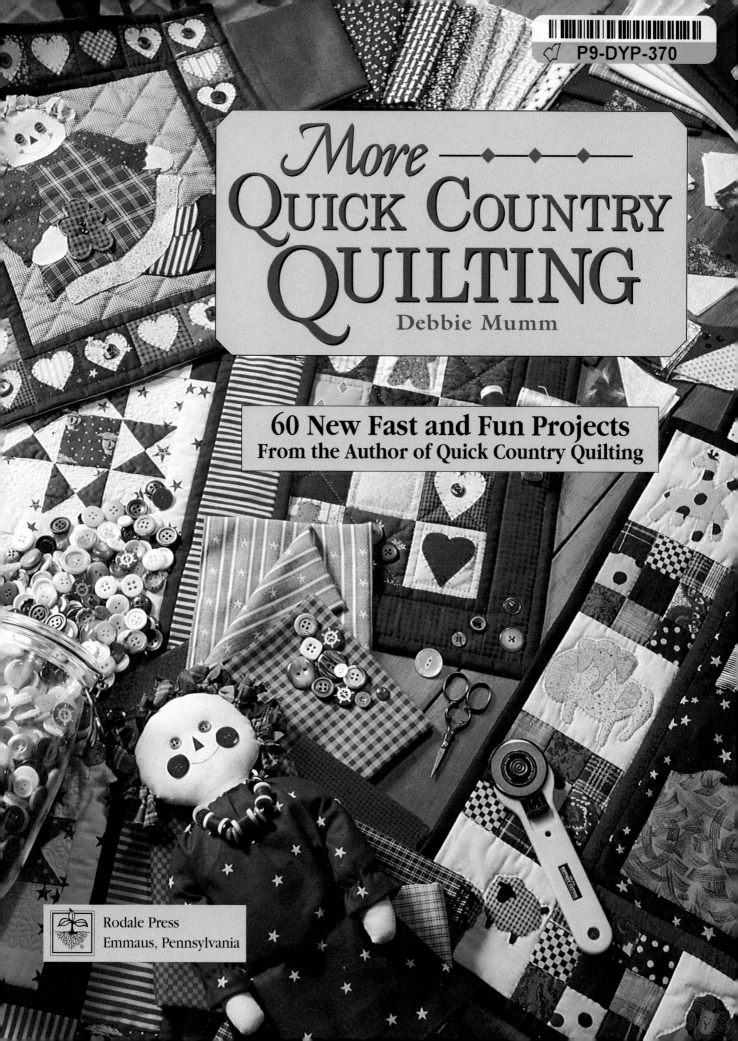

More QUICK COUNTRY QUILTING

Debbie Mumm

60 New Fast and Fun Projects
From the Author of Quick Country Quilting

Rodale Press
Emmaus, Pennsylvania

*To my mother and father, Ardis Kvare and Richard Kvare,
in appreciation of their unwavering support
and wholehearted enthusiasm.*

More Quick Country Quilting **Editorial
and Design Staff**

Editor: Ellen Pahl
Interior Designer: Sandy Freeman
Cover Designer: Lisa Palmer
Interior Layout: Robin M. Hepler and Lisa Palmer
Front Cover Photographer: John Hamel
Back Cover and Interior Photographer: Mitch Mandel
Photo Stylist: Marianne Grape Laubach
Copy Editors: Sarah Dunn and Maria Zator
Production Coordinators: Eileen Bauder and
    Melinda Rizzo
Administrative Assistant: Susan Nickol

If you have any questions or comments concerning this book, please write to:
    Rodale Press, Inc.
    Book Readers' Service
    33 East Minor Street
    Emmaus, PA 18098

Rodale Home and Garden Books

Editor-in-Chief, Rodale Books: William Gottlieb
Executive Editor: Margaret Lydic Balitas
Managing Editor, Quilt Books: Suzanne Nelson
Art Director: Michael Mandarano
Copy Manager: Dolores Plikaitis
Office Manager: Karen Earl-Braymer

Illustrations:
    Technique Illustrations: Janet Bohn
    Project Art Labels: Robin M. Hepler
    Project Diagrams: Kelly Fisher and Debbie Mumm
    All other illustrations are by Debbie Mumm.

Cover Quilts and Projects: Projects on the shelf—Shaker Box (page 157) and Rag Doll (page 206). Left to right below the shelf—Patriotic Sampler (page 153), Bow Tie Bears (page 28), and Patriotic Nine-Star Quilt (page 66).
Back Cover Quilts and Projects: Rag Doll Wallhanging (page 203), Doll's Quilt (page 208), All Aboard! (page 131), Rag Doll (page 206), and Patriotic Nine-Star Quilt (page 66).

Library of Congress Cataloging-in-Publication Data
Mumm, Debbie.
    More quick country quilting : 60 new fast and fun projects from the author of Quick country quilting / Debbie Mumm.
        p.   cm.
    ISBN 0-87596-627-6 hardcover
    ISBN 0-87596-757-4 paperback
    1. Quilting—Patterns. 2. Patchwork—Patterns. 3. Appliqué—Patterns. I. Title.
TT835.M83 1994
746.46—dc20   94-14993
                                                  CIP

Distributed in the book trade by St. Martin's Press

   4 6 8 10 9 7 5   hardcover
      6 8 10 9 7 5   paperback

Contents

Acknowledgments

For his never-ending love, support, and encouragement, I want to thank my husband, Steve Mumm. He is always there to boost my confidence when I need it—and he never complains, even though my schedule keeps getting busier and busier. I am so lucky to have such a wonderful partner!

And thank you to Murphy Mumm, my five-year-old son, for inspiring me to create bright, bold dinosaur quilts and for playing hopscotch on one of my quilts, sparking the idea for Game Quilts!

A special thank you goes to Kelly Fisher, who works closely with me as my assistant. Her contributions are so numerous, I would never be able to list them all! Kelly's many talents and her willingness to tackle any assignment are essential in turning my designs into finished quilts with complete, easy-to-follow instructions for making them.

I also want to acknowledge the wonderful talents of Jodi Gosse, whose contributions to the book include creative and technical writing.

My dedicated office manager and friend Kathy Grabowski keeps things running smoothly at the office and keeps me organized and on schedule. She's always a step ahead of me, whether I need a photocopy or a good laugh. Her good nature is appreciated by everyone in the office!

Many thanks to all the other women at the office: Barbara Carlson, Krista Dean, Carol Jesperson, Darlene Linahan, Theresa Stone, and Pat Walters. Their hard work and dedication make it possible for me to accomplish projects such as this book.

For sharing friendship as well as sewing and writing skills with me, I would like to thank Ann Weisbeck.

I miss working with her, but wish her all the best in her new career.

Jackie Wolff has been a friend for about ten years. She encouraged me to attend my first Quilt Market and deserves a big thank you for creating a quilting and fabric haven for us in Spokane. Friendship and quilts go hand in hand.

I am grateful for the many talented and creative people who help make my quilts, projects, and patterns. Carol Von Stubbe assisted in writing catchy titles and lively introductions to my patterns. Mairi Fischer did all the hand quilting for the projects in this book. Thank you for your exquisite workmanship and skill with the quilting needle. Your stitching remains flawless despite my demanding deadlines! Gayle Gregory is so much fun to be around. She shared her creativity and machine quilting skills in the Patriotic Nine-Star Quilt. Pam Clarke's machine quilting enhanced the Game Quilts, and Manya Powell's sewing skills are evident in the Scotties on Parade Quilt and all the Rub-a-Dub Ducks projects.

To Suzanne Nelson, many thanks for her generous support and enthusiasm for my projects and for her tremendous editorial creativity. It's fun to work with someone who has a similar vision and who makes the process of doing a book so fun and rewarding. And thanks also to Ellen Pahl for her keen eye for detail and for scrutinizing all the project directions to make sure they are all complete and accurate.

I would like to thank fabric manufacturers Fabri-Quilt and Benartex for providing fabrics for the Rub-A-Dub-Ducks projects, and Fabri-Quilt for providing the fabrics used in the Game Quilts.

Introduction

When my first book, *Quick Country Quilting,* came out, I was almost overwhelmed by the response it received from quiltmakers across the country who appreciated the fact that they could start *and* finish a project in much less time than they ever expected. I'm proud of the fact that my book enabled many people who had never made a quilt before to plunge right in and make a project they could be proud of. And I was also gratified that quilters with experience had *fun* making my quilts!

Since that book came out, many of you have asked for more. That's why I'm so pleased to welcome you to my second book. In *More Quick Country Quilting* you'll see the same quick-cutting and quick-sewing techniques that you found so handy, along with a whole new array of quilt designs that I hope will get you itching to start stitching. Plus, there are lots of new tips and suggestions to make your quilting experience fun and satisfying—all the way from selecting fabrics to displaying your finished project.

One of my goals in writing this book is to help you make quilts that create a cozy country style for your home. In *More Quick Country Quilting,* you'll find plenty of quilts to choose from that will be perfect to hang year-round, as well as special designs to use as holiday decorations. There's nothing that gives a heartwarming country kind of welcome so well as lots of handmade quilts displayed throughout all the rooms in your house. (My quilts are so easy and quick, you'll be able to fill every room without much effort.)

I'm especially excited about including a section in this book called "Country Color Guide for Quilters." In this chapter, which begins on page 216, I share with you my guidelines, suggestions, and ideas for choosing and coordinating fabrics in quilts. You'll be able to create the same warm, rich country look you see in the color photographs throughout the book.

You'll find a great summary of all the points you need to consider when selecting fabric in the "Quilter's Color and Fabric Checklist" on page 217. You can refer to this as you head out to the fabric store or while you're working in your sewing room and (perhaps) struggling with your fabric choices. A quick review of these points can help clarify the direction you need to take.

Please take time to read over the general techniques sections in the back of the book before you begin any of the projects. In those chapters I describe in detail the techniques and tools for cutting and piecing, appliquéing, and finishing. I provide tips for ever greater success and cover troubleshooting for problems that may arise.

Featured near the beginning of each project are fabric selection tips called "Sew Colorful." Here, I share my approach and suggestions on how to coordinate colors and fabrics for each specific project. Remember, I'm making suggestions for how to achieve the look you see in the photographs. Don't be afraid to try something different.

Sprinkled throughout the book you'll find "Sew Smart" tips. These extra suggestions, hints, and helpful reminders appear where they can make the technical aspects of quilt construction go a little more smoothly or quickly.

And, to get you thinking of even more possibilities, look for "Sew Creative" suggestions for ways to personalize your project, add your own special touches, or use the design to create something altogether different.

Part of the reason why I love what I do so much is that it's lots of fun to keep on the lookout for new ideas. Inspiration for my quilts and colors comes from many sources. I follow country home decorating styles and trends. I pore over magazines and catalogs on a regular basis. Sometimes even the colors of a piece of cloth may inspire me. Often a country folk-art object, even if it's done in another medium such as wood or metal, sparks new quilt designs. I also collect children's books and greeting cards. They are gold mines for charming and delightful illustrations and artwork. I love looking through quilting books and magazines and enjoy admiring the work of other quilters. Wherever I go I keep my eyes open— because I never know where inspiration for my next quilt design is likely to strike.

My hope is that you'll find as much joy as I do putting fabrics together to create your own quilt. It's such a thrill to see the pieces come together to become a quilt top and finished project. If you haven't already become hooked on quilting, I imagine that soon you'll find yourself "reprioritizing" your schedule, shortening your sleeping requirements, and loosening up on your housekeeping regimen as I have. You'll want to make sure you have time in your life to be creative and express yourself through quilting. Now, look through the book and pick out your first project!

Happy Quilting!

Debbie Mumm

Debbie Mumm

COUNTRY HOME COLLECTION

Add that special handmade touch of country to your home
by stitching one of these wonderful quilts. Pick your favorite
creature—they're all here, from cats and dogs to lovely
winged butterflies. There's also a properly attired bear all
ready for tea, a heavenly batch of shooting stars, and even a pen
of pigs. Whatever strikes your fancy, it's sure to go together quickly
and easily. You may even decide to make one of each just for fun!

Before you begin, take a minute to read through this checklist. These are important pointers you should keep in mind to make sure that each of your quilts is a success.

♥ Be sure you read "Techniques for More Quick Country Quilting," beginning on page 215, to familiarize yourself with fabric selection; the tools you'll need; time-saving techniques for cutting, piecing, and appliqué; as well as finishing instructions.

♥ Take advantage of the helpful hints in "Sew Colorful" at the start of each project. Here is where you'll find pointers on selecting colors and fabrics for each particular design.

♥ Prewash and press all of your fabrics.

♥ Read the step-by-step directions from start to finish, and look at all the diagrams before you cut and sew any fabric.

♥ Always use a ¼-inch seam allowance, unless there is a special note that tells you a different seam allowance is required.

♥ Refer to the **Fabric Key** for each project as a help in following the diagrams.

♥ Pay attention to the pressing directions given in the step-by-step text and to the pressing arrows shown in the diagrams.

Crazy for Cats II

32"

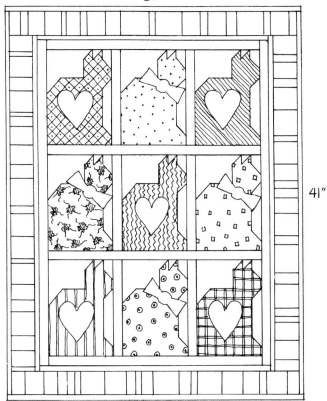

41"

QUILT LAYOUT

It's the cat's meow! This quilt is a perfect project for the quilt-crazy cat fancier! Each friendly feline in this delightful display is made of a different fabric and dressed up with either an appliquéd heart or bow for extra personality and pizzazz. The hearts, bows, and scrap border present a "purr"fect opportunity to use up your favorite scraps.

Finished Quilt: 32 × 41 inches
Finished Block: 7 × 10 inches

Materials

Obvious directional prints are not recommended.

FABRIC A

Use nine fabrics.
Cats and Scrap Border ¼ yard
each of *nine* fabrics

FABRIC B

Block Background ⅔ yard
Lattice and Scrap Border ½ yard
　TOTAL 1¼ yards

FABRIC C

Use nine fabrics.
Bows and Scrap Border ⅛ yard
each of *four* fabrics
Hearts and Scrap
　Border ⅙ yard (6 inches)
each of *five* fabrics

FABRIC D

Half-Inch Border
　and Binding ½ yard

BACKING 1⅛ yards

BATTING 1⅛ yards

SEW COLORFUL

Cats: Even though each cat is made of a different fabric, I suggest that you work with two or three basic colors. For example, in my quilt I chose a black-and-red color scheme. Within your color scheme, select fabrics in a variety of prints and with varied visual textures.

Background: Look for a background that provides good contrast with the cat fabrics. The background I found is a light neutral with a small pattern that adds just enough visual interest, yet doesn't overpower the cats.

Hearts and Bows: For these accents, stay in your color scheme and choose fabrics that contrast well with the cat fabrics. Have fun pairing cats with their "accessories." But don't be afraid to introduce a scrap of fabric that isn't used elsewhere in the quilt. As long as you pick up some of the colors within your established fabrics and the contrast is good, anything goes!

Borders and Binding: The scrap border ties the quilt together by incorporating all the different fabrics that make up the cats, bows, hearts, and background. Use a strong, solid color for the half-inch border and binding.

Cutting Directions

Prewash and press all of your fabrics. Using a rotary cutter, see-through ruler, and cutting mat, prepare the strips as described in the first column in the chart below. Then from those strips, cut the pieces listed in the second column. Some portions of the quilt need to be cut only once, so no additional cutting information will appear in the second column. Measurements for all pieces include ¼-inch seam allowances.

	FIRST CUT		SECOND CUT	
	NO. OF STRIPS	**DIMENSIONS**	**NO. OF PIECES**	**DIMENSIONS**
FABRIC A	**Cats:** from *each* of the *nine* fabrics, cut the following			
	1	4 × 8-inch piece		
	1	4½-inch square		
	1	6 × 6½-inch piece		
	1	2 × 5-inch piece		
	1	2½-inch square		
	2	1½-inch squares		
	Scrap Border: from *each* of the *nine* fabrics, cut the following			
	Before You Cut: Cut one or two scrap border strips in varying widths, from 1¼ inches to 3 inches wide.			
	1 or 2	1¼–3 × 28-inch strips		

	FIRST CUT		SECOND CUT	
	NO. OF STRIPS	DIMENSIONS	NO. OF PIECES	DIMENSIONS
FABRIC B	**Background**			
	1	8 × 44-inch strip	9	8 × 4-inch pieces
	1	4½ × 44-inch strip	9	4½-inch squares
	1	3½ × 44-inch strip	9	3½ × 4½-inch pieces
	2	1½ × 44-inch strips	9	1½ × 4½-inch pieces
			9	1½-inch squares
	Scrap Border			
	Before You Cut: Cut one or two scrap border strips in varying widths, from 1¼ inches to 3 inches wide.			
	1 or 2	1¼–3 × 28-inch strips		
	Lattice			
	Before You Cut: From *two* of the 44-inch strips, cut the pieces listed in the second column. The remaining six strips need no further cutting.			
	8	1½ × 44-inch strips	6	1½ × 10½-inch strips
FABRIC C	**Bows:** from *each* of the *four* fabrics, cut the following			
	2	3 × 6-inch pieces		
	Hearts: from *each* of the *five* fabrics, cut the following			
	2	5½ × 7-inch pieces		
	Scrap Border: from *each* of the *nine* fabrics, cut the following			
	Before You Cut: Cut the bows and hearts before you cut the strips for the scrap border. Cut the scrap border strips in varying widths, from 1¼ inches to 3 inches wide.			
	1	1¼–3 × 28-inch strip		
FABRIC D	**Half-Inch Border**			
	4	1 × 44-inch strips		
	Binding			
	4	2¾ × 44-inch strips		

Making Triangle Sets

Step 1. Refer to "Speedy Triangles" on page 231 for how to mark, sew, and cut.

Step 2. Position the 4 × 8-inch Fabric A and B pieces with right sides together. You will have nine sets. On each set draw a grid of three 1⅞-inch squares. See **Diagram 1.**

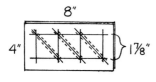

DIAGRAM 1

Step 3. After sewing and cutting are complete, press the seams toward Fabric A. You will have a total of 54 Fabric A/B 1½-inch triangle sets, six of each cat and background fabric. (You will use only five sets of each fabric combination to make the blocks.)

Step 4. Position the 4½-inch Fabric A and B squares with right sides together. You will have nine sets. On each set draw one 2⅜-inch square. See **Diagram 2.**

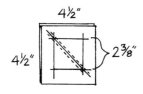

DIAGRAM 2

Step 5. After sewing and cutting are complete, press the seams toward Fabric A. You will have made a total of eighteen 2-inch Fabric A/B triangle sets, two of each cat and background fabric. (You will use only one set of each fabric combination to make the blocks.)

Making the Blocks

Throughout this section, refer to the **Fabric Key** to identify the fabric placements in the diagrams. Also, it's a good idea to review "Assembly Line Piecing" on page 233 before you get started. It's more efficient to do the same step for each block at the same time than to piece one entire block together at a time. Pay close attention to the triangle sets so that they are positioned exactly as shown in the diagrams. Be sure to press as you go and follow the arrows for pressing direction.

FABRIC KEY
FABRIC A (CATS)
FABRIC B (BACKGROUND)

Section One

Step 1. Sew one 1½-inch triangle set to another 1½-inch triangle set, as shown in **Diagram 3.** Position them right sides together and line the triangle sets up next to your sewing machine. Stitch the first set together, then butt the same set from the next block directly behind them and continue sewing each set without breaking your thread. Do a total of nine pairs of triangle sets, one for each cat block. Press the seams toward the triangle set on the left, as shown, and cut the joining threads.

DIAGRAM 3

In each of the remaining steps, use the same continuous-seam method. You will be making a total of nine blocks.

Step 2. Sew the Step 1 units to the nine 2½-inch Fabric A squares, as shown in **Diagram 4.** Press the seams toward Fabric A.

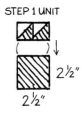

DIAGRAM 4

Step 3. Sew the Step 2 units to the nine 3½ × 4½-inch Fabric B pieces. Press the seams toward Fabric B. See **Diagram 5.**

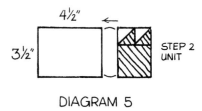

DIAGRAM 5

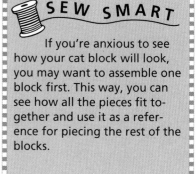

SEW SMART

If you're anxious to see how your cat block will look, you may want to assemble one block first. This way, you can see how all the pieces fit together and use it as a reference for piecing the rest of the blocks.

Section Two

Step 1. Sew nine 1½-inch Fabric B squares to nine 1½-inch triangle sets. See **Diagram 6.** Press the seams toward Fabric B.

DIAGRAM 6

Step 2. Sew nine 1½-inch Fabric A squares to the Step 1 units, as shown in **Diagram 7.** Press the seams toward Fabric A.

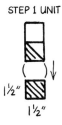

DIAGRAM 7

Step 3. Sew Section One to Section Two. Press the seams toward Section Two. See **Diagram 8.**

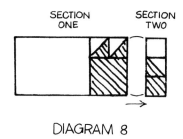

DIAGRAM 8

Section Three

Step 1. Sew nine 2 × 5-inch Fabric A pieces to nine 2-inch triangle sets. Press the seams toward Fabric A, as shown in **Diagram 9.**

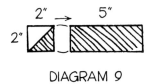

DIAGRAM 9

Step 2. Sew nine 6 × 6½-inch Fabric A pieces to the Step 1 units. Press the seams toward Fabric A, as shown in **Diagram 10.**

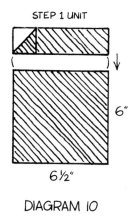

DIAGRAM 10

Section Four

Step 1. Sew nine 1½-inch triangle sets to nine 1½ × 4½-inch Fabric B pieces. See **Diagram 11.** Press the seams toward Fabric B.

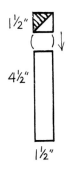

DIAGRAM 11

Step 2. Sew nine 1½-inch triangle sets to nine 1½-inch Fabric A squares. Press the seams toward Fabric A. See **Diagram 12.**

DIAGRAM 12

Step 3. Sew the Step 1 units to the Step 2 units. See **Diagram 13.** Press the seams toward the Step 1 units.

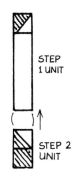

DIAGRAM 13

Section Assembly

Step 1. Sew Section Three to Section Four. See **Diagram 14.** Press the seams toward Section Three.

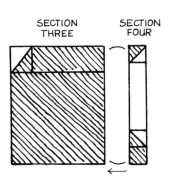

DIAGRAM 14

Step 2. Sew Sections Three and Four to Sections One and Two. See **Diagram 15.** Press the seams toward Sections One and Two.

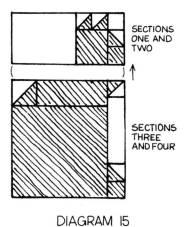

SECTIONS
ONE AND
TWO

SECTIONS
THREE
AND FOUR

DIAGRAM 15

Hearts and Bows

Step 1. Using the **Heart Appliqué Pattern** and **Bow Appliqué Pattern** on the opposite page, you will be cutting two hearts and two bows for each appliqué. Use the 3 × 6-inch Fabric C pieces for the bows and the 5½ × 7-inch pieces for the hearts. Place the fabric pieces right sides together. Trace the heart or bow onto the wrong side of the fabric. Cut both layers of fabric approximately ¼ inch from the tracing line (your sewing line). Sew with right sides together, clip the curves, and trim the seam allowances to ⅛ inch. Slit the back and turn. Press.

SEW SMART

To achieve trimming and clipping all in one quick step, use pinking shears to trim your seam allowance.

Step 2. Pin the hearts and bows in position and hand appliqué in place. Refer to "Hand Appliqué" on page 241 for directions.

SEW SMART

After appliquéing the hearts and bows to the quilt top, you may want to cut out the fabric behind the appliqué to eliminate the extra bulk. This must be done before layering your quilt.

Lattice

Step 1. Lay out your blocks in a pleasing arrangement with three rows of three blocks each. Keep track of your layout while sewing on the lattice.

Step 2. Sew a 1½ × 10½-inch Fabric B lattice strip to each side of the three center blocks from each row. See **Diagram 16.** Press all seams toward the lattice.

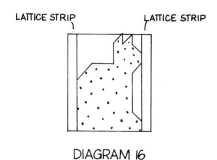

LATTICE STRIP   LATTICE STRIP

DIAGRAM 16

Step 3. Sew a block to each side of those lattice strips to make a row of three cats. See **Diagram 17.** Repeat for the two remaining rows. Press.

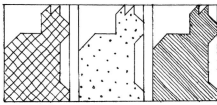

DIAGRAM 17

Step 4. Sew 1½ × 44-inch lattice strips to the bottom of all three rows and to the top of the top row. Trim the excess and press. Stitch the three rows together. Press.

Step 5. Sew 1½ × 44-inch lattice strips to the quilt sides. Trim and press.

Half-Inch Border

Step 1. Sew 1 × 44-inch Fabric D border strips to the quilt top and bottom. Trim the excess and press all seams toward the border.

Step 2. Sew the remaining two Fabric D border strips to the quilt sides. Trim and press.

Scrap Border

Step 1. Arrange the 28-inch scrap border strips cut in varying widths from Fabrics A, B, and C in a pleasing order. Sew them together to make an 18½ × 28-inch strip set. See **Diagram 18.**

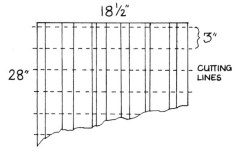

18½"

3"

28"   CUTTING LINES

DIAGRAM 18

Step 2. Cut this strip set into eight 3 × 18½-inch strips, referring to the cutting lines in **Diagram 18.** Piece together sets of two 3 × 18½-inch strips to make four 3 × 36½-inch strips.

Step 3. Sew a scrap border strip to each quilt side. Trim the excess and press all seams toward the half-inch border.

Step 4. Sew the scrap border strips to the top and bottom. Trim the excess and press.

Layering the Quilt

Arrange and baste the backing, batting, and quilt top together, following the directions for "Layering the Quilt" on page 249. Trim the batting and backing to ¼ inch from the raw edge of the quilt top.

Binding the Quilt

Using the four 2¾ × 44-inch Fabric D binding strips, follow the directions in "Binding the Quilt" on page 249.

Finishing Stitches

Outline the cats, hearts, and bows in hand quilting. Stitch a 1½-inch diagonal grid in the background.

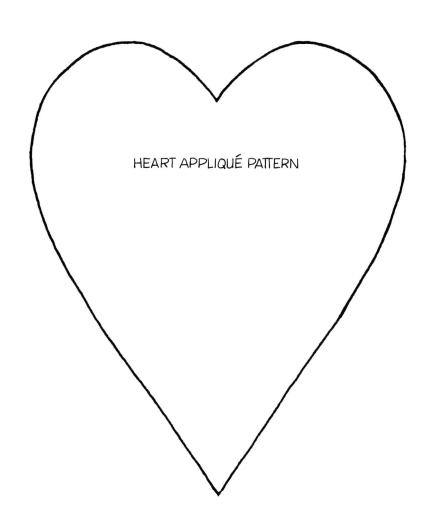

HEART APPLIQUÉ PATTERN

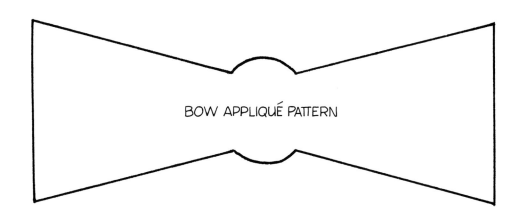

BOW APPLIQUÉ PATTERN

Patchwork Pigs

38"

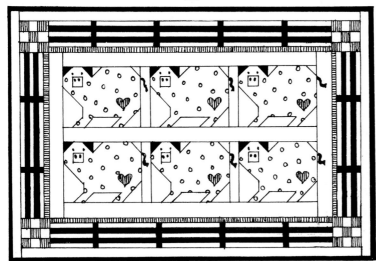

25½"

SIX PIGS QUILT LAYOUT

Look around and you'll find lovable, plump patchwork pigs popping up everywhere! You can piece together this patch of precocious pigs in no time at all. Corral a half-dozen pigs in a fence, or make a smaller scrap version of four pigs enclosed within a checkerboard border. Either way, you'll be sewing up your own little slice of pig heaven!

Six Pigs in a Pen

Finished Quilt: 38 × 25½ inches
Finished Block: 8 × 6 inches

Materials

Obvious directional prints are not recommended.

FABRIC A

Pigs	½ yard

FABRIC B

Block Background	⅓ yard
Lattice and Nine-Patch	
Corner Squares	⅓ yard
TOTAL	⅔ yard

FABRIC C

Ears and Tails	¼ yard
Fence Border	¼ yard
Binding	⅜ yard
TOTAL	⅞ yard

FABRIC D

Fence Border Background	½ yard

FABRIC E

Half-Inch Border	⅛ yard
Nine-Patch Corner Squares	
and Hearts	⅛ yard
TOTAL	¼ yard

BACKING	⅞ yard

BATTING	⅞ yard

NOTIONS AND SUPPLIES

Black embroidery floss for eyes
Twelve ³⁄₁₆-inch buttons for noses

SEW COLORFUL

Pigs: This quilt has a fairly simple color scheme. I used a dark tan fabric for the pig bodies and a black fabric for the ears and tails. For the pig to take shape, it's important that the ears and the nose have good contrast to the pig body fabric. Select a nice red solid or print for the heart. I think these muddy browns work very effectively and are quite appropriate for a pig quilt, but pink or gray could also work well.

Background: Select a light neutral for the background fabric—a tea-dyed look would be perfect for a pig pen!

Borders and Binding: Pick a fence background that echoes the color in the pig bodies, but is not exactly the same. Repeat the heart color in the nine-patch to create a visual accent. A dark solid, such as black, for the fence and binding provides a nice, sharp graphic boundary to the whole quilt.

Cutting Directions

Prewash and press all of your fabrics. Using a rotary cutter, see-through ruler, and cutting mat, prepare the strips as described in the first column in the chart below. Then from those strips, cut the pieces listed in the second column. Some portions of the quilt need to be cut only once, so no additional cutting information will appear in the second column. Measurements for all pieces include ¼-inch seam allowances.

	FIRST CUT		SECOND CUT	
	NO. OF STRIPS	DIMENSIONS	NO. OF PIECES	DIMENSIONS
FABRIC A	Pig Blocks			
	1	8 × 44-inch strip	1	8 × 12-inch piece
			1	8 × 11-inch piece
			1	8 × 6-inch piece
	3	1½ × 44-inch strips	12	1½-inch squares
			12	1½ × 3½-inch pieces
			6	1½ × 4½-inch pieces
	1	3½ × 44-inch strip	6	3½ × 5½-inch pieces
FABRIC B	Background			
	1	8 × 44-inch strip	1	8 × 12-inch piece
			1	8 × 11-inch piece
	2	1½ × 44-inch strips	12	1½-inch squares
			12	1½ × 2½-inch pieces

	FIRST CUT		SECOND CUT	
	NO. OF STRIPS	DIMENSIONS	NO. OF PIECES	DIMENSIONS
FABRIC B *(continued)*	**Lattice**			
	1	1½ × 44-inch strip	4	1½ × 6½-inch pieces
	Before You Cut: From *one* of the 44-inch strips, cut the pieces listed in the second column. The remaining three strips need no further cutting.			
	4	2 × 44-inch strips	2	2 × 22-inch strips
	Nine-Patch Corner Squares			
	1	1½ × 44-inch strip	1	1½ × 15-inch strip
			2	1½ × 8-inch strips
FABRIC C	**Ears**			
	1	6 × 8-inch piece		
	Tails			
	1	1¼ × 44-inch strip		
	Fence Border			
	Before You Cut: From *one* of the 44-inch strips, cut the pieces listed in the second column. The remaining six strips need no further cutting.			
	7	1 × 44-inch strips	12	1 × 3-inch pieces
	Binding			
	4	2¾ × 44-inch strips		
FABRIC D	**Fence Border Background**			
	9	1 × 44-inch strips		
	4	1½ × 44-inch strips		
FABRIC E	**Half-Inch Border**			
	Before You Cut: From *one* of the 44-inch strips, cut the pieces listed in the second column. The remaining two strips need no further cutting.			
	3	1 × 44-inch strips	2	1 × 22-inch strips
	Nine-Patch Corner Squares			
	1	1½ × 44-inch strip	2	1½ × 15-inch strips
			1	1½ × 8-inch strip
	Hearts			
	2	2 × 13-inch pieces		

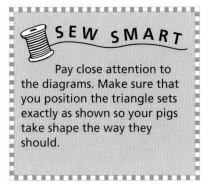

Making Triangle Sets

Step 1. Refer to "Speedy Triangles" on page 231 for how to mark, sew, and cut.

Step 2. Position the 8 × 12-inch Fabric A and B pieces with right sides together. Draw a grid of fifteen 1⅞-inch squares. See **Diagram 1.**

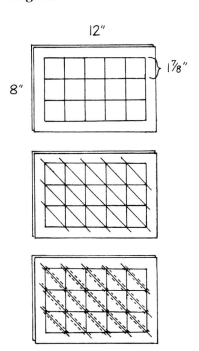

DIAGRAM 1

Step 3. After sewing and cutting are complete, press the seams toward Fabric A. You will have made a total of thirty 1½-inch Fabric A/B triangle sets.

Step 4. Position the 6 × 8-inch Fabric A and C pieces with right sides together. Draw a grid of six 1⅞-inch squares. See **Diagram 2.**

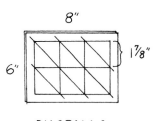

DIAGRAM 2

Step 5. After sewing and cutting are complete, press the seams toward Fabric C. You will have made a total of twelve 1½-inch Fabric A/C triangle sets.

Step 6. Position the 8 × 11-inch Fabric A and B pieces with right sides together. Draw a grid of six 2⅞-inch squares. See **Diagram 3.**

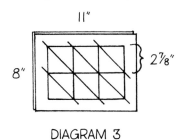

DIAGRAM 3

Step 7. After sewing and cutting are complete, press the seams toward Fabric A. You will have made a total of twelve 2½-inch Fabric A/B triangle sets.

Making the Blocks

Throughout this section, refer to the **Fabric Key** to identify the fabric placements in the diagrams. Also, it's a good idea to review "Assembly Line Piecing" on page 233 before you get started. It's more efficient to do the same step for each block at the same time than to piece one entire block to-

gether at a time. Be sure to press as you go, and follow the arrows for pressing direction.

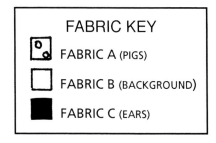

FABRIC KEY

FABRIC A (PIGS)

FABRIC B (BACKGROUND)

FABRIC C (EARS)

Section One

Step 1. Sew a 1½-inch Fabric A/C triangle set to each end of six 1½-inch Fabric A squares. Match the Fabric As in each. See **Diagram 4.** Position the pieces right sides together and line them up next to your sewing machine. Stitch the first set together, then butt the same set from the second block directly behind and continue sewing the second set without breaking your thread. Sew all six sets. Cut the threads. Press toward Fabric A.

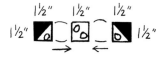

DIAGRAM 4

In each of the remaining steps, use this same continuous-seam method. You will be making a total of six pig blocks.

Step 2. Sew six 1½-inch Fabric A squares to six 1½-inch Fabric B squares. See **Diagram 5.** Press toward Fabric A.

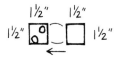

DIAGRAM 5

Step 3. Sew the six Step 2 units to six 2½-inch Fabric A/B triangle sets, as shown in **Diagram 6.** Press toward the triangle set.

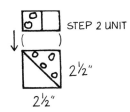

DIAGRAM 6

Step 4. Sew the six Step 3 units to six 1½ × 3½-inch Fabric A pieces. See **Diagram 7.** Press toward Fabric A.

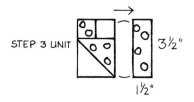

DIAGRAM 7

Step 5. Sew the six Step 1 units to the six Step 4 units, as shown in **Diagram 8.** Press toward the Step 1 unit.

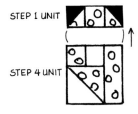

DIAGRAM 8

Section Two

Step 1. Sew a 1½-inch Fabric A/B triangle set to each side of six 1½ × 3½-inch Fabric A pieces. Match the Fabric As in each. See **Diagram 9.** Press toward Fabric A.

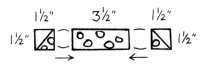

DIAGRAM 9

Step 2. Sew the six Step 1 units to six 3½ × 5½-inch Fabric A pieces. See **Diagram 10.** Press toward Fabric A.

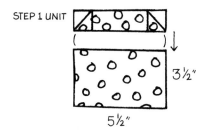

DIAGRAM 10

Section Three

Step 1. Sew six 1½-inch Fabric B squares to six 1½-inch Fabric A/B triangle sets, as shown in **Diagram 11.** Press toward Fabric B.

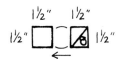

DIAGRAM 11

Step 2. Sew six Step 1 units to six 1½ × 2½-inch Fabric B pieces. See **Diagram 12.** Press toward the Step 1 unit.

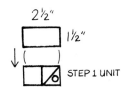

DIAGRAM 12

Step 3. Sew six 1½-inch Fabric A/B triangle sets to six 1½ × 2½-inch

Fabric B pieces. See **Diagram 13.** Press toward Fabric B.

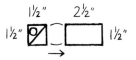

DIAGRAM 13

Step 4. Sew six 1½-inch Fabric A/B triangle sets to the six Step 3 units, as shown in **Diagram 14.** Press toward the Step 3 unit.

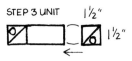

DIAGRAM 14

Step 5. Sew the six Step 4 units to six 1½ × 4½-inch Fabric A pieces. See **Diagram 15.** Press toward Fabric A.

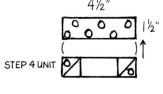

DIAGRAM 15

Step 6. Sew the six Step 2 units to the six Step 5 units, as shown in **Diagram 16.** Press toward the Step 2 unit.

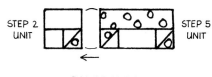

DIAGRAM 16

Step 7. Sew six 2½-inch Fabric A/B triangle sets to the six Step 6 units, as shown in **Diagram 17** on page 22. Press toward the triangle set.

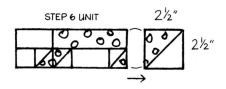

STEP 6 UNIT   2½″

2½″

DIAGRAM 17

Section Assembly

Step 1. Sew Section One to Section Two. See **Diagram 18.** Press toward Section Two.

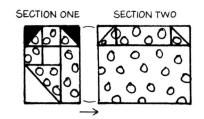

SECTION ONE   SECTION TWO

DIAGRAM 18

Step 2. Sew the Step 1 units to Section Three. Press toward the Step 1 units, as shown in **Diagram 19.** Your pigs are complete—minus their tails! The blocks will measure 6½ × 8½ inches. See **Diagram 20.**

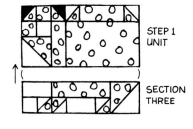

STEP 1 UNIT

SECTION THREE

DIAGRAM 19

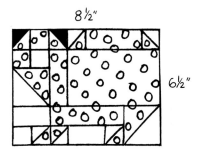

8½″

6½″

DIAGRAM 20

Tails

Step 1. Fold the 1¼ × 44-inch Fabric C tail strip in half lengthwise, right sides together. Sew along the length of the strip and trim the seam allowance to ⅛ inch. Cut the strip into six 5-inch lengths. Turn them right side out.

Step 2. Tie a knot approximately ½ inch from one cut end. Trim that end to ¼ inch beyond the knot. Then trim the entire tail to 2½ inches. Repeat for the remaining tails.

Step 3. Baste the tails to the pigs. See **Diagram 21** for placement.

Lattice

Step 1. Sew 1½ × 6½-inch Fabric B lattice strips to each side of the center blocks from each of the two rows. See **Diagram 21.** Press all seams toward the lattice, except the seams on the right side of the blocks where the tails are inserted. Press these seams toward the block, as shown in **Diagram 21.**

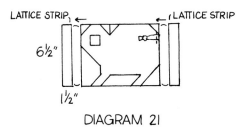

LATTICE STRIP   LATTICE STRIP

6½″

1½″

DIAGRAM 21

Step 2. Sew a block to each side of those lattice strips. Make two rows of three blocks. See **Diagram 22.** Press.

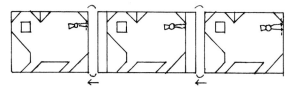

DIAGRAM 22

Step 3. Sew 2 × 44-inch lattice strips to the bottom of both rows and to the top of the top row. Trim the excess and press. Stitch the two rows together. Press.

Step 4. Sew 2 × 22-inch lattice strips to the sides. Trim and press.

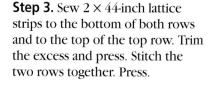

SEW SMART

Alternate the sewing direction each time you piece one strip to another. This will help avoid the warpage that occurs when sewing strips.

Fence Border

Step 1. Take three 1 × 44-inch Fabric D strips and two 1 × 44-inch Fabric C strips. Alternating fabrics, sew them together to make a 3 × 44-inch strip set, as shown in **Diagram 23.** Repeat with the remaining strips to make a total of three 3 × 44-inch strip sets.

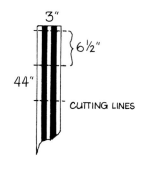

3″

6½″

44″

CUTTING LINES

DIAGRAM 23

Step 2. Cut the strip sets into sixteen 3 × 6½-inch sections.

Step 3. For the top and bottom borders, sew four 1 × 3-inch Fabric C pieces between five of the 3 × 6½-inch Step 2 sections. See **Diagram 24.** Make two of these borders. Press toward Fabric C.

Step 4. For each side border, sew two 1 × 3-inch Fabric C pieces between three 3 × 6½-inch Step 2 sections. Press toward Fabric C.

Step 5. Sew 1 × 44-inch Fabric E strips to one long edge of both the top and bottom border sections. Trim the excess and press toward Fabric E. Sew 1 × 22-inch Fabric E strips to one long edge of each side border section. Trim the excess and press toward Fabric E.

Nine-Patch Corner Squares

Step 1. To make nine-patch corner squares, take two 1½ × 15-inch Fabric E strips and one 1½ × 15-inch Fabric B strip. Alternating fabrics, sew together to make a 3½ × 15-inch strip set. See **Diagram 25.** Press all seams to the right. Cut this strip set into eight 1½ × 3½-inch sections.

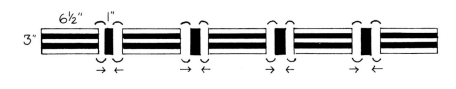

DIAGRAM 24

Step 2. Take two 1½ × 8-inch Fabric B strips and one 1½ × 8-inch Fabric E strip. Alternating fabrics, sew them together to make a 3½ × 8-inch strip set, as shown in **Diagram 26.** Press all seams to the left. Cut this strip set into four 1½ × 3½-inch sections.

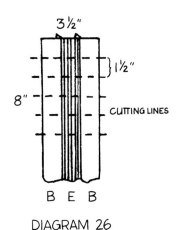

B E B

DIAGRAM 26

Step 3. Resew the 1½ × 3½-inch sections together to make four nine-patches, as shown in **Diagram 27.** Press.

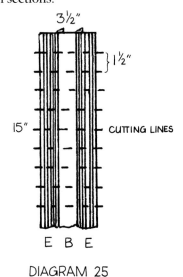

E B E

DIAGRAM 25

DIAGRAM 27

Making the Border Sections

Step 1. Fit the top and bottom fence borders to the quilt top by matching the centers of the borders to the centers of the top and bottom edges of the quilt top. Trim the excess from each end. Set the borders aside.

Step 2. Fit the side borders by matching the centers of the borders to the centers of the sides of the quilt top. Trim the excess from each end. Sew a nine-patch corner square to each end of each of the side borders. Press toward the nine-patches.

Step 3. Pin and sew the top and bottom borders to the quilt top. Press all seams toward the border. Pin and sew the side borders to the quilt top. Press.

Step 4. Sew 1½ × 44-inch Fabric D strips to the top and bottom of the quilt. Press the seams toward this border and trim. Sew 1½ × 44-inch Fabric D strips to the quilt sides. Trim the excess and press.

Heart Appliqué

Step 1. Position the two 2 × 13-inch Fabric E pieces with right sides together. Using the **Heart Appliqué Pattern** on page 27, trace six hearts onto the wrong side of the fabric, leaving a generous ½ inch between hearts. This tracing line is your sewing line. First sew along the tracing lines, keeping right sides together. Then cut out the hearts approximately $\frac{1}{8}$ inch from the sewing line. (You will find it easier to handle these small pieces if you sew first, then cut them out.) Clip the curves. Slit the back, as shown in **Diagram 28,** and turn right side out. Press.

DIAGRAM 28

Step 2. Pin the hearts in position and hand appliqué in place. Refer to "Hand Appliqué" on page 241 for directions. Use the **Six Pigs Quilt Layout** on page 17 as a placement guide.

Eyes and Noses

Step 1. Using three strands of embroidery floss, make French knots for eyes. See "Stitches for Special Touches" on page 248 if you are unfamiliar with French knots.

Step 2. Sew the $\frac{3}{16}$-inch buttons on for noses.

Layering the Quilt

Arrange and baste the backing, batting, and top together, following the directions for "Layering the Quilt" on page 249. Trim the batting and backing to $\frac{1}{4}$ inch from the raw edge of the quilt top.

Binding the Quilt

Using the four $2\frac{3}{4} \times 44$-inch Fabric C strips, follow the directions for "Binding the Quilt" on page 249.

Finishing Stitches

Give the tails a slight curl and tack them in position with a few stitches. Outline the pigs and fence border in quilting. Quilt a $1\frac{1}{2}$-inch diagonal grid on the background fabric.

Four-Pig Quilt

Finished Quilt: 27 × 23 inches
Finished Block: 8 × 6 inches

Materials

Obvious directional prints are not recommended.

FABRIC A

Use four fabrics.

Pigs and Corner Squares	$\frac{1}{6}$ yard *each* of *four* fabrics

FABRIC B

Block Background	$\frac{1}{3}$ yard
Lattice	$\frac{1}{6}$ yard
TOTAL	$\frac{1}{2}$ yard

FABRIC C

Ears	$\frac{1}{8}$ yard
Half-Inch Border and Binding	$\frac{1}{2}$ yard
TOTAL	$\frac{5}{8}$ yard

FABRIC D

Three-Inch Border	$\frac{1}{4}$ yard

Note: You may want to choose one of your pig fabrics.

BACKING	$\frac{7}{8}$ yard
BATTING	$\frac{7}{8}$ yard

NOTIONS AND SUPPLIES

Black embroidery floss for eyes
Eight $\frac{3}{16}$-inch buttons for noses

Cutting Directions

Prewash and press all of your fabrics. Using a rotary cutter, see-through ruler, and cutting mat, prepare the strips as described in the first column in the chart on the opposite page. Then from those strips, cut the pieces listed in the second column. Some portions of the quilt need to be cut only once, so no additional cutting information will appear in the second column. Measurements for all pieces include $\frac{1}{4}$-inch seam allowances.

SEW COLORFUL

Pigs: Look for four fun fabrics for the pig bodies; the "spotty" ones seem to impart a real-live pig personality. I chose a two-color scheme of black and rust. Select fabrics for the ears that will show up well against the background and next to the pig fabrics.

Background: For a very warm, country-farm look, I used a deep tan for the background. The background should contrast well with the pigs.

Borders and Binding: Use black or another strong coordinating color for the half-inch border and binding. For the three-inch border, I used checks since they always make me feel as though I'm down on the farm. Make sure you choose an interesting fabric since this is such a wide border. You may want to use one of your pig fabrics for this.

	FIRST CUT		SECOND CUT	
	NO. OF STRIPS	DIMENSIONS	NO. OF PIECES	DIMENSIONS
FABRIC A	**Pig Blocks:** from *each* of the *four* fabrics, cut the following			
	1	1¼ × 5-inch piece		
	2	1½-inch squares		
	2	1½ × 3½-inch pieces		
	1	1½ × 4½-inch piece		
	1	3½ × 5½-inch piece		
	1	4½-inch square		
	1	4-inch square		
	1	4 × 8-inch piece		
	Corner Squares (choose *one* Fabric A)			
	4	3½-inch squares		
FABRIC B	**Background**			
	1	1½ × 44-inch strip	8	1½-inch squares
			8	1½ × 2½-inch pieces
	4	4½-inch squares		
	4	4 × 8-inch pieces		
	Lattice			
	3	1½ × 44-inch strips	2	1½ × 6½-inch pieces
			3	1½ × 17½-inch pieces
			2	1½ × 15½-inch pieces
FABRIC C	**Ears**			
	4	4-inch squares		
	Half-Inch Border			
	2	1 × 44-inch strips	4	1 × 22-inch strips
	Binding			
	4	2¾ × 44-inch strips		
FABRIC D	**Three-Inch Border**			
	2	3½ × 44-inch strips	4	3½ × 22-inch strips

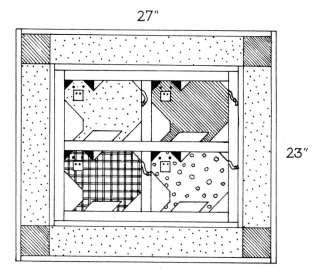

27"

23"

FOUR PIGS QUILT LAYOUT

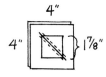

♡ SEW CREATIVE ♡

You may choose to vary the fabrics used for the pigs' ears. For each set of ears, you will need one 4-inch square of fabric.

Making Triangle Sets

Step 1. Refer to "Speedy Triangles" on page 231 for how to mark, sew, and cut.

Step 2. Position the 4-inch Fabric A and C squares with right sides together. You will have four sets. On each set draw a 1⅞-inch square. See **Diagram 29.**

4"

4" 1⅞"

DIAGRAM 29

Step 3. After sewing and cutting are complete, press the seams toward Fabric A. You will have made a total of eight 1½-inch Fabric A/C triangle sets, two of each pig and ear fabric.

Step 4. Position the 4 × 8-inch Fabric A and B pieces with right sides together. You will have four sets. On each set draw a grid of three 1⅞-inch squares. See **Diagram 30.**

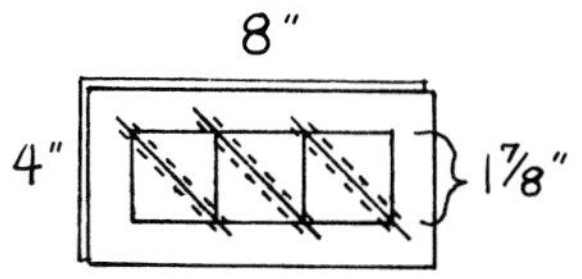

8"

4" 1⅞"

DIAGRAM 30

Step 5. After sewing and cutting are complete, press the seams toward Fabric A. You will have a total of twenty-four 1½-inch Fabric A/B triangle sets, six of each pig and background fabric. You will use only five of each of these triangle sets in the quilt.

Step 6. Position the 4½-inch Fabric A and B squares with right sides together. You will have four sets. On each set draw a 2⅞-inch square. See **Diagram 31.**

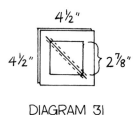

4½"

4½" 2⅞"

DIAGRAM 31

Step 7. After sewing and cutting are complete, press the seams toward Fabric A. You will have a total of eight 2½-inch Fabric A/B triangle sets, two of each pig and background fabric.

Making the Blocks

Refer to "Section One," "Section Two," "Section Three," and "Section Assembly" for Six Pigs in a Pen, beginning on page 20. Follow all these steps. You will be making a total of four pig blocks, one of each Fabric A. Make sure to match the Fabric As within each block.

Tails

Step 1. Fold the 1¼ × 5-inch tail strips in half lengthwise with right sides together. Sew along the length of the strip and trim the seam allowance to ⅛ inch. Turn right side out.

Step 2. Tie a knot approximately ½ inch from one cut end. Trim that end to ¼ inch beyond the knot. Then trim the entire tail to 2½ inches. Repeat for the remaining three tails.

Step 3. Baste the tails to the pigs. See **Diagram 32** for placement.

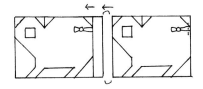

DIAGRAM 32

Lattice

Step 1. Lay out your pig blocks in a pleasing arrangement, with two rows of two pigs each. Keep track of your layout while sewing on the lattice.

Step 2. Sew a 1½ × 6½-inch lattice strip to the right side of each left block. Press the seams toward the blocks.

Step 3. Sew the right blocks to the lattice to make two rows of two blocks each. See **Diagram 32.** Press all seams toward the lattice except the seams on the right side of the blocks where the tails are inserted. Press these seams toward the block.

Step 4. Sew a 1½ × 17½-inch lattice strip to the top of both rows

of blocks, and one to the bottom of the bottom row. Sew the rows together. Press.

Step 5. Sew 1½ × 15½-inch lattice strips to the sides of the quilt top. Press.

Half-Inch Border

Step 1. Sew 1 × 22-inch Fabric C strips to the quilt top and bottom. Trim the excess and press all seams toward the border.

Step 2. Sew 1 × 22-inch Fabric C strips to the quilt sides. Trim the excess and press.

Three-Inch Border

Step 1. Compare and fit the 3½ × 22-inch Fabric D strips to the top and bottom of the quilt top. Trim the excess and set these strips aside.

Step 2. Compare and fit the remaining two 3½ × 22-inch Fabric D strips to the quilt sides. Trim the excess. Sew 3½-inch Fabric A corner squares to each end of these two border strips. Press the seams toward the corner squares. Set aside.

Step 3. Pin and sew the top and bottom borders to the quilt top. Press all seams toward the half-inch border. Pin and sew the side borders to the quilt top. Press.

Completing the Quilt

Refer to the instructions for Six Pigs in a Pen from "Eyes and Noses" through "Finishing Stitches," beginning on page 24.

♡ **SEW CREATIVE** ♡

Use the **Heart Appliqué Pattern** on this page as a template and quilt hearts on your pigs' thighs.

HEART APPLIQUÉ PATTERN

Bow Tie Bears

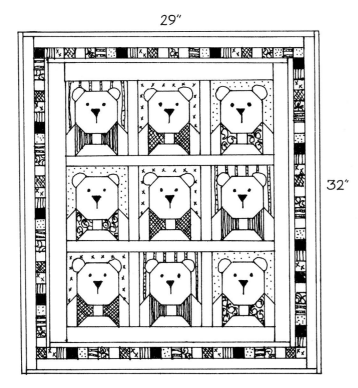

29"

32"

QUILT LAYOUT

Sift through your favorite scraps and stitch up a batch of bright-eyed bears! With button eyes and colorful bow ties, these irresistible and oh-so-proper bears are a cinch to sew. Embroider the noses and present this quilt as a gift to a bear-loving friend. Or give yourself a treat of nine new bear buddies to display on the wall.

Finished Quilt: 29 × 32 inches
Finished Block: 6 × 7 inches

Materials

Obvious directional prints are not recommended.

FABRIC A

Use three fabrics.
Bears and Scrap Border   ⅓ yard
each of *three* fabrics

FABRIC B

Use three fabrics.
Background
   and Scrap Border   ¼ yard
each of *three* fabrics
Note: If you prefer to use only one background fabric for all blocks, a total of ½ yard is needed.

FABRIC C

Use three fabrics.
Bow Ties
   and Scrap Border   ¼ yard
each of *three* fabrics

FABRIC D

Use three fabrics.
Bow Tie Centers
   and Scrap Border   ⅛ yard
each of *three* fabrics
(or one 2 × 44-inch strip of each)

FABRIC E

Lattice
   and One-Inch Border   ½ yard

FABRIC F

Half-Inch Border   ⅛ yard
Binding   ⅜ yard
   TOTAL   ½ yard

(continued)

Materials–Continued

BACKING   1 yard

BATTING   1 yard

NOTIONS AND SUPPLIES

Eighteen ⁵⁄₁₆-inch buttons for eyes
Black embroidery floss for noses

Cutting Directions

Prewash and press all of your fabrics. Using a rotary cutter, see-through ruler, and cutting mat, prepare the strips as described in the first column in the chart below. Then from those strips, cut the pieces listed in the second column. Some portions of the quilt need to be cut only once, so no additional cutting information will appear in the second column. Measurements for all pieces include ¼-inch seam allowances.

SEW COLORFUL

This design requires 15 different fabrics. Don't let these numbers overwhelm you! Just coordinate the fabrics in the order I suggest, and you'll be done before you can say "teddy bears' picnic."

Background: First choose three light, neutral fabrics, either plain or with a subtle pattern. I prefer the look of different background fabrics used together in this quilt but, to simplify fabric selection, you could choose to use just one background.

Bear Fabrics: Choose three medium to dark fabrics for the bears; you will make three bears from each fabric you select. Lay each of these bear fabrics on one of the background fabrics. Pair them up, keeping in mind that you want good contrast between the fabrics and variety in the prints.

Bow Ties: When choosing fabrics for the bow ties and centers, think of these as accent colors. The red centers I've used in three of the bow ties add just the right touch of brightness to the quilt. The colors you choose for these accents shouldn't be too bright because they might overpower the more muted country coloring used throughout the rest of the quilt.

Lattice: The lattice should give some contrast to the background fabrics but should not be so dark that it overpowers the bears.

Borders and Binding: These should be the last fabrics you select. A solid works well for the half-inch border and binding, and the scrap border ties all the fabrics of the quilt together.

	FIRST CUT		SECOND CUT	
	NO. OF STRIPS	**DIMENSIONS**	**NO. OF PIECES**	**DIMENSIONS**
FABRIC A	**Bears:** from *each* of the *three* fabrics, cut the following			
	1	1½ × 44-inch strip	15	1½ × 2½-inch pieces
	1	4 × 8-inch piece		
	1	6 × 8-inch piece		
	3	1⅞-inch squares		
	3	2½ × 4½-inch pieces		
	Note: Remainder of fabric will be used for bears' ears.			
	Scrap Border: from *each* of the *three* fabrics, cut the following			
	1	1½ × 44-inch strip	2	1½ × 22-inch strips

	FIRST CUT		SECOND CUT	
	NO. OF STRIPS	**DIMENSIONS**	**NO. OF PIECES**	**DIMENSIONS**
FABRIC B	**Background:** from *each* of the *three* fabrics, cut the following			
	1	1½ × 44-inch strip	9	1½ × 4½-inch pieces
	1	4 × 8-inch piece		
	3	1⅞-inch squares		
	Scrap Border: from *each* of the *three* fabrics, cut the following			
	1	1½ × 44-inch strip	1	1½ × 22-inch strip
	Note: If you choose to use only one background fabric, cut three times as many pieces as directed.			
FABRIC C	**Bow Tie:** from *each* of the *three* fabrics, cut the following			
	1	1½ × 22-inch strip	6	1½ × 2-inch pieces
	1	6 × 8-inch piece		
	Scrap Border: from *each* of the *three* fabrics, cut the following			
	1	1½ × 22-inch strip		
FABRIC D	**Bow Tie Centers:** from *each* of the *three* fabrics, cut the following			
	1	1½ × 22-inch strip	3	1½-inch squares
	Scrap Border: from *each* of the *three* fabrics, cut the following			
	1	1½ × 22-inch strip		
FABRIC E	**Lattice**			
	3	1½ × 44-inch strips	6	1½ × 7½-inch pieces
			2	1½ × 22-inch strips
	Before You Cut: From *one* of the 44-inch strips, cut the pieces listed in the second column. The remaining two strips need no further cutting.			
	3	2 × 44-inch strips	2	2 × 22-inch strips
	One-Inch Border			
	4	1½ × 44-inch strips		
FABRIC F	**Half-Inch Border**			
	4	1 × 44-inch strips		
	Binding			
	4	2¾ × 44-inch strips		

Making Triangle Sets

Step 1. Refer to "Speedy Triangles" on page 231 for how to mark, sew, and cut.

Step 2. You are going to make three bears each of three different Fabric A and B color combinations for a total of nine bear blocks. Determine your three color combinations for bears and backgrounds.

Step 3. Position the 4 × 8-inch Fabric A and B pieces with right sides together. You will have three sets. On each set draw a grid of three 1⅞-inch squares. See **Diagram 1.**

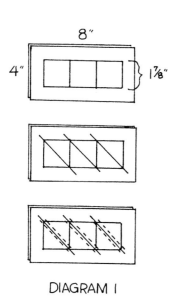

DIAGRAM 1

Step 4. After sewing and cutting are complete, press the seams toward Fabric A. You will have made a total of eighteen 1½-inch Fabric A/B triangle sets, six of each bear and background fabric.

Step 5. Of the nine bear blocks, you are going to make three bears each of three different Fabric A and C color combinations.

Determine your three color combinations for bears and bow ties.

Step 6. Position the 6 × 8-inch Fabric A and C pieces with right sides together. You will have three sets. On each set draw a grid of six 1⅞-inch squares. See **Diagram 2.**

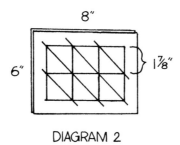

DIAGRAM 2

Step 7. After sewing and cutting are complete, press the seams toward Fabric A. You will have made a total of thirty-six 1½-inch Fabric A/C triangle sets, twelve of each bear and bow tie fabric.

Ear Assembly

Step 1. Make a template by tracing the **Ear Pattern** on page 36. Position the remainder of one Fabric A with right sides together. Trace six ears onto the wrong side of the fabric, leaving a generous ½ inch between ears. This tracing line is your sewing line. First, sew through the two layers of fabric along the tracing lines, having right sides together. Leave the bottom edge open. Then cut out the ears approximately ⅛ inch from the sewing line. (You will find it's easier to handle these small pieces if you sew first, then cut out.) Clip curves. Turn right side out and press. Repeat Step 1 to make six ears from each of your three bear fabrics.

Step 2. Sew a row of machine basting along the bottom, ⅛ inch

from the raw edge, backstitching two or three stitches at one end. Pull the basting thread until the bottom measures 1⅛ inches. Tie the threads to hold. Distribute the gathers evenly. See **Diagram 3.**

←1⅛→

DIAGRAM 3

Step 3. Take the eighteen 1⅞-inch Fabric A and B squares (three of each Fabric A, and three of each Fabric B). Cut each square diagonally once into two triangles. See **Diagram 4.** You will be making six 1½-inch Fabric A/B triangle sets with ears sandwiched between for each Fabric A/B combination.

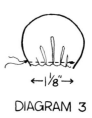

DIAGRAM 4

Step 4. Align the straight, gathered edge of the ear even with the bias edge of a matching Fabric A triangle. Baste the ear to the triangle, being careful not to stretch the bias edge of the triangle. See **Diagram 5.**

DIAGRAM 5

Step 5. Sew a Fabric B triangle to the Fabric A triangle, with the ear sandwiched between. See **Diagram 6**. Press the seam toward the Fabric A triangle.

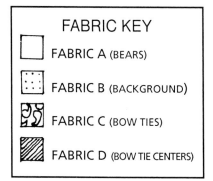

DIAGRAM 6

Making the Blocks

Throughout this section, refer to the **Fabric Key** to identify the fabric placements in the diagrams. Also, it's a good idea to review "Assembly Line Piecing" on page 233 before you get started. It is more efficient to do the same step for each block at the same time than to piece one entire block together at a time. Pay close attention to the triangle sets so that they are positioned exactly as shown in the diagrams. Be sure to press as you go and follow the arrows for pressing direction.

FABRIC KEY

 FABRIC A (BEARS)

 FABRIC B (BACKGROUND)

FABRIC C (BOW TIES)

FABRIC D (BOW TIE CENTERS)

You will be making a total of nine bear blocks, three each of three different fabric combinations. Before you start sewing, coordinate bear, background, and bow tie fabrics for each of the three combinations. Keep track of the combinations as you sew.

Section One (Head)

Step 1. Sew nine Fabric A/B triangle sets (with attached ears) to nine 1½ × 2½-inch Fabric A pieces. Position them right sides together and line them up next to your sewing machine. See **Diagram 7**. Stitch the first set together, then butt the next set directly behind them and continue sewing each set without breaking your seam. Sew all nine sets. Press the seams toward Fabric A. Cut the threads.

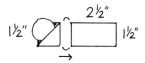

DIAGRAM 7

In each of the remaining steps, use this same continuous-seam method to complete the blocks.

Step 2. Sew nine Fabric A/B triangle sets (with attached ears) to the opposite ends of the nine Step 1 units. See **Diagram 8**. Press the seams toward Fabric A.

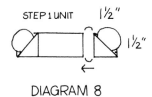

DIAGRAM 8

Step 3. Sew nine Step 2 units to nine 1½ × 4½-inch Fabric B pieces, as shown in **Diagram 9**. Press the seams toward Fabric B.

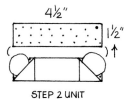

STEP 2 UNIT

DIAGRAM 9

Step 4. Sew nine Step 3 units to nine 2½ × 4½-inch Fabric A pieces. Press the seams toward Fabric A, as shown in **Diagram 10.**

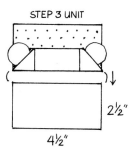

DIAGRAM 10

Step 5. Sew eighteen 1½ × 4½-inch Fabric B pieces to the sides of the nine Step 4 units, as shown in **Diagram 11**. Press the seams toward the Step 4 units.

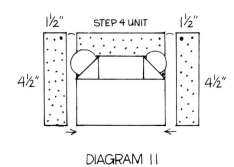

DIAGRAM 11

Section Two (Body and Bow Tie)

Step 1. Sew eighteen 1½ × 2-inch Fabric C pieces to the sides of nine

1½-inch Fabric D squares. See **Diagram 12.** Press the seams toward Fabric C.

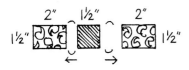

DIAGRAM 12

Step 2. Sew eighteen Fabric A/C triangle sets to the ends of nine 1½ × 2½-inch Fabric A pieces, as shown in **Diagram 13.** Press the seams toward Fabric A.

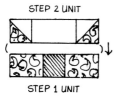

DIAGRAM 13

Step 3. Sew nine Step 1 units to nine Step 2 units. See **Diagram 14.** Press the seams toward the Step 1 units.

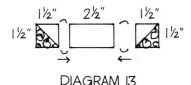

DIAGRAM 14

Step 4. Sew eighteen Fabric A/C triangle sets to the ends of nine 1½ × 2½-inch Fabric A pieces. Press the seams toward Fabric A. See **Diagram 15.**

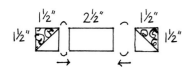

DIAGRAM 15

Step 5. Sew nine Step 3 units to nine Step 4 units, as shown in **Diagram 16.** Press the seams toward the Step 3 units.

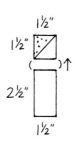

DIAGRAM 16

Step 6. Sew nine Fabric A/B triangle sets to nine 1½ × 2½-inch Fabric A pieces, as shown in **Diagram 17.** Press the seams toward the triangle sets.

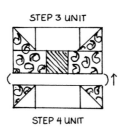

DIAGRAM 17

Step 7. Sew nine Fabric A/B triangle sets to nine 1½ × 2½-inch Fabric A pieces, as shown in **Diagram 18.** Press the seams toward the triangle sets.

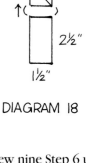

DIAGRAM 18

Step 8. Sew nine Step 6 units to the left side of nine Step 5 units. See **Diagram 19.** Sew nine Step 7 units to the right side of these nine units. Press the seams toward the Fabric A/B units.

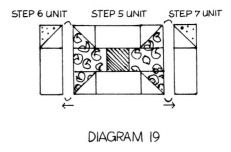

DIAGRAM 19

Section Assembly

Sew Section One to Section Two, as shown in **Diagram 20.** Press the seams toward Section One. Your block will now measure 6½ × 7½ inches.

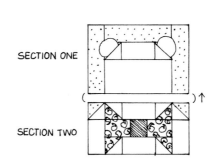

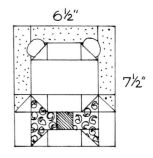

DIAGRAM 20

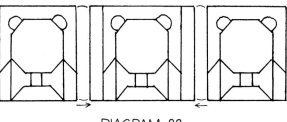

DIAGRAM 22

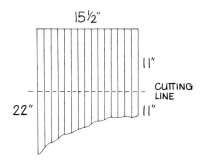

DIAGRAM 23

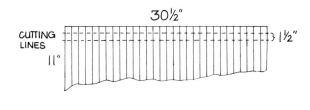

DIAGRAM 24

Lattice

Step 1. Lay out your quilt blocks in a pleasing arrangement, with three rows of three blocks each. Keep track of your layout while sewing on the lattice.

Step 2. Sew the 1½ × 7½-inch Fabric E lattice strips to each side of the center blocks from each of the three rows. See **Diagram 21.** Press all seams toward the lattice.

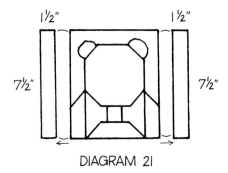

DIAGRAM 21

Step 3. Sew a block to each side of those lattice strips to make three rows of three blocks. See **Diagram 22.** Press.

Step 4. Sew the 1½ × 22-inch lattice strips to the top and bottom of the middle row only. Trim the excess and press. Stitch the three rows together. Press.

Step 5. Add the 2 × 22-inch lattice strips to the top and bottom of the quilt top. Trim the excess and press.

Step 6. Sew a 2 × 44-inch lattice strip to each side of the quilt top. Trim the excess and press.

Half-Inch Border

Step 1. Sew 1 × 44-inch Fabric F border strips to the quilt top and bottom. Trim the excess and press all seams toward the border.

Step 2. Sew 1 × 44-inch Fabric F border strips to the quilt sides. Trim the excess and press.

Scrap Border

Step 1. Take the fifteen 1½ × 22-inch scrap border strips (two of each Fabric A and one of each Fabrics B, C, and D), and arrange them in a pleasing order. Sew the strips together, alternating sewing direction with each strip sewn, to make a 15½ × 22-inch strip set. See **Diagram 23.** Press all the seams in the same direction as you go.

Step 2. Cut this strip set in half widthwise, referring to the cutting line in **Diagram 23.** Resew the halves together to make an 11 × 30½-inch strip set. See **Diagram 24.** From this, cut four 1½ × 30½-inch strips.

Step 3. Fit and sew the scrap border to the top and bottom of the quilt, removing any excess squares. Press all seams toward the half-inch border.

Step 4. Fit and sew the scrap border to the sides of the quilt, removing excess squares as necessary. Press.

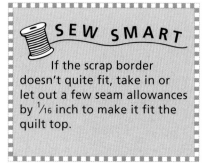

SEW SMART

If the scrap border doesn't quite fit, take in or let out a few seam allowances by $1/16$ inch to make it fit the quilt top.

One-Inch Border

Step 1. Sew a $1\frac{1}{2} \times 44$-inch Fabric E strip to the top and bottom of the quilt top. Trim the excess and press all seams toward the one-inch border.

Step 2. Sew $1\frac{1}{2} \times 44$-inch Fabric E strips to the sides of the quilt top. Trim the excess and press.

Bringing Your Bears to Life

Step 1. Sew the $3/16$-inch buttons on for the bears' eyes.

Step 2. Using three strands of embroidery floss, embroider the noses using the satin stitch. See **Diagram 25.** Use the stem stitch for the vertical line. See "Stitches for Special Touches" on page 248 if you are unfamiliar with these stitches.

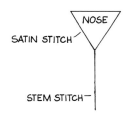

SATIN STITCH

NOSE

STEM STITCH

DIAGRAM 25

Layering the Quilt

Arrange and baste the backing, batting, and quilt top together as described in "Layering the Quilt" on page 249. Trim the batting and backing to $1/4$ inch from the raw edge of the quilt top.

Binding the Quilt

Using the four $2\frac{3}{4} \times 44$-inch Fabric F binding strips, bind the quilt as described in "Binding the Quilt" on page 249.

Finishing Stitches

Outline the bears, bow ties, and blocks in the seam line with quilting. The lattice is quilted with a one-inch diagonal grid, and the scrap border and one-inch border are quilted with straight lines stitched perpendicular to the binding.

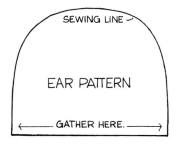

SEWING LINE

EAR PATTERN

GATHER HERE.

Butterfly Collection

Butterfly Collection

It's easy to become a butterfly collector!
Using speedy strip-piecing techniques, you
can quickly put together a brilliant collection of butterflies to mount on your wall or
use as a throw for an impromptu picnic.
You have two choices—a tropical version
with a two-color checkerboard or a pastel
version with a three-color checkerboard.

Tropical Butterflies

Materials

Finished Quilt: 57 × 40 inches
Finished Block: 13 × 12 inches

Obvious directional prints may be
used for Fabric A only; they are
not recommended for Fabrics B, C,
or D. See "Sew Colorful" on page
41 before you select your fabrics.

FABRIC A

Wings	⅞ yard
	(1¼ yards if directional
	print is used)

FABRIC B

Block Background	½ yard
Lattice	⅝ yard
Checkerboard Border	½ yard
Binding	⅞ yard
TOTAL	2½ yards

FABRIC C

Butterfly Body and	
Corner Squares	⅜ yard
One-Inch Border	⅓ yard
TOTAL	¾ yard

FABRIC D

Checkerboard Border	⅓ yard

BACKING 1¾ yards

BATTING 1¾ yards

57"

40"

QUILT LAYOUT

Cutting Directions

Prewash and press all of your fabrics. Using a rotary cutter, see-through ruler, and cutting mat, prepare the strips as described in the two tables that follow. The first table tells you how to cut the strips for the lattice, borders, and binding. The second table explains how to cut the strips for the butterfly blocks. Measurements for all pieces include ¼-inch seam allowances.

Cutting the Quilt Pieces	FIRST CUT		SECOND CUT	
	NO. OF STRIPS	DIMENSIONS	NO. OF PIECES	DIMENSIONS
FABRIC B	**Lattice**			
	Before You Cut: From *two* of the 44-inch strips, cut the pieces listed in the second column. The remaining five strips need no further cutting.			
	7	2½ × 44-inch strips	4	2½ × 12½-inch strips
	Checkerboard Border			
	11	1½ × 44-inch strips		
	Binding			
	5	5½ × 44-inch strips		
FABRIC C	**Corner Squares**			
	4	3½-inch squares		
	One-Inch Border			
	5	1½ × 44-inch strips		
FABRIC D	**Checkerboard Border**			
	11	1½ × 44-inch strips		

Cutting the Strips

Refer to the fabric requirements for blocks *only.* For Fabrics A and B, cut the block yardage in half lengthwise (on the fold) so you will have two approximately 22-inch-wide pieces. It is very important to remember this cutting applies to block yardages only. Referring to the lists of strips to be cut, cut the 22-inch strips first. When all the 22-inch strips have been cut, cut the remaining blocks of fabric in half lengthwise. (This means you will have two 11-inch-wide pieces for each 22-inch-wide piece.) From those pieces, cut the 11-inch strips.

GUIDE FOR CUTTING STRIPS
OF DIRECTIONAL FABRIC

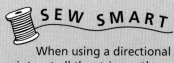

When using a directional print, cut all the strips so the direction of the print is parallel to the length of the strip. Keep the pattern running in the same direction on all the strip sets.

Cutting the Strips

	FIRST CUT		SECOND CUT	
	NO. OF STRIPS	DIMENSIONS	NO. OF PIECES	DIMENSIONS
FABRIC A	Wings			
	1	13 × 22-inch strip		
	1	9 × 22-inch strip		
	1	11-inch square		
	1	7 × 11-inch strip		
	2	5½ × 11-inch strips		
	2	3½ × 11-inch strips		
	4	2½ × 11-inch strips		
	4	1½ ×11-inch strips		
FABRIC B	Background			
	2	2½ × 22-inch strips		
	2	7 × 11-inch strips		
	2	5 × 11-inch strips		
	4	3½ × 11-inch strips		
	2	3 × 11-inch strips		
	8	2½ × 11-inch strips		
	4	1½ × 11-inch strips		
FABRIC C	Body			
	1	8½ × 11-inch quitrip		

SEW COLORFUL

Create totally different effects by using pretty pastels or exotic, brilliantly colored tropical prints.

Butterflies: Look for a cheerful multicolor print for the wings. With the wide array of beautiful floral prints to choose from, it may be difficult to decide which fabric to transform into your butterfly collection! Pick an accent color from the wing fabric to use for the butterfly body. The same fabric will be used in the one-inch accent border, checkerboard, and binding, so make it your favorite. (I needed to pull some of the black background into the border area, so I chose black for the binding on the tropical version.)

Background: For the tropical version, black can be the perfect background to set off the brilliant colors. However, if black does not suit your decorating style, a light neutral could be substituted. For a pastel version, use a soft, neutral fabric with a subtle pattern for the background.

Checkerboard Border: For the two-color checkerboard, combine the background fabric with one of the colors in your multicolor print. Repeat the one-inch border fabric in the corner squares. You'll need one additional accent color if you make the three-color checkerboard. Select it from the multicolor print fabric. It will be combined with the background fabric and the fabric from the butterfly bodies. This third color can also be used for the corner squares.

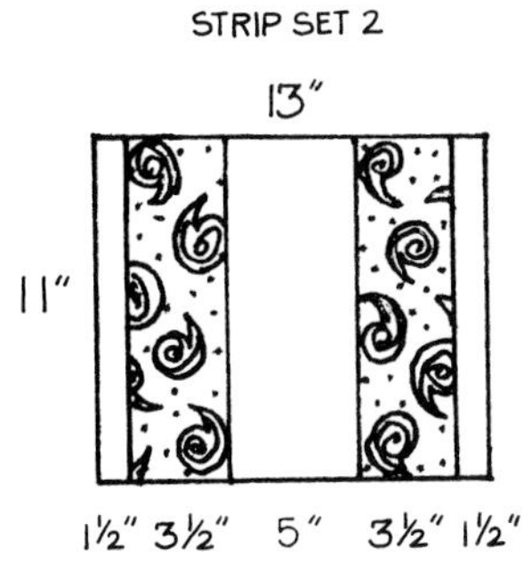

STRIP SET 2

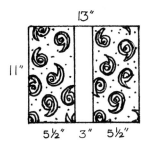

DIAGRAM 2

Strip Set 3. Use two 5½ × 11-inch Fabric A strips and one 3 × 11-inch Fabric B strip. See **Diagram 3.**

STRIP SET 3

13″

11″

5½″   3″   5½″

DIAGRAM 3

Sewing the Strip Sets

Sew the strips together following **Diagrams 1 through 11** and the directions below. Use accurate ¼-inch seam allowances. Press as you go, pressing all seams toward Fabric A except in sets 8 and 9; for those two exceptions follow the arrows in the diagrams. Refer to the **Fabric Key** for fabric identification. All finished strip sets will be 13 inches wide except Strip Set 11. This will be 12½ inches wide.

FABRIC KEY

🔳 FABRIC A (WINGS)

⬜ FABRIC B (BACKGROUND)

▦ FABRIC C (BODY)

Strip Set 1. Use two 1½ × 11-inch Fabric A strips, two 2½ × 11-inch Fabric B strips, and one 7 × 11-inch Fabric B strip. See **Diagram 1.**

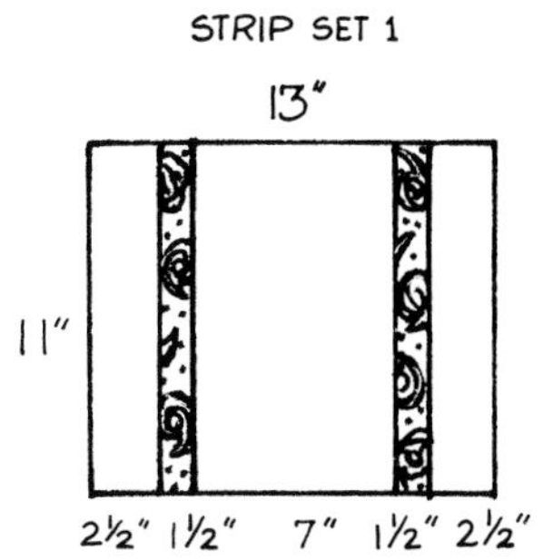

STRIP SET 1

13″

11″

2½″ 1½″   7″   1½″ 2½″

DIAGRAM 1

Strip Set 2. Use two 3½ × 11-inch Fabric A strips, two 1½ × 11-inch Fabric B strips, and one 5 × 11-inch Fabric B strip. See **Diagram 2.**

Strip Set 4. Use one 13 × 22-inch Fabric A strip, as shown in **Diagram 4.** No sewing here!

STRIP SET 4

13″

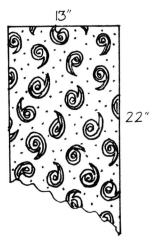

22″

DIAGRAM 4

Strip Set 5. Use one 11-inch Fabric A square and two 1½ × 11-inch Fabric B strips. See **Diagram 5.**

STRIP SET 5

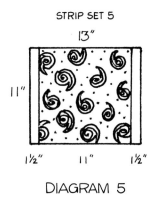

DIAGRAM 5

Strip Set 6. Use one 9 × 22-inch Fabric A strip and two 2½ × 22-inch Fabric B strips. See **Diagram 6.**

STRIP SET 6

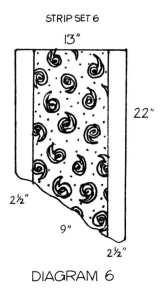

DIAGRAM 6

Strip Set 7. Use one 7 × 11-inch Fabric A strip and two 3½ × 11-inch Fabric B strips. See **Diagram 7.**

Strip Set 8. Use two 2½ × 11-inch Fabric A strips, one 3 × 11-inch Fabric B strip, and two 3½ × 11-inch Fabric B strips. Follow the arrows in **Diagram 8** for pressing direction.

STRIP SET 7

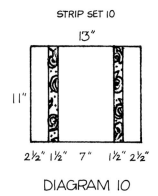

DIAGRAM 7

STRIP SET 8

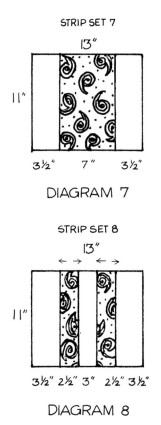

DIAGRAM 8

Strip Set 9. Use two 2½ × 11-inch Fabric A strips, one 5 × 11-inch Fabric B strip, and two 2½ × 11-inch Fabric B strips. Follow the arrows in **Diagram 9** for pressing direction.

STRIP SET 9

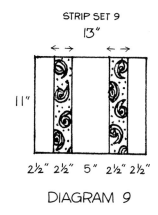

DIAGRAM 9

Strip Set 10. Use two 1½ × 11-inch Fabric A strips, one 7 × 11-inch Fabric B strip, and two 2½ × 11-inch Fabric B strips. See **Diagram 10.**

STRIP SET 10

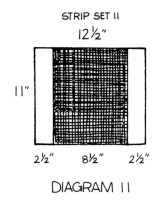

DIAGRAM 10

Strip Set 11. Use two 2½ × 11-inch Fabric B strips and one 8½ × 11-inch Fabric C strip. See **Diagram 11.** Set aside Strip Set 11 for later use.

STRIP SET 11

DIAGRAM 11

Stacking and Cutting the Strip Sets

Step 1. Stack the strip sets in order, with Strip Set 10 on the bottom and Strip Set 1 on the top of the pile. (Remember that you are holding Strip Set 11 aside for a later step.) Remove from the pile the 22-inch-long Strip Sets 4 and 6.

Step 2. Take the top half of the pile of 11-inch strip sets (Sets 1 through 5, setting aside Strip Set 4), and cut six 1½ × 13-inch strips. See **Diagram 12.** Then take the bottom half of your stack (Strip Sets 7 through 10) and cut six 1½ × 13-inch strips.

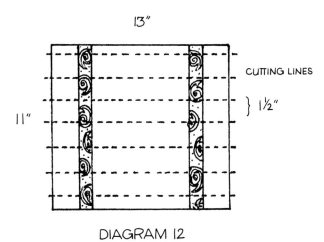

13"

11"

CUTTING LINES

} 1½"

DIAGRAM 12

Step 3. From the 22-inch Strip Sets 4 and 6, cut six 2½ × 13-inch strips of each.

Step 4. After all the strips are cut, put them back in order. You will make six piles and each pile will have one strip from each strip set. They must be in sequence, with Strip Set 10 on the bottom and Strip Set 1 on the top of each pile. (Remember that you are holding Strip Set 11 aside for a later step.) Each pile will make one block.

Making the Blocks

Sew the blocks together, following **Diagrams 13 through 19** and the directions below. Use accurate ¼-inch seam allowances. Press as you go, pressing the seams toward the strip you just added.

Wings

Step 1. Line up your six piles of strips next to your sewing machine.

Step 2. From the first pile, sew Strip Set 1 to Strip Set 2, right sides together. From the second pile, again sew Strip Set 1 to Strip Set 2. Repeat until you have sewn all Strip Sets 1 and 2 together from all six piles. Butt the pairs of strips behind one another and sew together in a continuous seam. Do not backstitch or cut threads. See **Diagram 13.** Press the seams toward Strip Set 2. You will end up with six joined pieces that look like those in **Diagram 14.** Resist the temptation to cut them apart!

Step 3. Sew the Strip Set 3 pieces to the Step 2 units. Remember, do not cut the connecting threads. Press the seams toward Strip Set 3. See **Diagram 15.**

Step 4. Sew the Strip Set 4 pieces to the Step 3 units. Press the seams toward Strip Set 4.

Step 5. Sew the remaining strips together, through Strip 10, using the same method. Be sure to add your strips in sequence and do not cut the threads. Press in the direction of the piece you have just added. Once all the strips have been sewn together, you can cut the threads that join your completed butterfly blocks. The blocks should look like the one in **Diagram 16.** At this point, the block will measure 13 × 12½ inches.

STRIP SET 1

STRIP SET 2

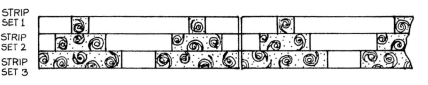

DIAGRAM 13

STRIP SET 1

STRIP SET 2

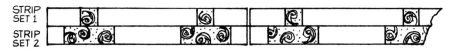

DIAGRAM 14

STRIP SET 1

STRIP SET 2

STRIP SET 3

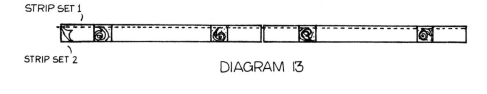

DIAGRAM 15

13"

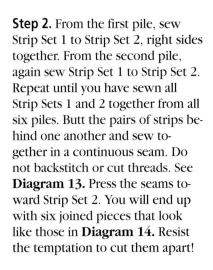

12½"

DIAGRAM 16

Body

Step 1. Cut six 1½ × 12½-inch strips from Strip Set 11. These will become the bodies.

Step 2. To add the body, cut your wing blocks in half down the center, as shown in **Diagram 17.** Use a see-through ruler to find the center of each block, mark the center, then cut along the line.

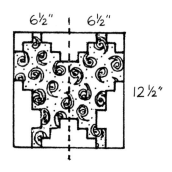

6½″   6½″

12½″

DIAGRAM 17

Step 3. Sew a 1½ × 12½-inch body strip to the left side of a wing section, with right sides together. See **Diagram 18.** Press the seam toward the center strip. Next sew the right side of the matching wing section to the body. Press toward the center strip. Repeat for all six blocks. The blocks should measure 13½ × 12½ inches and look like the one shown in **Diagram 19.** The blocks are now done!

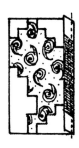

DIAGRAM 18

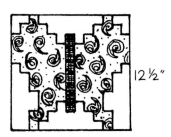

13½″

12½″

DIAGRAM 19

Lattice

Step 1. Sew 2½ × 12½-inch Fabric B lattice strips to each side of two blocks. Press all seams toward the lattice.

Step 2. Make a row of three butterflies by sewing one block with lattice strips between two blocks without lattice strips, as shown in **Diagram 20.** Press. Repeat to make a second row of three butterflies.

Step 3. On one row of butterflies, sew a 2½ × 44-inch lattice strip to the bottom. On the second row, sew a lattice strip to both the top and bottom. This row with two lattices will become the top row of butterflies in the quilt. Trim the excess and press. Sew the rows together.

Step 4. Sew 2½ × 44-inch lattice strips to both sides of the quilt top. Trim the excess and press.

One-Inch Border

Step 1. Sew 1½ × 44-inch Fabric C border strips to the quilt sides. Trim the excess and press all seams toward the border.

Step 2. The 44-inch-long border strips will not be long enough for the top and bottom of the quilt, so you must use the fifth strip to add the needed length. Cut the fifth strip in half, then sew each half to one 44-inch strip. Sew the lengthened border strips to the top and bottom. Trim the excess and press.

Two-Color Checkerboard Border

Step 1. Sew together 11 Fabric B and 11 Fabric D 1½ × 44-inch strips, alternating the fabrics, as shown in **Diagram 21.** Press all seams toward Fabric D as you go.

Step 2. From this strip set, cut twenty-four 1½ × 22½-inch strips. Refer to **Diagram 21** when you cut.

Step 3. For the top and bottom borders, sew three 1½ × 22½-inch strips together end to end to create one 1½ × 66½-inch strip. Repeat to make a total of six 1½ × 66½-inch strips.

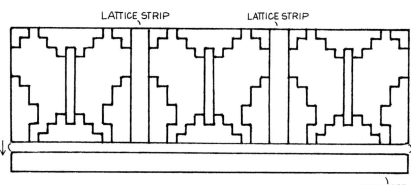

LATTICE STRIP   LATTICE STRIP

LATTICE STRIP

DIAGRAM 20

Step 4. See "Hints on Fitting a Checkerboard Border" on page 245. Fit one strip to the top of the quilt, measuring from raw edge to raw edge. Use a seam ripper to remove the excess checkerboard. You will be removing 17 squares. Save all excess checkerboard. Fit and match up two more rows of checkerboard to equal the one fitted to the quilt top edge. Each strip should have 49 squares. Sew the three strips together to create the triple checkerboard. See **Diagram 22.** Pin the checkerboard in position and stitch to the quilt top. Repeat for the bottom of the quilt.

Step 5. For the side borders, sew one 1½ × 22½-inch checkerboard strip to the excess of one strip of 17 leftover squares from the top and bottom borders. Repeat to make six of these strips. Remove 7 excess squares from each strip to

end up with six strips of 32 squares. Fit the checkerboard strips to the sides of the quilt. Measure up to but do not include the borders you just added to the top and bottom. Then add ¼ inch on each end of the strips before trimming so they will fit correctly after the corner squares are added. Sew the three strips together to make the triple checkerboard for each side.

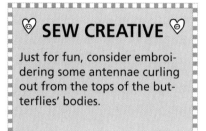

♡ **SEW CREATIVE** ♡

Just for fun, consider embroidering some antennae curling out from the tops of the butterflies' bodies.

Step 6. For the corner squares, sew a 3½-inch Fabric C square to each end of the two side checker-

board strips. Press. Pin the strips in position and sew them to the quilt sides.

Layering the Quilt

Arrange and baste the backing, batting, and quilt top together, following the directions for "Layering the Quilt" on page 249. Trim the batting and backing to ¾ inch from the raw edge of the quilt top.

Binding the Quilt

Step 1. Two of the Fabric B binding strips will need to be lengthened to fit across the top and bottom of the quilt. Cut the fifth strip in half and sew each half to one 44-inch strip.

Step 2. Follow the directions on page 249 for "Binding the Quilt."

Finishing Stitches

Outline your collection of butterflies by quilting either in the ditch or ¼ inch from the seam line. Add extra detailing with a 1½-inch grid quilted in the background. You can also quilt diagonal lines through the checkerboard. See **Diagram 23** for suggested quilting patterns.

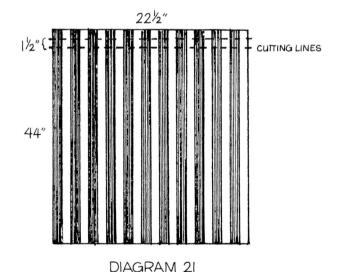

DIAGRAM 21

DIAGRAM 22

DIAGRAM 23

Pastel Butterflies

Materials

Obvious directional prints may be used for Fabric A only; they are not recommended for Fabrics B, C, or D. See "Sew Colorful" on page 41 before you select your fabrics.

FABRIC A

Wings	7/8 yard (1 1/4 yards if directional print is used)

FABRIC B

Block Background	1/2 yard
Lattice	5/8 yard
Checkerboard Border	1/2 yard
TOTAL	1 5/8 yards

FABRIC C

Butterfly Body	1/4 yard
One-Inch Border	1/3 yard
Checkerboard Border	1/3 yard
Binding	7/8 yard
TOTAL	1 7/8 yards

FABRIC D

Checkerboard Border	1/3 yard
Corner Squares	1/8 yard
TOTAL	1/2 yard

BACKING 1 3/4 yards

BATTING 1 3/4 yards

Before You Begin

Throughout these directions, you will be referred back to the Tropical Butterflies for steps that are identical. Specific assembly directions needed for the Pastel Butterflies are given in detail here.

Cutting Directions

Prewash and press all of your fabrics. Using a rotary cutter, see-through ruler, and cutting mat, prepare the strips for the butterfly blocks as described in "Cutting the Strips" for Tropical Butterflies, beginning on page 40. The chart below explains how to cut the pieces for the rest of the quilt. Measurements for all pieces include 1/4-inch seam allowances.

Cutting the Quilt Pieces

		FIRST CUT		SECOND CUT	
		NO. OF STRIPS	DIMENSIONS	NO. OF PIECES	DIMENSIONS
FABRIC B	Lattice				
	Before You Cut: From *two* of the 44-inch strips, cut the pieces listed in the second column. The remaining five strips need no further cutting.				
		7	2 1/2 × 44-inch strips	4	2 1/2 × 12 1/2-inch strips
	Checkerboard Border	11	1 1/2 × 44-inch strips		
FABRIC C	One-Inch Border	5	1 1/2 × 44-inch strips		
	Checkerboard Border	6	1 1/2 × 44-inch strips		
	Binding	5	5 1/2 × 44-inch strips		
FABRIC D	Checkerboard Border	5	1 1/2 × 44-inch strips		
	Corner Squares	4	3 1/2-inch squares		

Making the Blocks

Refer to "Sewing the Strip Sets" through "Making the Blocks" for Tropical Butterflies, beginning on page 41. Follow all the steps.

Lattice

Refer to "Lattice" for Tropical Butterflies, beginning on page 44.

One-Inch Border

Refer to "One-Inch Border" for Tropical Butterflies, beginning on page 44.

Three-Color Checkerboard Border

Step 1. Sew together eleven Fabric B, six Fabric C, and five Fabric D

1½ × 44-inch strips, alternating fabrics in the order shown in **Diagram 24.** Press all seams toward Fabric B as you go.

B C B D B C B D B C B D B C B D B C B D B C

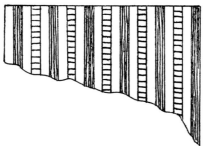

DIAGRAM 24

Step 2. To complete the checkerboard border, follow Steps 2 through 5 of "Two-Color

Checkerboard Border" for Tropical Butterflies, beginning on page 44. Your completed checkerboard should look like the one in the photograph on page 37.

Step 3. For the corner squares, sew a 3½-inch Fabric D square to each end of the side checkerboard strips. Press. Pin the strips in position and sew to the quilt sides.

Completing the Quilt

Refer to "Layering the Quilt" through "Finishing Stitches" for Tropical Butterflies, beginning on page 45. You will use Fabric C for the binding of the Pastel Butterflies.

Scotties on Parade

37″

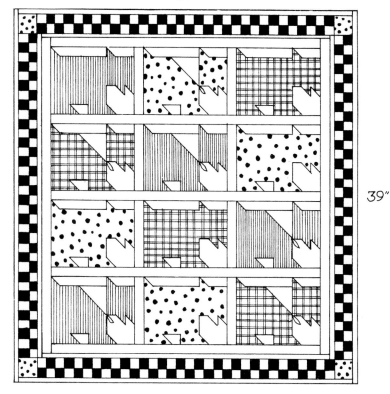

39″

QUILT LAYOUT

Great Scot! A whole quilt full of Scottie dogs! These proud pups are all ready to stand watch over your home and serve as faithful but quiet companions. Some of the pooches are wearing red shawls to keep them snug and warm inside the cheerful checkerboard border. Sew up this easy-to-make clan of Scotties, and it's almost as good as having the real thing by your side!

Finished Quilt: 37 × 39 inches
Finished Block: 9 × 7 inches

Materials

Obvious directional prints are not recommended.

FABRIC A

Use three fabrics.
Dogs and Corner Squares   ⅜ yard
each of *three* fabrics

FABRIC B

Block Background	½ yard
Lattice	½ yard
Checkerboard Border	⅓ yard
TOTAL	1⅓ yards

FABRIC C

Checkerboard Border	⅓ yard

FABRIC D

Half-Inch Border	⅛ yard
Binding	⅓ yard
TOTAL	½ yard

FABRIC E

Use six fabrics.
Shawls   5 × 6-inch piece
each of *six* fabrics

BACKING   1¼ yards

BATTING   1¼ yards

SEW COLORFUL

Scottie Dogs: I held on to tradition and chose black for a classic Scottie dog appeal. Look for three dog fabrics with different visual textures. I found one with a great "hairy" texture, then complemented it with one plaid and one spotty print. The dogs should stand out well against the background.

Background: I chose a light tan print for the background, but you can experiment with other colors. Just be sure that you lay all the choices for the dogs on top to see if they are compatible.

Half-Inch Border and Binding: Use a solid dark fabric for the half-inch border and the binding. I used black for mine.

Shawls: I found a variety of playful reds for the dogs' shawls. Plaids, of course, are perfect, but you'll need to vary the scale of the plaids to keep things lively. Using some stripes and checks as well will add interest.

Border: With all the geometric prints in the shawls, I looked for a different texture print or a solid to use in the checkerboard. For the corner squares, the "spotty" fabric was fun and gave the best contrast to the black solid.

Cutting Directions

Prewash and press all of your fabrics. Using a rotary cutter, see-through ruler, and cutting mat, prepare the strips as described in the first column in the chart below. Then from those strips, cut the pieces listed in the second column. Some portions of the quilt only need to be cut once, so no additional cutting information will appear in the second column. Measurements for all pieces include ¼-inch seam allowances.

	FIRST CUT		SECOND CUT	
	NO. OF STRIPS	DIMENSIONS	NO. OF PIECES	DIMENSIONS
FABRIC A	**Dogs:** from *each* of the *three* fabrics, cut the following			
	1	3½ × 44-inch strip	4	3½ × 9½-inch pieces
	1	6 × 14-inch piece		
	1	2½ × 44-inch strip	4	2½ × 6½-inch pieces
			8	2½ × 1½-inch pieces
	Corner Squares (choose *one* Fabric A)			
	4	2½-inch squares		
FABRIC B	**Background**			
	1	5½ × 22-inch strip	12	5½ × 1½-inch pieces
	1	3½ × 22-inch strip	12	3½ × 1½-inch pieces
	1	1½ × 44-inch strip	24	1½-inch squares
	1	2½ × 44-inch strip	24	2½ × 1½-inch pieces
	1	6 × 44-inch strip	3	6 × 14-inch pieces

| FIRST CUT | | SECOND CUT | |
NO. OF STRIPS	DIMENSIONS	NO. OF PIECES	DIMENSIONS
FABRIC B *(continued)*	**Lattice**		
	Before You Cut: From *two* of the 44-inch strips, cut the pieces listed in the second column. The remaining seven strips need no further cutting.		
9	1½ × 44-inch strips	8	1½ × 7½-inch pieces
	Checkerboard Border		
6	1½ × 44-inch strips		
FABRIC C	**Checkerboard Border**		
6	1½ × 44-inch strips		
FABRIC D	**Half-Inch Border**		
4	1 × 44-inch strips		
	Binding		
4	2¾ × 44-inch strips		

Making Triangle Sets

Step 1. Refer to "Speedy Triangles" on page 231 for how to mark, sew, and cut.

Step 2. Use three 6 × 14-inch pieces each of Fabrics A and B. Position one Fabric A piece with one Fabric B piece, right sides together. Repeat for a total of three sets. On each set, mark a grid of twelve 1⅞-inch squares. See **Diagram 1.**

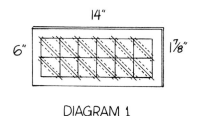

DIAGRAM 1

Step 3. After sewing and cutting are complete, press the seams toward Fabric A. You will have made a total of seventy-two 1½-inch triangle sets, twenty-four of each Fabric A/B combination.

Making the Blocks

Throughout this section, refer to the **Fabric Key** to identify the fabric placements in the diagrams. Also, it's a good idea to review "Assembly Line Piecing" on page 233 before you get started. It is more efficient to do the same step for each block at the same time than to piece one entire block together at a time. Be sure to press as you go and follow the arrows for pressing direction.

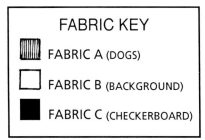

FABRIC KEY
- FABRIC A (DOGS)
- FABRIC B (BACKGROUND)
- FABRIC C (CHECKERBOARD)

Section One

Step 1. Sew twelve 1½ × 5½-inch Fabric B strips to twelve Fabric A/B triangle sets. See **Diagram 2.** Position them right sides together

and line them up next to your sewing machine. Stitch the first set together, then butt the next set directly behind it and continue sewing each set without breaking the thread. Do all twelve sets using this continuous-seam technique. Remember, sew four of each of the three different Fabric As. Press the seams toward Fabric B and then cut the joining threads.

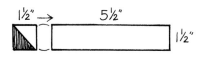

DIAGRAM 2

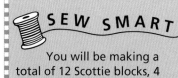

SEW SMART

You will be making a total of 12 Scottie blocks, 4 each of the 3 Fabric As. When piecing your blocks together, be careful to use the same Fabric A for each individual Scottie block.

In each of the remaining steps, use the same continuous-seam method. You will be making a total of twelve blocks.

Step 2. Sew twelve 1½ × 2½-inch Fabric B pieces to twelve Fabric A/B triangle sets. Press toward Fabric B. See **Diagram 3.**

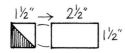

DIAGRAM 3

Step 3. Sew the Step 1 units to the Step 2 units. Press toward the Step 1 units. See **Diagram 4.**

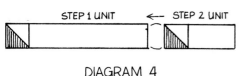

DIAGRAM 4

Section Two

The second section is the 3½ × 9½-inch Fabric A piece. Section Two is complete as is!

Section Three

Step 1. Sew twelve Fabric A/B triangle sets to twelve 1½-inch Fabric B squares. Press toward Fabric B. See **Diagram 5.**

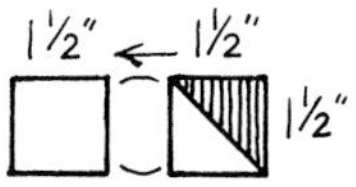

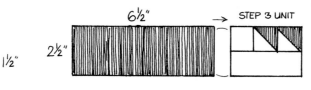

DIAGRAM 5

SEW SMART

Pay close attention so that the triangle sets are positioned exactly as shown in the diagrams.

Step 2. Sew twelve Fabric A/B triangle sets to the Step 1 units, as shown in **Diagram 6.** Press toward the triangle sets just added.

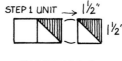

DIAGRAM 6

Step 3. Sew the Step 2 units to twelve 1½ × 3½-inch Fabric B pieces. Press toward Fabric B. See **Diagram 7.**

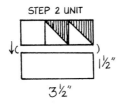

DIAGRAM 7

Step 4. Sew the Step 3 units to twelve 2½ × 6½-inch Fabric A pieces. Press toward the Step 3 units. See **Diagram 8.**

DIAGRAM 8

Section Four

Step 1. Sew twelve Fabric A/B triangle sets to twelve 1½ × 2½-inch Fabric A pieces. Press toward Fabric A. See **Diagram 9.**

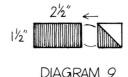

DIAGRAM 9

Step 2. Sew twelve 1½ × 2½-inch Fabric A pieces to twelve 1½-inch Fabric B squares. Press toward Fabric A. See **Diagram 10.**

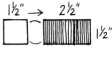

DIAGRAM 10

Step 3. Sew twelve 1½ × 2½-inch Fabric B pieces to twelve Fabric A/B triangle sets. Press toward Fabric B. See **Diagram 11.**

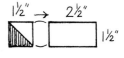

DIAGRAM II

Step 4. Sew the Step 1 units to the Step 2 units, as shown in **Diagram 12.** Press toward the Step 2 units.

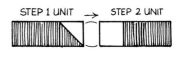

DIAGRAM 12

Step 5. Sew the Step 3 units to the Step 4 units. Press toward the Step 4 units. See **Diagram 13.**

Section Assembly

Step 1. Sew Section One to Section Two, referring to **Diagram 14.** Press toward Section Two.

Step 2. Sew Section Three to Section Four. Press toward Section Three. See **Diagram 15.**

Step 3. Sew the Step 1 units to the Step 2 units. Press toward the Step 1 units. See **Diagram 16.** Now your Scottie blocks are complete! The blocks will now measure 7½ × 9½ inches.

Lattice

Step 1. Lay out your blocks in a pleasing arrangement, with four rows of three Scotties each (refer to the **Quilt Layout** on page 49). Keep track of your layout while sewing on the lattice.

Step 2. Sew the 1½ × 7½-inch Fabric B lattice strips to both sides of the four center blocks from each row. Press all seams toward the lattice. See **Diagram 17.**

Step 3. Sew a block to each side of those strips to make four rows of three blocks. Press. See **Diagram 18.**

Step 4. Sew 1½ × 44-inch lattice strips to the bottom of each row. Trim and press. Sew the four rows together. Press.

Step 5. Sew a lattice strip to the top of the quilt. Trim and press. Sew a strip to each quilt side. Trim and press.

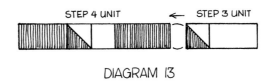

DIAGRAM 13

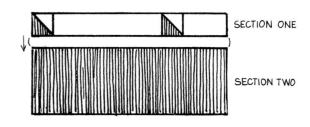

DIAGRAM 14

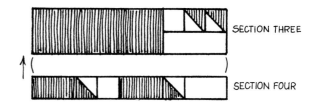

DIAGRAM 15

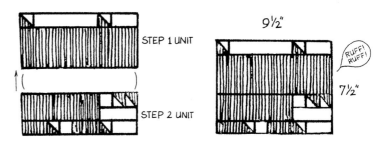

DIAGRAM 16

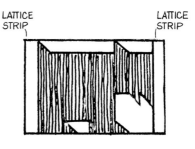

DIAGRAM 17

DIAGRAM 18

Half-Inch Border

Step 1. Sew 1 × 44-inch Fabric D strips to the quilt top and bottom. Trim the excess and press all seams toward the border.

Step 2. Sew the two remaining strips to the quilt sides. Trim and press.

Checkerboard Border

Step 1. Sew together six 1½ × 44-inch strips each of Fabrics B and C, alternating the fabrics. See **Diagram 19.** Press all seams toward Fabric C as you go.

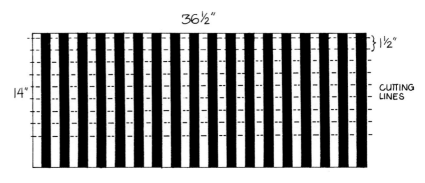

DIAGRAM 20

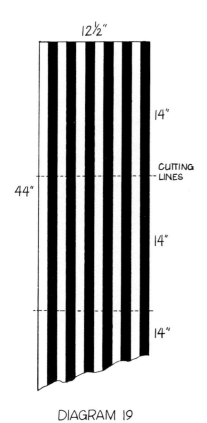

DIAGRAM 19

Step 2. Cut this strip set into thirds across the width, as shown in **Diagram 19.** Resew the thirds together to make a 14 × 36½-inch strip set. See **Diagram 20.**

Step 3. From the Step 2 strip set, cut eight 1½ × 36½-inch strips, following the cutting lines in **Diagram 20.**

Step 4. Fit one strip to the top of the quilt top (raw edge to raw edge). Use a seam ripper to remove the excess checkerboard. See "Hints on Fitting a Checkerboard Border" on page 245. Match up a second row of checkerboard to equal the one fitted to the quilt edge. Sew the two strips together to create the checkerboard pattern. Pin in position and sew to the quilt top. Press all seams toward the half-inch border. Repeat for the bottom of the quilt.

Step 5. Fit a checkerboard strip to the quilt sides in the same manner as in Step 4. Measure up to the outside seam line of the half-inch border, but do not include the top and bottom checkerboard borders that you just added. Then add ¼ inch to the ends of each strip so they will fit correctly after the corner squares are added.

Step 6. Sew a 2½-inch Fabric A corner square to each end of the two side checkerboards. Pin the borders to the quilt sides and sew in place.

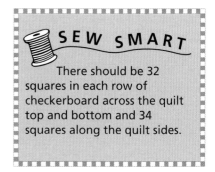

SEW SMART

There should be 32 squares in each row of checkerboard across the quilt top and bottom and 34 squares along the quilt sides.

Shawls

Decide how many Scotties will wear shawls and cut that number using the **Shawl Appliqué Pattern** on the opposite page. Follow the directions in "Hand Appliqué" on page 241. I appliquéd six shawls from six different red plaids and stripes. For a more interesting look, position the shawls so they are balanced on the quilt, but in an unpredictable way.

Layering the Quilt

Arrange and baste the backing, batting, and quilt top together, following the directions in "Layering the Quilt" on page 249. Trim the batting and backing to ¼ inch from the raw edge of the quilt.

Binding the Quilt

Using the 2¾ × 44-inch Fabric D strips, follow the directions on page 249 for "Binding the Quilt."

Finishing Stitches

Outline the Scotties and shawls by quilting in the ditch. Quilt a heart on the dogs not wearing shawls, as shown in **Diagram 21,** using the **Heart Quilting Template** on this page. Stitch a 1½-inch diagonal grid to fill in the background.

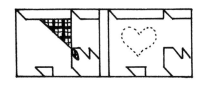

DIAGRAM 21

SEW CREATIVE

Look around the house and rummage through your draw-ers—you may find other fun things, such as a collar or a bell, to hang around one of your Scottie's necks.

HEART QUILTING TEMPLATE

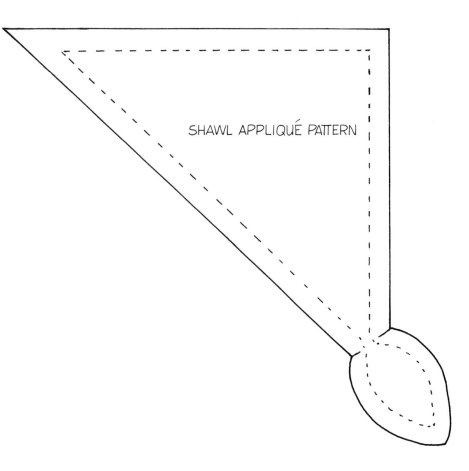

SHAWL APPLIQUÉ PATTERN

Shooting Stars

32″

24″

SIX-STAR QUILT LAYOUT

I wish I may, I wish I might . . . " Make a wish come true with a quilt of sophisticated stars! Create a variation on the Ohio Star pattern with your own special sampling of festive fabrics. The two versions on the opposite page have a formal and classic appeal. If you're in a patriotic mood, try the red, white, and blue variation shown in the photo on page 66—it sparkles with an extra bonus of stars in the background fabric. No matter which version you choose, you're sure to end up with a star-spangled winner!

Six-Star Quilt

Finished Quilt: 32 × 24 inches
Finished Block: 6 inches square
(does not include border around
each block)

Materials

Obvious directional prints are not recommended.

FABRIC A

Use three fabrics.
Main stars ⅛ yard
each of *three* fabrics

FABRIC B

Block Background	⅝ yard
Lattice	¼ yard
TOTAL	¾ yard

FABRIC C

Use three fabrics.
Secondary Stars ¼ yard
each of *three* fabrics

FABRIC D

Block Border and
Half-Inch Border ¼ yard

FABRIC E

Two-and-a-Half-Inch Border
and Binding ¾ yard

BACKING ⅞ yard

BATTING ⅞ yard

SEW COLORFUL

Borders and Binding: First select an interesting multicolor print for the two-and-a-half-inch border and binding. Then choose coordinating fabrics for your stars. Look for a strong solid for the block border and half-inch border.

Stars: I used a two-color scheme of purple and teal to coordinate with the border. The basic star shape (meaning the points of the stars) is created by what I call the main star fabric (Fabric A). If you look closely at my quilt, you'll see that some of these stars stand out more prominently than others. The contrast between the main fabric and the sec-ondary star fabric (Fabric C) determines how prominent the stars will be. You will need three main star and three secondary star fabrics. (There are two purple Fabric As in the quilt shown on page 56. The difference between them is subtle and may not be obvious in the photograph.) To really make the basic star shape stand out from the rest of the quilt, pair two fabrics with a high level of contrast. I would suggest a dark color for the main star fabric and a medium color for the secondary star fabric.

Background: Use a warm neutral for the background fabric.

Cutting Directions

Prewash and press all of your fabrics. Using a rotary cutter, see-through ruler, and cutting mat, prepare the strips as described in the first column in the chart below. Then from those strips, cut the pieces listed in the second column. Some portions of the quilt need to be cut only once, so no additional cutting information will appear in the second column. Measurements for all pieces include ¼-inch seam allowances.

	FIRST CUT		SECOND CUT	
	NO. OF STRIPS	**DIMENSIONS**	**NO. OF PIECES**	**DIMENSIONS**
FABRIC A	**Main Stars:** from *each* of the *three* fabrics, cut the following			
	Before You Cut: The strip below does not need to be exactly 4½ inches wide. Use the width of your ⅛-yard piece.			
	1	4½ × 15-inch piece		
FABRIC B	**Background**			
	2	4½ × 44-inch strips	3	4½ × 15-inch pieces
	1	8½ × 44-inch strip	3	8½-inch squares
	Lattice			
	Before You Cut: From *one* of the 44-inch strips, cut the pieces listed in the second column. The remaining four strips need no further cutting.			
	5	1½ × 44-inch strips	4	1½ × 7½-inch pieces
FABRIC C	**Secondary Stars:** from *each* of the *three* fabrics, cut the following			
	1	8½-inch square		
	2	2½-inch squares		

	FIRST CUT		SECOND CUT	
	NO. OF STRIPS	DIMENSIONS	NO. OF PIECES	DIMENSIONS
FABRIC D	Block Border			
	5	1×44-inch strips	12	$1 \times 6\frac{1}{2}$-inch pieces
			12	$1 \times 7\frac{1}{2}$-inch pieces
	Half-Inch Border			
	4	1×44-inch strips		
FABRIC E	Two-and-a-Half-Inch Border			
	4	3×44-inch strips		
	BINDING			
	4	$2\frac{3}{4} \times 44$-inch strips		

Making Triangle Sets

Step 1. Refer to "Speedy Triangles" on page 231 for how to mark, sew, and cut.

Step 2. Position the $8\frac{1}{2}$-inch Fabric B and C squares with right sides together. You will have three sets. On each set draw a grid of four $2\frac{7}{8}$-inch squares. See **Diagram 1.**

Step 3. After sewing and cutting are complete, press the seams toward Fabric C. You will have made a total of twenty-four $2\frac{1}{2}$-inch Fabric B/C triangle sets, eight of each Fabric C.

Quarter-Square Speedy Triangles

Step 1. For the quarter-square triangle sets, position the $4\frac{1}{2} \times 15$-inch Fabric A and B pieces with right sides together. You will have three sets. Using a ballpoint pen and see-through ruler, draw a grid of four $3\frac{1}{4}$-inch squares. Mark on the wrong side of the lighter fabric. See **Diagram 2.** Next, draw a diagonal line across the squares, intersecting the corners exactly. Draw a second diagonal across each square in the opposite direc-

tion. (Each square will be marked with an ✕.) See **Diagram 3.**

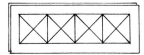

DIAGRAM 3

Step 2. Using a $\frac{1}{4}$-inch seam allowance, stitch along both sides of the diagonal lines of half of the ✕. See **Diagram 4.**

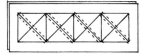

DIAGRAM 4

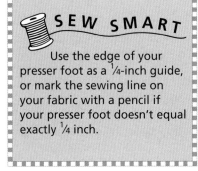

SEW SMART

Use the edge of your presser foot as a $\frac{1}{4}$-inch guide, or mark the sewing line on your fabric with a pencil if your presser foot doesn't equal exactly $\frac{1}{4}$ inch.

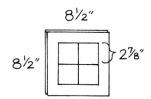

$8\frac{1}{2}''$

$8\frac{1}{2}''$

$2\frac{7}{8}''$

DIAGRAM 1

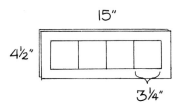

$15''$

$4\frac{1}{2}''$

$3\frac{1}{4}''$

DIAGRAM 2

Step 3. Use your rotary cutter to cut along all pen lines. (You need to cut along the unstitched diagonals also.) Each square will make four triangle sets.

Step 4. Press the seams toward Fabric A, being very careful to keep the iron away from the bias edge of the triangle set. See **Diagram 5.** You will have made a total of forty-eight Fabric A/B triangle sets, sixteen of each Fabric A.

DIAGRAM 5

Making the Triangle Units

Step 1. From the first Fabric A/B color combination, match up pairs of quarter-square triangles, as shown in **Diagram 6.** Stitch the first pair together, then butt the next pair directly behind and continue sewing each pair without breaking your thread. Sew eight pairs. Cut the joining threads and press the seams to either side. *Pay close attention not to stretch the bias as you sew.* (See "Sew Smart" on page 64 for hints on handling the quarter-square triangles.)

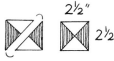

DIAGRAM 6

Step 2. Repeat Step 1 for each of the two remaining Fabric A/B color combinations. Sew eight pairs of each. You will have a total of eight 2½-inch squares of each Fabric A/B combination.

SEW SMART

Each triangle set will match up correctly with one that looks the same. Triangle sets that are mirror images of each other will not work together. Keep switching sets until you have eight pairs that will match up.

Making the Blocks

Throughout this section, refer to the **Fabric Key** to identify the fabric placements in the diagrams. Also, it's a good idea to review "Assembly Line Piecing" on page 233 before you get started.

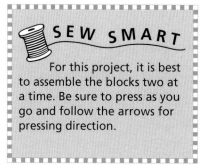

SEW SMART

For this project, it is best to assemble the blocks two at a time. Be sure to press as you go and follow the arrows for pressing direction.

You will be making a total of six star blocks, two of each fabric combination. Lay out the blocks, trying a variety of fabric combinations until you have determined a pleasing arrangement.

Complete two blocks of the same fabric combination at the same time. You will be sewing them in three sets of two blocks each. Follow the steps from each section for both blocks of the same color combination at the same time.

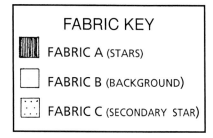

FABRIC KEY

FABRIC A (STARS)
FABRIC B (BACKGROUND)
FABRIC C (SECONDARY STAR)

Section One

Step 1. Sew two Fabric B/C triangle sets to two Fabric A/B quarter-square triangle sets. Position them right sides together and line them up next to your sewing machine. Stitch the first set together, then butt the next set directly behind and continue sewing without breaking your thread. Pay close attention so that the triangle sets are positioned as shown in **Diagram 7.** Press the seams toward the Fabric B/C triangle set and cut the joining threads.

DIAGRAM 7

In each of the remaining steps, use the same continuous-seam method.

Step 2. Sew two Fabric B/C triangle sets to two Step 1 units. See **Diagram 8.** Press the seams toward the Fabric B/C triangle set.

Repeat Steps 1 and 2 to make a total of six of Section One.

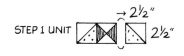

DIAGRAM 8

Section Two

Step 1. Sew two Fabric A/B quarter-square triangle sets to two 2½-inch Fabric C center squares. (Match the center square color to the Fabric B/C triangle set in Section One.) See **Diagram 9.** Press toward the center squares.

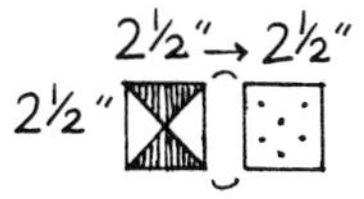

DIAGRAM 9

Step 2. Sew two Fabric A/B quarter-square triangle sets to two Step 1 units. See **Diagram 10.** Press toward the center squares.

Repeat Steps 1 and 2 to make a total of six of Section Two.

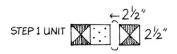

DIAGRAM 10

Section Three

Step 1. Sew two Fabric B/C triangle sets to two Fabric A/B quarter-square triangle sets. See **Diagram 11.** Press toward the Fabric B/C triangle sets.

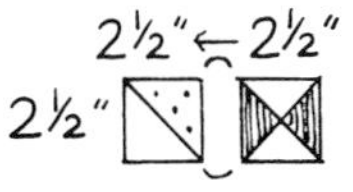

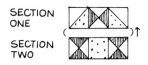

DIAGRAM 11

Step 2. Sew two Fabric B/C triangle sets to two Step 1 units. See **Diagram 12.** Press toward the Fabric B/C triangle sets.

Repeat Steps 1 and 2 to make a total of six of Section Three.

DIAGRAM 12

Section Assembly

Step 1. Sew Section One to Section Two, as shown in **Diagram 13.** Press toward Section One.

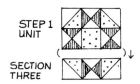

DIAGRAM 13

Step 2. Sew Section Three to the Step 1 units, as shown in **Diagram 14.** Press toward Section Three. The blocks will measure 6½ inches square (including seam allowances).

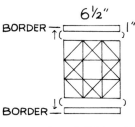

DIAGRAM 14

Block Borders

Step 1. Sew 1 × 6½-inch Fabric D pieces to the top and bottom of each of the six star blocks. See **Diagram 15.** Press all seams toward the border.

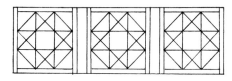

DIAGRAM 15

Step 2. Sew 1 × 7½-inch Fabric D pieces to each side of the six star blocks. See **Diagram 16.** Press.

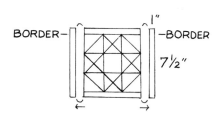

DIAGRAM 16

Lattice

Step 1. Lay out the star blocks according to the **Six-Star Quilt Layout** on page 57, with two rows of three blocks each. Keep track of your layout while sewing on the lattice.

Step 2. Sew the 1½ × 7½-inch Fabric B lattice strips to each side of the center blocks from each of the two rows. See **Diagram 17.** Press all seams toward the lattice.

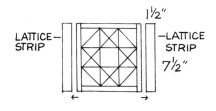

DIAGRAM 17

Step 3. Sew a block to each side of those lattice strips to make two rows of three stars. See **Diagram 18.** Press.

DIAGRAM 18

Step 4. Sew 1½ × 44-inch lattice strips to the bottom of each row of blocks and to the top of the top row. Trim the excess and press. Sew the two rows together. Press.

Step 5. Use the last 1½ × 44-inch lattice strip for both sides of the quilt. Cut the strip in half, then sew those strips to the sides, trimming the excess. Press.

Half-Inch Border

Step 1. Sew 1 × 44-inch Fabric D strips to the quilt top and bottom. Trim the excess and press all seams toward the border.

Step 2. Sew the remaining two border strips to the sides. Trim and press.

Two-and-a-Half-Inch Border

Step 1. Sew 3 × 44-inch Fabric E strips to the top and bottom of the quilt. Trim the excess and press all seams toward the half-inch border.

Step 2. Sew the remaining two border strips to the sides of the quilt. Trim and press all seams toward the half-inch border.

Layering the Quilt

Arrange and baste the backing, batting, and quilt top together, following the directions for "Layering the Quilt" on page 249. Trim the batting and backing to ¼ inch from the raw edge of the quilt top.

Binding the Quilt

Using the four 2¾ × 44-inch Fabric D binding strips, follow the directions for "Binding the Quilt" on page 249.

Finishing Stitches

Outline the triangles by quilting ¼ inch away from the seam line, as shown in **Diagram 19**. Stitch a 1-inch diagonal grid on the lattice and the two-and-a-half-inch border.

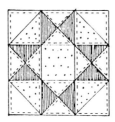

DIAGRAM 19

Nine-Star Quilt

Finished Quilt: 28 inches square
Finished Block: 6 inches square

Materials

Obvious directional prints are not recommended.

FABRIC A

Use five fabrics.
Stars ⅛ yard
each of *five* fabrics

FABRIC B

Block Background	⅔ yard
Lattice	⅓ yard
TOTAL	1 yard

FABRIC C

One-Inch Corner Squares
and Lattice Squares ⅛ yard
(or one 1½ × 44-inch strip)

FABRIC D

Half-Inch Border
and Binding ½ yard

FABRIC E

Two-and-a-Half-Inch Border ½ yard

BACKING 1 yard

BATTING 1 yard

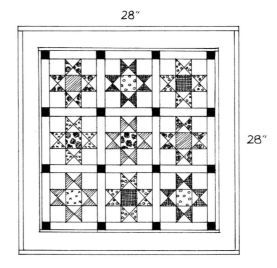

28″

28″

NINE-STAR QUILT LAYOUT

Cutting Directions

Prewash and press all of your fabrics. Using a rotary cutter, see-through ruler, and cutting mat, prepare the strips as described in the first column in the chart below. Then from those strips, cut the pieces listed in the second column. Some portions of the quilt need to be cut only once, so no additional cutting information will appear in the second column. Measurements for all pieces include ¼-inch seam allowances.

SEW COLORFUL

Borders: First select an interesting multicolor print for the two-and-a-half-inch border. Then choose coordinating fabrics for your stars. Look for a strong, solid accent color for the half-inch border and the binding.

Stars: I have the same purple and teal color scheme as in the Six-Star Quilt, but with more fabrics. I have interchanged the squares in the middle of the block with different star fabrics. I've used the accent color from the half-inch border in the squares between the blocks.

Background: Since there is a large area of background in this quilt, choose a neutral color with a subtle print.

	FIRST CUT		SECOND CUT	
	NO. OF STRIPS	DIMENSIONS	NO. OF PIECES	DIMENSIONS
FABRIC A	**Stars:** from *each* of the *five* fabrics, cut the following			
	1	4½ × 15-inch piece		
	2	2½-inch squares		
FABRIC B	**Background**			
	3	4½ × 44-inch strips	5	4½ × 15-inch pieces
	3	2½ × 44-inch strips	40	2½-inch squares
	Lattice			
	1	6½ × 44-inch strip	1	6½ × 27-inch piece
	2	1½ × 44-inch strips	12	1½ × 6½-inch pieces
FABRIC C	**One-Inch Corner Squares and Lattice Squares**			
	1	1½ × 44-inch strip	1	1½ × 27-inch strip
			4	1½-inch squares
FABRIC D	**Half-Inch Border**			
	4	1 × 44-inch strips		
	Binding			
	4	2¾ × 44-inch strips		
FABRIC E	**Two-and-a-Half-Inch Border**			
	4	3 × 44-inch strips		

Quarter-Square Speedy Triangles

Step 1. Refer to "Quarter-Square Speedy Triangles" for the Six-Star Quilt, beginning on page 59, for how to mark, sew, and cut.

Step 2. Position the 4½ × 15-inch Fabric A and B pieces with right sides together. You will have five sets. On each set draw a grid of four 3¼-inch squares. See **Diagram 20.**

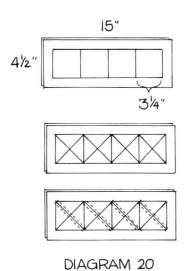

DIAGRAM 20

Step 3. After sewing and cutting are complete, press the seams toward Fabric A, being very careful to keep the iron away from the bias edge of the triangle set. See **Diagram 21.** You will have made a total of 80 Fabric A/B quarter-square triangle sets, 16 of each Fabric A.

← BIAS EDGE

DIAGRAM 21

Making the Triangle Units

Refer to "Making the Triangle Units" for the Six-Star Quilt, beginning on page 60, for complete directions. Sew eight 2½-inch squares of each of the five Fabric A/B combinations.

Making the Blocks

Throughout this section, refer to the **Fabric Key** to identify the fabric placements in the diagrams. Also, it's a good idea to review "Assembly Line Piecing" on page 233 before you get started. It's more efficient to do the same step for each block at the same time than to piece one entire block together at a time. Be sure to press as you go and follow the arrows for pressing direction. You will be making two blocks of each Fabric A, for a total of ten blocks. (You will use nine out of the ten blocks for the quilt.)

FABRIC KEY
▓ FABRIC A (STARS)
☐ FABRIC B (BACKGROUND)

Section One

Step 1. Sew ten Fabric A/B quarter-square triangle sets to ten 2½-inch Fabric B squares. Position them right sides together and line them up next to your sewing machine. Stitch the first set together, then butt the next set directly behind and continue sewing each set without breaking your thread. Press toward Fabric B and cut the joining threads. Pay close attention

so that the triangle sets are positioned as shown in **Diagram 22.** Press toward Fabric B.

DIAGRAM 22

In each of the remaining steps, use the same continuous-seam method.

Step 2. Sew ten 2½-inch Fabric B squares to the ten Step 1 units. See **Diagram 23.** Press toward Fabric B.

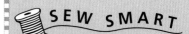

DIAGRAM 23

SEW SMART

Be careful not to stretch the bias edges of the quarter-square triangles. Treat these pieces with tender loving care when you press; use an up-and-down motion with the iron and don't slide it along the bias edges. When you move from sewing machine to ironing board, carry them flat instead of holding them by their edges. And when you sew, be sure to treat them gently. Any tugging or pulling will stretch them out of shape, making it harder for you to piece accurately.

Section Two

Step 1. Sew ten Fabric A/B quarter-square triangle sets to ten 2½-inch Fabric A squares. Mix and match different Fabric A center squares with different Fabric A star fabrics for a more "scrappy" look. See **Diagram 24.** Press toward Fabric A.

DIAGRAM 24

Step 2. Sew ten Fabric A/B quarter-square triangle sets to ten Step 1 units. Match Fabric As in each. See **Diagram 25.** Press toward Fabric A.

DIAGRAM 25

Section Three

Step 1. Sew ten Fabric A/B quarter-square triangle sets to ten 2½-inch Fabric B squares. See **Diagram 26.** Press toward Fabric B.

DIAGRAM 26

Step 2. Sew ten 2½-inch Fabric B squares to ten Step 1 units, as shown in **Diagram 27.** Press toward Fabric B.

DIAGRAM 27

Section Assembly

Step 1. Sew Section One to Section Two. See **Diagram 28.** Press toward Section One.

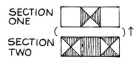

DIAGRAM 28

Step 2. Sew Section Three to the Step 1 unit. See **Diagram 29.** Press toward Section Three. The blocks will measure 6½ inches square (including seam allowances). You will have ten star blocks, one more than needed for the quilt.

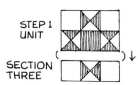

DIAGRAM 29

Lattice

Step 1. Lay out your star blocks in a pleasing arrangement, with three rows of three blocks each. Keep track of your layout while sewing on the lattice.

Step 2. Sew 1½ × 6½-inch Fabric B lattice strips to each side of the center block in each of the three rows. See **Diagram 30.** Press all seam allowances toward the lattice.

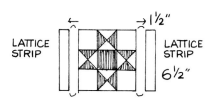

DIAGRAM 30

Step 3. Sew a star block to each side of those lattice strips to make three rows of three stars each. Sew the remaining 1½ × 6½-inch lattice strips to each end of each row. See **Diagram 31.** Press.

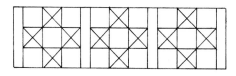

DIAGRAM 31

Step 4. To assemble the horizontal lattice strips, sew the 1½ × 27-inch Fabric C strip to the 6½ × 27-inch Fabric B strip. Press toward Fabric B and cut into thirds. See **Diagram 32.**

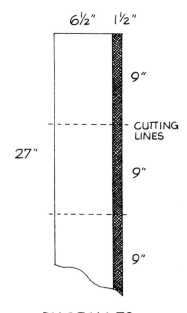

DIAGRAM 32

Resew the sections together to make a 9 × 21½-inch strip set, as shown below in **Diagram 33.** From this strip set, cut four 1½ × 21½-inch strips. Sew a 1½-inch Fabric C square to each strip, at the end without a corner square. See **Diagram 34.** Press.

Step 5. Pin in position and sew one of these horizontal lattice strips to the bottom of each row of stars and to the top of the top row. Press all seams toward the lattice.

Step 6. Sew the three rows together. Press.

Half-Inch Border

Step 1. Sew 1 × 44-inch Fabric D strips to the quilt top and bottom. Trim the excess and press all seams toward the border.

Step 2. Sew the remaining two border strips to the sides. Trim and press.

Two-and-a-Half-Inch Border

Step 1. Sew 3 × 44-inch Fabric E border strips to the top and bot-

tom of the quilt. Trim the excess and press all seams toward the half-inch border.

Step 2. Sew the remaining two border strips to the sides of the quilt. Trim the excess and press all seams toward the half-inch border.

Layering the Quilt

Arrange and baste the backing, batting, and quilt top together, following the directions for "Layering the Quilt" on page 249. Trim the batting and backing to ¼ inch from the raw edge of the quilt top.

Binding the Quilt

Using the four 2¾ × 44-inch Fabric D binding strips, follow the directions for "Binding the Quilt" on page 249.

Finishing Stitches

Outline the background pieces by quilting ¼ inch away from the seam line, as shown in **Diagram 35.**

 SEW CREATIVE ♡

Turn that extra star block into a potholder and add it to a hostess gift basket. Or bind and quilt it, put it in a handsome frame, and you have a delightful small wallhanging ready for last-minute gift-giving.

Patriotic Nine-Star Quilt

To create a quilt bursting with patriotic pride, follow the directions for the Nine-Star Quilt beginning on page 62 up through "Half-Inch Border" on this page. The yardages and cutting are the same for both quilts.

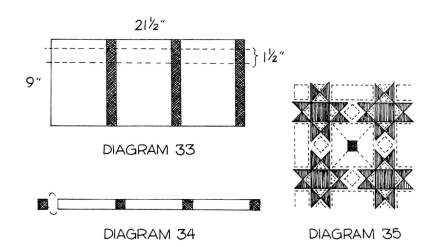

DIAGRAM 33

DIAGRAM 34

DIAGRAM 35

SEW COLORFUL

Be on the lookout for energetic, flag-waving reds, whites, and blues for this one!

Stars: To create a pleasing scrap quilt look, I alternated red and blue for the stars and then mixed and matched red and blue for the centers. This symmetry adds just the right touch of organization to this informal arrangement of fabrics. Strive for variety in the textures of your prints. All star-print fabrics would be too much, but if you want to use more than one, as I did, be sure to vary the scale of the stars.

Borders, Corner Squares, and Binding: Since navy is a strong color, this was my choice for the lattice squares, accent border, and binding. A red print or stripe for the border creates a good contrast next to the solid navy and carries out the patriotic color theme. For the corner squares, choose a fabric that contrasts well with the wide border. A solid navy would have blended in with the binding, so I picked a navy print.

Background: The stipple quilting really fills in the space on the background of this one, but it is still a good idea to look for a subtle print instead of a solid. The star print I used works well because the stars are placed randomly and there is plenty of negative space around them.

Two-and-a-Half-Inch Border

Step 1. Cut four 3-inch corner squares of one Fabric A.

Step 2. Sew 3 × 44-inch Fabric E border strips to the quilt top and bottom. Trim the excess and press all seams toward the border.

Step 3. Compare two border strips to the sides and fit to the correct length. Measure up to, but do not include, the borders you just added to the quilt top and bottom. Then add ¼ inch to each end of the strips before trimming so they will fit correctly after the corner squares are added.

Step 4. Sew the Fabric A corner squares to each end of the side border strips. Press the seams toward the border. Pin in position and sew the border strips with the corner squares to the sides of the quilt. Press.

Completing the Quilt

Refer to "Layering the Quilt" and "Binding the Quilt" for the Nine-Star Quilt, on the opposite page.

Quilt as for the Nine-Star Quilt, or fill the block background pieces with stipple quilting, as I did on the quilt in the photograph. See "Machine Stipple Quilting" on this page for instructions on this technique.

MACHINE STIPPLE QUILTING

Stipple quilting is closely spaced quilting that fills in a background area with random curving lines. The sewing line constantly changes directions, and stitches never cross or touch. The purpose of stipple quilting is to create visual texture. The stipple-quilted area is flattened, making other areas stand out more.

To do stipple quilting by machine, drop your machine's feed dog and use the darning foot. Begin in one corner of the block, working toward the center and then back out to the corners to fill in the space. Use both hands to guide the quilt back and forth under the needle. It helps to imagine that you are drawing on the quilt with the needle. Curve your stitching in winding, random, stair-step–type patterns. Remember, don't let your stitching lines cross. Stipple quilting should appear random and spontaneous.

Even though this is machine quilting, it is still a time-consuming process, so try not to overdo on your first project. Also, be careful not to get cornered!

STIPPLE QUILTING

A COUNTRY CHRISTMAS

Deck the halls with one or more of these quick country Christmas quilts! There are scrappy-looking pine trees and red-and-green holiday wreaths to stitch for the season. Patriotic Santas and Santa gnomes lend a festive Americana Christmas look to any part of your house, while the appliqué wallhangings and ornaments will keep your home and tree well decorated for many holidays to come. Make a set of charming Christmas stockings to line your mantel, then use the same appliqué designs on handmade cards, packages, and boxes. The only difficult part is deciding what to make first!

Before you begin, take a minute to read through this checklist. These are important pointers you should keep in mind to make sure that each of your quilts is a success.

♥ Be sure you read "Techniques for More Quick Country Quilting," beginning on page 215, to familiarize yourself with fabric selection; the tools you'll need; time-saving techniques for cutting, piecing, and appliqué; as well as finishing instructions.

♥ Take advantage of the helpful hints in "Sew Colorful" at the start of each project. Here is where you'll find pointers on selecting colors and fabrics for each particular design.

♥ Prewash and press all of your fabrics.

♥ Read the step-by-step directions from start to finish, and look at all the diagrams before you cut and sew any fabric.

♥ Always use a ¼-inch seam allowance, unless there is a special note that tells you a different seam allowance is required.

♥ Refer to the **Fabric Key** for each project as a help in following the diagrams.

♥ Pay attention to the pressing directions given in the step-by-step text and to the pressing arrows shown in the diagrams.

Whispering Pines

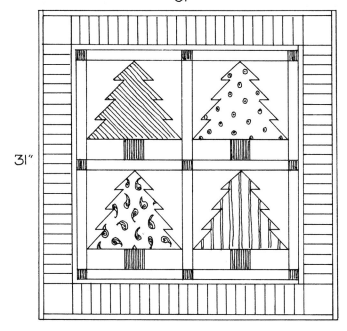

31"

31"

FOUR-TREE QUILT LAYOUT

It's hard to resist daydreaming about a walk in the woods on a bright, sunny day. The fragrance of pine and the murmur of breezes rustling through the trees are some of the most soothing sensations imaginable. Capture the quiet and contentment of moments spent in a pine-filled forest with these soothing patchwork trees. Perfectly suited for display year-round, these four- or twelve-tree wall quilts can also be used as part of your holiday decor.

Four-Tree Quilt

Finished Quilt: 31 inches square
Finished Block: 10 inches square

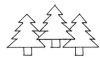

Materials

Obvious directional prints are not recommended.

FABRIC A

Use four fabrics.
Trees and Scrap Border ⅓ yard
each of *four* fabrics

FABRIC B

Block Background,
  Large Corner Squares, and
  Scrap Border ¾ yard
Lattice ¼ yard
  TOTAL 1 yard

FABRIC C

Trunks and
  Lattice Corner Squares ⅛ yard

FABRIC D

Half-Inch Border and
  Binding ½ yard

BACKING 1 yard

BATTING 1 yard

Cutting Directions

Prewash and press all of your fabrics. Using a rotary cutter, see-through ruler, and cutting mat, prepare the strips as described in the first column in the chart below. Then from those strips, cut the pieces listed in the second column. Some portions of the quilt need to be cut only once, so no additional cutting information will appear in the second column. Measurements for all pieces include ¼-inch seam allowances.

	FIRST CUT		SECOND CUT	
	NO. OF STRIPS	DIMENSIONS	NO. OF PIECES	DIMENSIONS
FABRIC A	**Trees:** from *each* of the *four* fabrics, cut the following			
	1	5 × 44-inch strip	1	5 × 14-inch piece
			1	2½ × 6½-inch piece
			1	2½ × 4½-inch piece
			1	2½-inch square
	Scrap Border: from *each* of the *four* fabrics, cut the following			
	3	1½ × 44-inch strips		
FABRIC B	**Block Background**			
	3	2½ × 44-inch strips	8	2½ × 4½-inch pieces
			8	2½ × 3½-inch pieces
			8	2½-inch squares
			8	2½ × 1½-inch pieces
	2	5 × 44-inch strips	4	5 × 14-inch pieces
	Lattice			
	4	1½ × 44-inch strips	12	1½ × 10½-inch pieces
	Corner Squares (for outside borders)			
	1	3½ × 44-inch strip	4	3½-inch squares
	Scrap Border			
	2	1½ × 44-inch strips		
FABRIC C	**Trunks**			
	4	2½-inch squares		
	Lattice Corner Squares			
	9	1½-inch squares		

FIRST CUT		SECOND CUT	
NO. OF STRIPS	DIMENSIONS	NO. OF PIECES	DIMENSIONS
FABRIC D	**Half-Inch Border**		
4	1 × 44-inch strips		
	Binding		
4	2¾ × 44-inch strips		

SEW COLORFUL

The fabrics you select will determine whether these quilts have a strong Christmas feel or a more general "woodsy" look for everyday use. The color scheme I used is mainly green and tan with a red accent.

Trees: You'll probably want to stick with greens, and you'll want a nice variety. Most of my greens were all darks, with maybe one or two mediums. Look for different visual textures to keep the greens lively. For the four-tree quilt, look for interesting, more active prints since the pieces are so large. One or two multicolor fabrics that incorporate your accent color work great.

Background: My choice was a warm neutral solid for the background, but a subtle print would be equally effective.

Borders and Binding: I used a red solid for the half-inch accent border and binding, but for a less Christmassy look, you might use a dark brown or black. For the corner squares, repeat either the accent or background color. The scrap border uses all the colors in the quilt and ties it all together.

Making Triangle Sets

Step 1. Refer to "Speedy Triangles" on page 231 for how to mark, sew, and cut.

Step 2. Position the 5 × 14-inch Fabric A and B pieces with right sides together. You will have four sets. On each set, draw a grid of four 2⅞-inch squares. See **Diagram 1**.

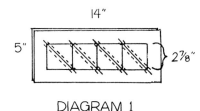

DIAGRAM 1

Step 3. After sewing and cutting are complete, press the seams toward Fabric B on one of the triangle sets for each Fabric A. Press toward Fabric A on the remaining triangle sets. You will have made a total of thirty-two 2½-inch Fabric A/B triangle sets, eight of each Fabric A.

Making the Blocks

Throughout this section, refer to the **Fabric Key** to identify the fabric placements in the diagrams. Also, it's a good idea to review "Assembly Line Piecing" on page

233 before you get started. It's more efficient to do the same step for each block at the same time than to piece one entire block together at a time. Be sure to press as you go and follow the arrows for pressing direction.

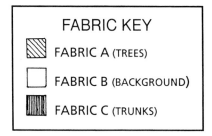

FABRIC KEY

FABRIC A (TREES)

FABRIC B (BACKGROUND)

FABRIC C (TRUNKS)

Section One

Step 1. For each of the four tree blocks, sew one 2½-inch Fabric A/B triangle set (pressed toward Fabric B) to another 2½-inch Fabric A/B triangle set (pressed toward Fabric A). Position them as shown in **Diagram 2,** with right sides together. Sew the first set together, then butt the next set directly behind them and continue sewing each set without breaking your thread. Press the seams as shown and cut the joining threads.

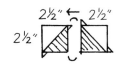

DIAGRAM 2

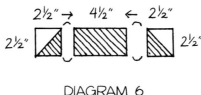

In each of the remaining steps, use the same continuous-seam method. You will be making a total of four blocks. Match the Fabric As within each block.

Step 2. Sew 2½ × 3½-inch Fabric B pieces to both ends of the four Step 1 units. See **Diagram 3.** Press toward Fabric B.

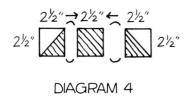

DIAGRAM 3

Section Two

Step 1. Sew 2½-inch Fabric A/B triangle sets to both ends of four 2½-inch Fabric A squares. See **Diagram 4.** Press toward Fabric A. Pay close attention so that the triangle sets are positioned exactly as shown in the diagrams.

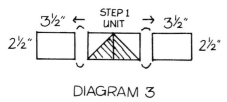

DIAGRAM 4

Step 2. Sew 2½-inch Fabric B squares to both ends of the four Step 1 units. See **Diagram 5.** Press toward Fabric B.

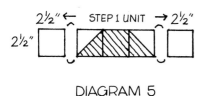

DIAGRAM 5

Section Three

Step 1. Sew 2½-inch Fabric A/B triangle sets to both ends of four 2½ × 4½-inch Fabric A pieces. See **Diagram 6.** Press toward Fabric A.

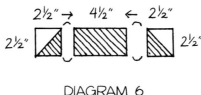

DIAGRAM 6

Step 2. Sew 1½ × 2½-inch Fabric B pieces to both ends of the four Step 1 units. See **Diagram 7.** Press toward Fabric B.

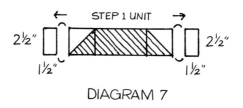

DIAGRAM 7

Section Four

Sew 2½-inch Fabric A/B triangle sets to both ends of four 2½ × 6½-inch Fabric A pieces. See **Diagram 8.** Press toward Fabric A.

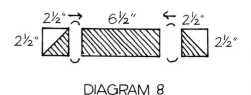

DIAGRAM 8

Section Five

Sew 2½ × 4½-inch Fabric B pieces to both ends of four 2½-inch Fabric C squares. See **Diagram 9.** Press toward Fabric C.

Section Assembly

Referring to **Diagram 10**, sew all the sections together in order. Press all seams toward Section Five. The blocks will measure 10½ inches square.

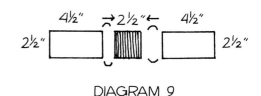

DIAGRAM 9

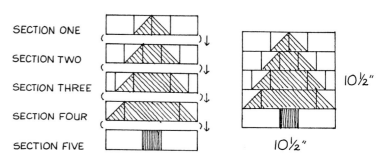

DIAGRAM 10

Lattice

Step 1. Lay out the tree blocks in a pleasing arrangement, with two rows of two blocks each. Keep track of your layout while sewing on the lattice.

Step 2. Sew one 1½ × 10½-inch Fabric B lattice strip between the two blocks in the top row. Press all seams toward the lattice. Sew lattice strips to each end of the row. Press. See **Diagram 11.** Repeat for the bottom row.

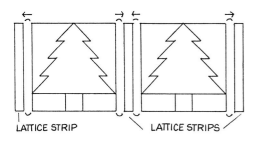

DIAGRAM 11

Step 3. To assemble the horizontal lattice strips, sew a 1½-inch Fabric C square between two 1½ × 10½-inch Fabric B lattice strips. Sew a 1½-inch Fabric C square to each end of that strip. Press the seams toward the lattice strip, as shown

in **Diagram 12.** Repeat to make a total of three horizontal lattice strips.

Step 4. Fit and pin a horizontal lattice strip to the top of each row of blocks, as shown in **Diagram 13.** Stitch. Fit, pin, and sew a horizontal lattice strip to the bottom of the bottom row of blocks. Press the seams toward the lattice strips.

Step 5. Fit and sew the two rows together. Press.

Half-Inch Border

Sew 1 × 44-inch Fabric D strips to the quilt top and bottom. Trim the excess and press all seams toward the border. Sew 1 × 44-inch Fabric D strips to the sides of the quilt. Trim and press.

Scrap Border

Step 1. Use twelve of the fourteen 1½ × 44-inch strips that you cut for the scrap border (three of each Fabric A and two of Fabric B), and arrange them in a pleasing order. (You will have two extra Fabric A strips.) Sew the twelve strips

together to make a 12½ × 44-inch strip set. Press all seams in the same direction.

Step 2. Cut this strip set in half. See **Diagram 14.**

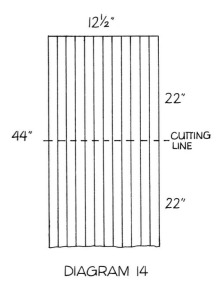

DIAGRAM 14

Step 3. Resew the two halves together to make a 22 × 24½-inch strip set. From this, cut four 3½ × 24½-inch strips, as shown in **Diagram 15.**

Step 4. See "Hints on Fitting a Scrap Border" on page 244 for details on how to fit a scrap border to the quilt. Sew the borders to the top and bottom of the quilt. Press toward the half-inch border.

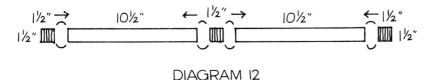

DIAGRAM 12

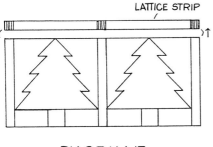

DIAGRAM 13

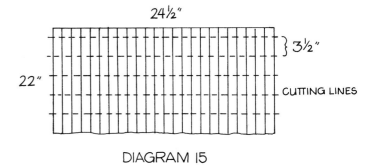

DIAGRAM 15

Step 5. Compare the remaining scrap borders to the sides of the quilt and fit to the correct length. Measure up to the outside seam line of the half-inch border, but do not include the top and bottom borders that you just added. Then add ¼ inch to each end of the strips so they will fit correctly after the corner squares are added.

Step 6. Sew the 3½-inch Fabric B corner squares to each end of the side borders. Press the seams toward the corner squares. See **Diagram 16.** Pin the border strips with corner squares to the sides of the quilt; sew and press toward the half-inch border.

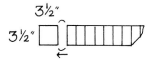

DIAGRAM 16

Layering the Quilt

Arrange and baste the backing, batting, and quilt top together, as described in "Layering the Quilt" on page 249. Trim the batting and backing to ¼ inch from the raw edge of the quilt top.

Binding the Quilt

Using the strips cut from Fabric D, follow directions in "Binding the Quilt" on page 249.

Finishing Stitches

Outline your trees by quilting in the ditch or ¼ inch from the seam lines. For the background, stitch a 1½-inch diagonal grid.

Twelve-Tree Quilt

Finished Quilt: 23 × 28½ inches
Finished Block: 5 inches square

Materials

Obvious directional prints are not recommended.

FABRIC A

Use six fabrics.
Trees and Scrap Border   ⅓ yard
each of *six* fabrics

FABRIC B

Block Background
  and Scrap Border   ⅔ yard
Lattice   ¼ yard
  TOTAL   ⅞ yard

FABRIC C

Trunks and Scrap Border   ⅛ yard

FABRIC D

Half-Inch Border, Corner Squares,
  and Binding   ½ yard

BACKING   ⅞ yard

BATTING   ⅞ yard

Cutting Directions

Prewash and press all of your fabrics. Using a rotary cutter, see-through ruler, and cutting mat, prepare the strips as described in the first column in the chart on the opposite page. Then from those strips, cut the pieces listed in the second column. Some portions of the quilt need to be cut only once, so no additional cutting information will appear in the second column. Measurements for all pieces include ¼-inch seam allowances.

♡ **SEW CREATIVE** ♡

If you are making a quilt with a Christmas theme, you could embellish it by sewing buttons, stars, and other small ornaments on your trees and in the corner squares.

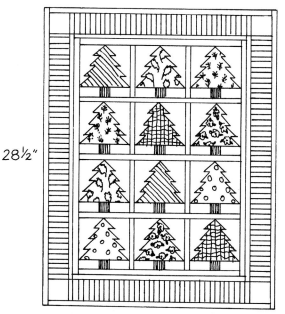

TWELVE-TREE QUILT LAYOUT

	FIRST CUT		SECOND CUT	
	NO. OF STRIPS	**DIMENSIONS**	**NO. OF PIECES**	**DIMENSIONS**
FABRIC A	**Trees:** from *each* of the *six* fabrics, cut the following			
	1	5½ × 44-inch strip	1	5½ × 10-inch piece
	1	1½ × 44-inch strip	2	1½ × 3½-inch pieces
			2	1½ × 2½-inch pieces
			2	1½-inch squares
	Scrap Border: from *each* of the *six* fabrics, cut the following			
	2	1 × 44-inch strips		
FABRIC B	**Block Background**			
	2	5½ × 44-inch strips	6	5½ × 10-inch pieces
	5	1½ × 44-inch strips	24	1½ × 2½-inch pieces
			24	1½ × 2-inch pieces
			24	1½-inch squares
			24	1½ × 1-inch pieces
	Lattice			
	Before You Cut: From *four* of the 44-inch strips, cut the pieces listed in the second column. The remaining two strips need no further cutting.			
	6	1 × 44-inch strips	8	1 × 5½-inch pieces
			5	1 × 22-inch strips
	Scrap Border			
	2	1 × 44-inch strips		
FABRIC C	**Trunks**			
	1	1½ × 44-inch strip	12	1½-inch squares
	Scrap Border			
	2	1 × 44-inch strips		
FABRIC D	**Half-Inch Border**			
	Before You Cut: From *one* of the 44-inch strips, cut the pieces listed in the second column. The remaining two strips need no further cutting.			
	3	1 × 44-inch strip	2	1 × 22-inch strips
	Corner Squares			
	1	2½ × 44-inch strip	4	2½-inch squares
	Binding			
	4	2¾ × 44-inch strips		

Making Triangle Sets

Step 1. Refer to "Speedy Triangles" on page 231 for how to mark, sew, and cut.

Step 2. Position the 5½ × 10-inch Fabric A and B pieces with right sides together. You will have six sets. On each set draw a grid of eight 1⅞-inch squares. See **Diagram 17.**

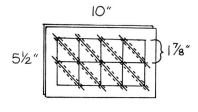

DIAGRAM 17

Step 3. After sewing and cutting are complete, press the seams toward Fabric A on two triangle sets from each combination and toward Fabric B on the remaining triangle sets. You will have made a total of ninety-six 1½-inch Fabric A/B triangle sets, sixteen of each Fabric A.

Making the Blocks

Throughout this section, refer to the **Fabric Key** to identify the fabric placements in the diagrams. Also, it's a good idea to review "Assembly Line Piecing" on page 233 before you get started. It's more efficient to do the same step for each block at the same time than to piece one entire block together at a time. Be sure to press as you go and follow the arrows for pressing direction.

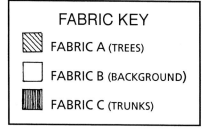

FABRIC KEY

FABRIC A (TREES)

FABRIC B (BACKGROUND)

FABRIC C (TRUNKS)

Section One

Step 1. For each of the 12 tree blocks, sew one 1½-inch Fabric A/B triangle set (pressed toward Fabric B) to another 1½-inch Fabric A/B triangle set (pressed toward Fabric A). See **Diagram 18.** Position them right sides together. Sew the first set together, then butt the next set directly behind them and continue sewing each set without breaking your thread. Press the seams and cut the joining threads.

DIAGRAM 18

In each of the remaining steps, use the same continuous-seam method. You will be making a total of 12 blocks. Match the Fabric As within each block.

Step 2. Sew 1½ × 2-inch Fabric B pieces to both ends of the 12 Step 1 units. See **Diagram 19.** Press toward Fabric B.

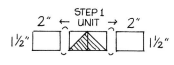

DIAGRAM 19

Section Two

Step 1. Sew 1½-inch Fabric A/B triangle sets to both ends of twelve 1½-inch Fabric A squares. See **Diagram 20.** Press toward Fabric A.

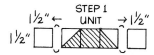

DIAGRAM 20

Step 2. Sew 1½-inch Fabric B squares to both ends of the twelve Step 1 units. See **Diagram 21.** Press toward Fabric B.

DIAGRAM 21

Section Three

Step 1. Sew 1½-inch Fabric A/B triangle sets to both ends of twelve 1½ × 2½-inch Fabric A pieces. See **Diagram 22.** Press toward Fabric A.

DIAGRAM 22

Step 2. Sew 1 × 1½-inch Fabric B pieces to both ends of the 12 Step 1 units. See **Diagram 23.** Press toward Fabric B.

DIAGRAM 23

Section Four

Sew 1½-inch Fabric A/B triangle sets to both ends of twelve 1½ × 3½-inch Fabric A pieces. See **Diagram 24.** Press toward Fabric A.

DIAGRAM 24

Section Five

Sew 1½ × 2½-inch Fabric B pieces to both ends of twelve 1½-inch Fabric C squares. See **Diagram 25.** Press toward Fabric C.

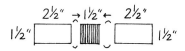

DIAGRAM 25

Section Assembly

Referring to **Diagram 26,** sew all the sections together in order. Press all seams toward Section Five. The tree blocks will measure 5½ inches square.

Lattice

Step 1. Lay out the tree blocks in a pleasing arrangement, with four rows of three blocks each. Keep track of your layout while sewing on the lattice.

Step 2. Sew the 1 × 5½-inch lattice strips to each side of the center blocks from each of the four rows. See **Diagram 27.** Press all seams toward the lattice.

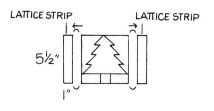

DIAGRAM 27

Step 3. Sew a block to each side of those lattice strips to make four rows of three blocks. See **Diagram 28.** Press.

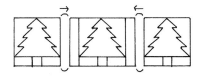

DIAGRAM 28

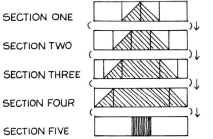

DIAGRAM 26

Step 4. Sew 1 × 22-inch lattice strips to the bottom of all four rows, and to the top of the top row. Trim the excess and press. Stitch the four rows together. Press.

Step 5. Sew the 1 × 44-inch lattice strips to the sides of the quilt. Trim and press.

Half-Inch Border

Sew 1 × 22-inch Fabric D border strips to the quilt top and bottom. Trim the excess and press all seams toward the border. Sew the 1 × 44-inch border strips to the sides of the quilt. Trim and press.

Scrap Border

Step 1. Take the sixteen 1 × 44-inch strips cut for the scrap border (two of each Fabric A, two of Fabric B, and two of Fabric C) and arrange them in a pleasing order. Sew the sixteen strips together to make an 8½ × 44-inch strip set.

Step 2. Cut this strip set into thirds, as shown in **Diagram 29.**

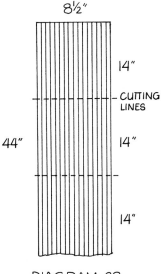

DIAGRAM 29

Step 3. Resew the thirds together to make a 14 × 24½-inch strip set. From this, cut four 2½ × 24½-inch strips. See **Diagram 30.**

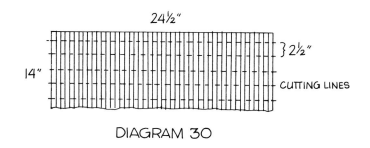

DIAGRAM 30

Step 4. See "Hints on Fitting a Scrap Border" on page 244 for details on how to fit a scrap border to the quilt. Sew the borders to the top and bottom of the quilt. Press toward the half-inch border.

Step 5. Compare the remaining scrap borders to the sides of the quilt and fit to the correct length. Measure up to the outside seam line of the half-inch border, but do not include the top and bottom borders that you just added. Then add ¼ inch to each end of the strips so they will fit correctly after the corner squares are added.

Step 6. Sew the 2½-inch Fabric D corner squares to each end of the borders. Press the seams toward the

corner squares. See **Diagram 31.** Pin the border strips with attached corner squares to the sides of the quilt; sew and press toward the half-inch border.

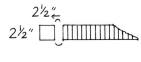

DIAGRAM 31

Completing the Quilt

Refer to "Layering the Quilt" and "Binding the Quilt" for the Four-Tree Quilt, beginning on page 76.

Finishing Stitches

Outline your trees by quilting in the ditch. Stitch a 1-inch diagonal grid in the background. Another simple option would be to outline your trees ¼ inch from the seam line and skip the background grid.

Homecoming Wreaths

Homecoming Wreaths

Come home to all the joys of the season—home-baked cookies, soft twinkling lights, and a wealth of wreaths. Choose between the Seasonal Wreath Quilt and a scrap interpretation of this design. Both feature a striking triple-checkerboard border that looks complex but is really very simple to sew.

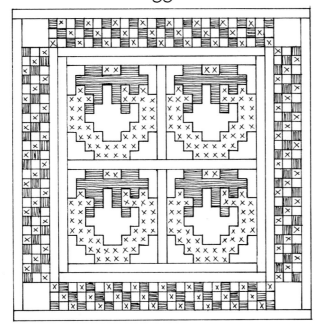

QUILT LAYOUT

Seasonal Wreath Quilt

Finished Quilt: 33 inches square
Finished Block: 10 inches square

Materials

Obvious directional prints may be used for Fabrics A, C, or D; they are not recommended for Fabric B or Fabric E.

FABRIC A

Wreaths	⅝ yard
Checkerboard Border	¼ yard
TOTAL	⅞ yard
	(1¼ yards if directional print is used)

FABRIC B

Block Background	½ yard
Lattice	⅓ yard
Checkerboard Border	¼ yard
TOTAL	1⅛ yards

FABRIC C

Bows	¼ yard
Checkerboard Border	¼ yard
TOTAL	½ yard
	(1¼ yards if directional print is used)

FABRIC D

Corner Squares	⅛ yard

FABRIC E

One-Inch Border	¼ yard
Binding	⅝ yard
TOTAL	⅞ yard

BACKING	1¼ yards
BATTING	1¼ yards

SEW COLORFUL

I used my favorite rich reds, greens, and tan in this quilt.

Background: A light tan is perfect for the background fabric. It gives a warm antique country look to the finished project. White would also work—the look would be brighter and crisper.

Wreaths and Bows: Look for an interesting multicolored green and red print for the wreaths. The print I used also has black in it, enhancing the rich feel. Avoid a print with a light background, as it won't show up against the background fabric. If the print you select for the wreath is bold and active, look for a red with a more subtle print for the bow. Two active prints would make the quilt look too busy.

Half-Inch Border and Binding: Select a medium green solid for the half-inch border and binding.

Corner Squares: Pick a deep, dark red or green or even black for the corner squares to give those elements a real visual punch.

Cutting Directions

Prewash and press all of your fabrics. Using a rotary cutter, see-through ruler, and cutting mat, prepare the strips as described in the two charts that follow. The first chart tells you how to cut the pieces for the lattice, borders, corner squares, and binding. The second chart explains how to cut strips for the blocks. Measurements for all pieces include ¼-inch seam allowances.

Cutting the Quilt Pieces	FIRST CUT		SECOND CUT	
	NO. OF STRIPS	DIMENSIONS	NO. OF PIECES	DIMENSIONS
FABRIC A	Checkerboard Border			
	5	1½ × 44-inch strips		
FABRIC B	Lattice			
	Before You Cut: From *one* of the 44-inch strips, cut the pieces listed in the second column. The remaining five strips need no further cutting.			
	6	1½ × 44-inch strips	2	1½ × 10½-inch strips
	Checkerboard Border			
	5	1½ × 44-inch strips		
FABRIC C	Checkerboard Border			
	5	1½ × 44-inch strips		
FABRIC D	Corner Squares			
	4	3½-inch squares		
FABRIC E	One-Inch Border			
	4	1½ × 44-inch strips		
	Binding			
	4	5½ × 44-inch strips		

Cutting the Strips

Refer to the fabric requirements for the *blocks only.* Cut the block yardage in half lengthwise (on the fold) so you will have two approximately 22-inch-wide pieces. Then cut each of those pieces in half again, making each piece approximately 11 inches wide. Do this for Fabrics A, B, and C. It is very important to remember this cutting applies to block yardages only. If you are using a directional print for Fabric C, cut one 11 × 44-inch strip and cut all the 11-inch strips from this.

for Fabric A, cut two 11 × 44-inch strips, and cut all the 11-inch strips from these. If you're using a directional print for Fabric C, cut one 11 × 44-inch strip and cut all the 11-inch strips from this.

Cutting the Strips	FIRST CUT		SECOND CUT	
	NO. OF STRIPS	DIMENSIONS	NO. OF PIECES	DIMENSIONS
FABRIC A	Wreaths			
	3	1½ × 11-inch strips		
	5	2½ × 11-inch strips		
	5	3½ × 11-inch strips		
	2	4½ × 11-inch strips		
	1	6½ × 11-inch strip		
FABRIC B	Background			
	9	1½ × 11-inch strips		
	5	2½ × 11-inch strips		
	3	3½ × 11-inch strips		
	1	4½ × 11-inch strip		
	1	6½ × 11-inch strip		
FABRIC C	Bows			
	6	1½ × 11-inch strips		
	3	2½ × 11-inch strips		
	1	8½ × 11-inch strip		

Sewing the Strip Sets

Sew the strips together following **Diagrams 1** through **10**. Use accurate ¼-inch seam allowances. Press all seams as you go; all seams will be pressed the same direction in each strip set, and each set will alternate directions. Follow the arrows for pressing direction for each strip set and refer to the **Fabric Key** for fabric identification. All finished strip sets will be 10½ × 11 inches long. If you are using a directional print, keep the pattern running in the same direction for all the strip sets.

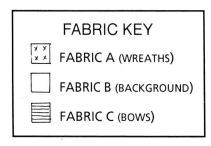

FABRIC KEY

FABRIC A (WREATHS)

FABRIC B (BACKGROUND)

FABRIC C (BOWS)

Strip Set 1. Use two 2½-inch Fabric B strips, two 2½-inch Fabric C strips, and one 2½-inch Fabric A strip. See **Diagram 1.**

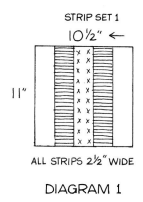

STRIP SET 1

10½" ←

11"

ALL STRIPS 2½" WIDE

DIAGRAM 1

Strip Set 2. Use two 1½-inch Fabric B strips and one 8½-inch Fabric C strip. See **Diagram 2.**

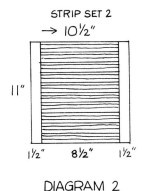

STRIP SET 2

→ 10½"

11"

1½"   8½"   1½"

DIAGRAM 2

Strip Set 3. Use three 1½-inch Fabric A strips, three 1½-inch Fabric B strips, two 1½-inch Fabric C strips, and one 2½-inch Fabric C strip. See **Diagram 3.**

STRIP SET 3

10½" ←

11"

2½"

ALL OTHER STRIPS 1½" WIDE

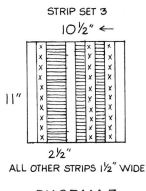

DIAGRAM 3

Strip Set 4. Use one 3½-inch and one 4½-inch Fabric A strip, two 1½-inch Fabric C strips, and one 1½-inch Fabric B strip. See **Diagram 4.**

STRIP SET 4

→ 10½"

11"

3½"   4½"

ALL OTHER STRIPS 1½" WIDE

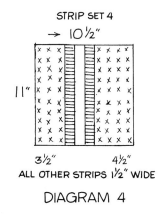

DIAGRAM 4

Strip Set 5. Use two 2½-inch Fabric A strips, two 1½-inch Fabric C strips, and one 3½-inch and one 1½-inch Fabric B strip. See **Diagram 5.**

STRIP SET 5

10½" ←

11"

2½"   3½"   2½"

ALL OTHER STRIPS 1½" WIDE

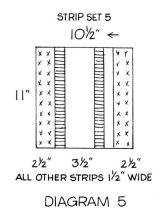

DIAGRAM 5

Strip Set 6. Use one 6½-inch Fabric B strip and two 2½-inch Fabric A strips. See **Diagram 6.**

STRIP SET 6

→ 10½"

11"

2½"   6½"   2½"

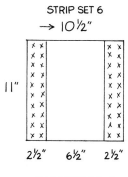

DIAGRAM 6

Strip Set 7. Use two 3½-inch Fabric A strips and one 4½-inch Fabric B strip. See **Diagram 7.**

STRIP SET 7

10½" ←

11"

3½"   4½"   3½"

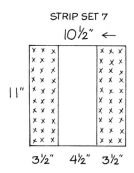

DIAGRAM 7

Strip Set 8. Use two 3½-inch Fabric A strips, and one 2½-inch and two 1½-inch Fabric B strips. See **Diagram 8.**

STRIP SET 8

→ 10½"

11"

1½" 3½" 2½" 3½" 1½"

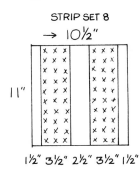

DIAGRAM 8

Strip Set 9. Use one 6½-inch Fabric A strip and two 2½-inch Fabric B strips. See **Diagram 9.**

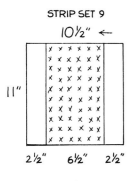

DIAGRAM 9

Strip Set 10. Use one 4½-inch Fabric A strip and two 3½-inch Fabric B strips. See **Diagram 10.**

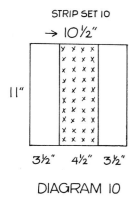

DIAGRAM 10

Stacking and Cutting the Strip Sets

Step 1. Stack the strip sets in order, with Strip Set 10 on the bottom and Strip Set 1 on the top of the pile.

Step 2. Divide this stack into three piles. Take the bottom pile (Sets 7 through 10) from your stack and cut these into four 1½ × 10½-inch strips. Cut through all the layers at once. Then cut the middle pile (Sets 4 through 6) into four 1½ × 10½-inch strips. Last, take the top pile (Sets 1 through 3) and cut into four 1½ × 10½-inch strips.

Step 3. After all the strips are cut, put them back in order. You will have four piles and each pile will have ten strips, one of each strip set. They must be in sequence, with Strip Set 10 on the bottom and Strip Set 1 on the top of each pile.

Making the Blocks

Step 1. Line up the four piles of 1½-inch strips next to your sewing machine.

Step 2. From the first pile, sew one Strip Set 1 to one Strip Set 2 (right sides together). From the second pile, again sew one Strip Set 1 to one Strip Set 2. Repeat until you have sewn all Strip Sets 1 and 2 together in all four piles. Butt all strips behind one another and sew together in a continuous seam. Do not backstitch or cut threads. Press the seams toward Strip Set 2. You will end up with four joined pieces that look like those in **Diagram 11.** Resist the temptation to cut them apart!

Step 3. Sew all Strip Set 3 pieces to the Step 2 units. Remember, do not cut the connecting threads. Press the seams toward Strip Set 3. See **Diagram 12.**

Step 4. Sew all Strip Set 4 pieces to the Step 3 units. Press the seams toward Strip Set 4.

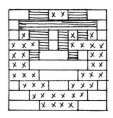
♡ **SEW CREATIVE** ♡

You need four blocks for either of the quilts, but you may choose to cut six strips (instead of four) from each strip set and make two extra blocks. Make a reusable fabric gift bag by adding borders and extra fabric. Or use your imagination to turn them into gifts or accessories!

Step 5. Sew all the remaining strips together through Strip Set 10 using the same method. Be sure to add your strips in sequence, and do not cut threads. Be careful not to flip-flop the strips when sewing them together. Most of the strips are not symmetrical from left to right. Press all seams in the direction of the piece you have just added. Once all the strips have been sewn together, you can cut the threads that join your completed wreath blocks. See **Diagram 13.** The block will now measure 10½ × 10½ inches.

DIAGRAM 13

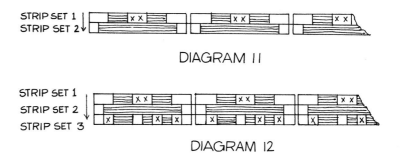

STRIP SET 1
STRIP SET 2

DIAGRAM 11

STRIP SET 1
STRIP SET 2
STRIP SET 3

DIAGRAM 12

Lattice

Step 1. Sew one $1\frac{1}{2} \times 10\frac{1}{2}$-inch Fabric B lattice strip between each pair of blocks to make two rows of two wreaths. Press all seams toward the lattice. See **Diagram 14.**

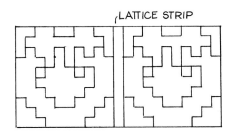

DIAGRAM 14

Step 2. Sew $1\frac{1}{2} \times 44$-inch lattice strips below each row of blocks and across the top of the top row of wreaths. Trim the excess and press.

Step 3. Sew the two rows together. Press.

Step 4. Sew $1\frac{1}{2} \times 44$-inch lattice strips to the quilt sides. Trim the excess and press.

One-Inch Border

Step 1. Sew $1\frac{1}{2} \times 44$-inch Fabric E border strips to the quilt top and bottom. Trim the excess and press all seams toward the border.

Step 2. Sew $1\frac{1}{2} \times 44$-inch border strips to the quilt sides. Trim the excess and press.

Triple-Checkerboard Border

Step 1. Sew together fifteen $1\frac{1}{2} \times 44$-inch strips of Fabrics A, B, and C, alternating fabrics, as shown in **Diagram 15.** Press all seams to the right as you go.

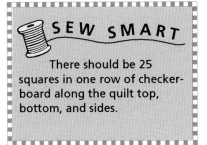

DIAGRAM 15

Step 2. Cut the strip set in half. Each half will be approximately 22 inches. Refer to the cutting line in **Diagram 15.** Resew the halves together to make a $22 \times 30\frac{1}{2}$-inch strip set. See **Diagram 16.**

Step 3. From this $22 \times 30\frac{1}{2}$-inch strip set, cut twelve $1\frac{1}{2} \times 30\frac{1}{2}$-inch strips. Refer to the cutting lines shown in **Diagram 16.**

Step 4. Fit one strip to the top of the quilt top (raw edge to raw edge). Use a seam ripper to remove the excess checkerboard. See "Hints on Fitting a Checkerboard Border" on page 245. Match up two more rows of checkerboard to equal the one fitted to the quilt edge. Sew the three strips together to create the triple checkerboard. Pin in position and sew to the quilt top. Press all seams toward the one-inch border. Repeat for the bottom of the quilt.

Step 5. Fit the remaining two checkerboard strips to the quilt sides in the same manner. Compare the strips to the quilt sides and measure up to but do not include the checkerboard borders you just added to the top and bottom. Then allow $\frac{1}{4}$ inch on both ends of each strip so they will fit correctly after the corner squares are added.

SEW SMART

There should be 25 squares in one row of checkerboard along the quilt top, bottom, and sides.

Step 6. After you have fit the strips and assembled the checkerboard borders, sew $3\frac{1}{2}$-inch corner squares to each end of the side checkerboards. Pin the borders in position and sew them to the quilt sides.

SEW SMART

If you are using a directional print for the corner squares, make sure they are positioned with the design facing the right direction.

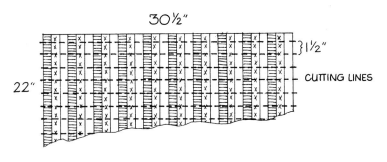

DIAGRAM 16

Layering the Quilt

Arrange and baste the backing, batting, and quilt top together, following the directions for "Layering the Quilt" on page 249. Trim the batting and backing to ¾ inch from the raw edge of the quilt top.

Binding the Quilt

Using the 5½ × 44-inch Fabric E binding strips, follow the directions on page 249 for "Binding the Quilt." Bind the sides first, then the top and bottom.

Finishing Stitches

Outline the wreaths and bows by quilting either in the ditch or ¼ inch from the seam line. Quilt a 1½-inch diagonal grid in the background.

Scrap Wreath Quilt

Finished Quilt: 36 inches square
Finished Block: 10 inches square

Materials

Obvious directional prints are not recommended.

FABRIC A

Wreaths and	
Checkerboard Border	⅛ yard
(or scraps) *each* of *ten* fabrics	

FABRIC B

Block Background	½ yard
Lattice	⅓ yard
Checkerboard Border	¼ yard
TOTAL	1⅛ yards

FABRIC C

Bows	¼ yard
Checkerboard Border	¼ yard
TOTAL	½ yard

FABRIC D

Corner Squares	⅛ yard

FABRIC E

One-Inch Border	¼ yard
Binding	⅝ yard
TOTAL	⅞ yard

BACKING	1¼ yards

BATTING	1¼ yards

Before You Begin

Many of the assembly techniques for the Scrap Wreath Quilt are the same as those given earlier for the Seasonal Wreath Quilt. Throughout these directions, you will be referred back to the Seasonal Wreath Quilt for steps that are identical. Specific assembly directions needed for the Scrap Wreath Quilt are given in detail here.

SEW COLORFUL

Wreaths and Bows: This version uses ten different green fabrics. Choose seven or eight similar shades of medium greens and two or three darker greens for the wreath. Five of these fabrics will be used in the checkerboard border. For the bow, look for a red with a subtle print.

Background: A light, warm tan makes a perfect background fabric for an antique country look. If you want more of a bright, crisp look, use white, or a white-on-white print.

One-Inch Border and Binding: Look for a medium green solid fabric.

Corner Squares: Use a dark green or any darker fabric that goes well with the fabrics and colors you've already chosen.

Cutting Directions

Prewash and press all of your fabrics. Using a rotary cutter, see-through ruler, and cutting mat, prepare the strips as described in the two charts that follow. The first chart tells you how to cut the strips for the blocks. The second chart explains how to cut the pieces for the rest of the quilt. Measurements for all pieces include ¼-inch seam allowances.

Cutting the Strips

Refer to the fabric requirements for the *blocks* only. Cut the block yardage in half lengthwise (on the fold) so you will have two approximately 22-inch-wide pieces. Then cut each of those pieces in half again, making each piece approximately 11 inches wide. Do this for Fabrics A, B, and C. It is very important to remember this cutting applies to block yardages only.

Cutting the Strips

	FIRST CUT		SECOND CUT	
	NO. OF STRIPS	DIMENSIONS	NO. OF PIECES	DIMENSIONS
FABRIC A	Wreaths			
	Before You Cut: You will be cutting a total of 42 Fabric A strips.			
	4	1½ × 11-inch strips from *each* of *eight* Fabric As		
	5	1½ × 11-inch strips from *each* of *two* Fabric As		
FABRIC B	Background			
	9	1½ × 11-inch strips		
	5	2½ × 11-inch strips		
	3	3½ × 11-inch strips		
	1	4½ × 11-inch strip		
	1	6½ × 11-inch strip		
FABRIC C	Bows			
	6	1½ × 11-inch strips		
	3	2½ × 11-inch strips		
	1	8½ × 11-inch strip		

Cutting the Quilt Pieces

	FIRST CUT		SECOND CUT	
	NO. OF STRIPS	DIMENSIONS	NO. OF PIECES	DIMENSIONS
FABRIC A	**Checkerboard Border:** from *five* of the *ten* fabrics, cut the following			
	1	1½ × 44-inch strip		
FABRIC B	Lattice			
	Before You Cut: From *one* of the 44-inch strips, cut the pieces listed in the second column. The remaining five strips need no further cutting.			
	6	1½ × 44-inch strips	2	1½ × 10½-inch strips
	Checkerboard Border			
	5	1½ × 44-inch strips		
FABRIC C	Checkerboard Border			
	5	1½ × 44-inch strips		
FABRIC D	Corner Squares			
	4	3½-inch squares		
FABRIC E	One-Inch Border			
	4	1½ × 44-inch strips		
	Binding			
	4	5½ × 44-inch strips		

Sewing the Strip Sets

Sew the strips together, following **Diagrams 17** through **26**. Intermix the ten different Fabric As. Press all seams as you go in the same direction for each strip set. Each set will alternate pressing directions; follow the arrows. Refer to the **Fabric Key** for fabric identification.

Strip Set 1. Use two 2½-inch Fabric B strips, two 2½-inch Fabric C strips, and two different 1½-inch Fabric A strips. See **Diagram 17.**

Strip Set 2. Use two 1½-inch Fabric B strips and one 8½-inch Fabric C strip. See **Diagram 18.**

Strip Set 3. Use three different 1½-inch Fabric A strips, three 1½-

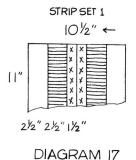

STRIP SET 1

10½" ←

11"

2½" 2½" ½"

DIAGRAM 17

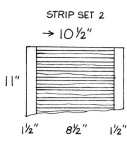

STRIP SET 2

→ 10½"

11"

½"   8½"   ½"

DIAGRAM 18

inch Fabric B strips, and two 1½-inch and one 2½-inch Fabric C strip. See **Diagram 19.**

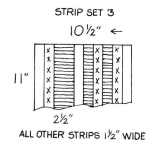

STRIP SET 3

10½" ←

11"

2½"

ALL OTHER STRIPS ½" WIDE

DIAGRAM 19

Strip Set 4. Use seven different 1½-inch Fabric A strips , two 1½-inch Fabric C strips, and one 1½-inch Fabric B strip. See **Diagram 20.**

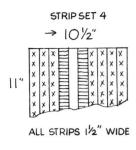

STRIP SET 4

→ 10½"

11"

ALL STRIPS 1½" WIDE

DIAGRAM 20

Strip Set 5. Use four different 1½-inch Fabric A strips, two 1½-inch Fabric C strips, and one 3½-inch and one 1½-inch Fabric B strip. See **Diagram 21.**

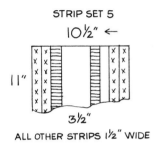

STRIP SET 5

10½" ←

11"

3½"

ALL OTHER STRIPS 1½" WIDE

DIAGRAM 21

Strip Set 6. Use one 6½-inch Fabric B strip and four different 1½-inch Fabric A strips. See **Diagram 22.**

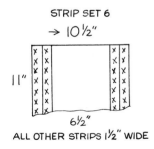

STRIP SET 6

→ 10½"

11"

6½"

ALL OTHER STRIPS 1½" WIDE

DIAGRAM 22

Strip Set 7. Use six different 1½-inch Fabric A strips and one 4½-inch Fabric B strip. See **Diagram 23.**

Strip Set 8. Use six different 1½-inch Fabric A strips, and one 2½-inch and two 1½-inch Fabric B strips. See **Diagram 24.**

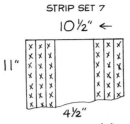

STRIP SET 7

10½" ←

11"

4½"

ALL OTHER STRIPS 1½" WIDE

DIAGRAM 23

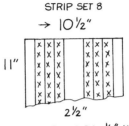

STRIP SET 8

→ 10½"

11"

2½"

ALL OTHER STRIPS 1½" WIDE

DIAGRAM 24

Strip Set 9. Use six different 1½-inch Fabric A strips and two 2½-inch Fabric B strips. See **Diagram 25.**

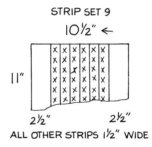

STRIP SET 9

10½" ←

11"

2½"   2½"

ALL OTHER STRIPS 1½" WIDE

DIAGRAM 25

Strip Set 10. Use four different 1½-inch Fabric A strips and two 3½-inch Fabric B strips. See **Diagram 26.**

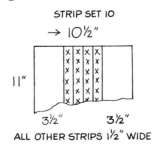

STRIP SET 10

→ 10½"

11"

3½"   3½"

ALL OTHER STRIPS 1½" WIDE

DIAGRAM 26

Making the Blocks

Follow the steps in "Stacking and Cutting the Strip Sets" through "Making the Blocks" for the Seasonal Wreath Quilt, beginning on page 86.

Lattice

Using the 1½-inch Fabric B lattice strips, follow Steps 1 through 5 in "Lattice" for the Seasonal Wreath Quilt, beginning on page 87.

One-Inch Border

Step 1. Sew 1½ × 44-inch Fabric E border strips to the quilt top and bottom. Trim the excess and press all seams toward the border.

Step 2. Sew the remaining two 44-inch border strips to the quilt sides. Trim the excess and press.

Triple-Checkerboard Border

Using the 15 checkerboard strips (one each of five different Fabric As and five each of Fabrics B and C), follow all the steps under "Triple-Checkerboard Border" for the Seasonal Wreath Quilt, beginning on page 87.

Completing the Quilt

Refer to "Layering the Quilt" through "Finishing Stitches" for the Seasonal Wreath Quilt, beginning on page 88.

Starlight Stockings and Appliqué Magic

Create a joyous collection of Christmas stockings and appliqué pleasures for family and friends! While you have your appliqué fabrics out to make the Starlight Stockings, cut extra shapes to apply to paper gift bags, wrapping paper, greeting cards, and even wooden boxes, as shown in the photograph above. Penstitch appliqué (no-sew!) makes each design fast and fun—a real timesaver during the hectic holidays. Have a Merry Christmas, and may all your stockings be full!

Stocking

Finished Size: 6½ × 21½ inches

Materials

STOCKING

Stocking Bottom and Backing	⅓ yard
Stocking Top	¼ yard (or 7-inch square)
Accent Strip	⅛ yard (or 1 × 7-inch strip)
Lining	⅓ yard (or ⅔ yard, if fabric is less than 44 inches wide)

APPLIQUÉ DESIGNS

Coordinated scraps (approximately 5 × 9-inch pieces), or ⅛ yard *each* of several coordinated fabrics

NOTIONS AND SUPPLIES

Nonsewable appliqué film
Black, extra-fine point, permanent felt-tip pen

SEW COLORFUL

For a country Christmas look, rely on deep greens and dark, muted reds, with accents of tan and black. If you are making several stockings, select a variety of colors and prints so they will look attractive when lined up next to each other. Make sure the fabrics used on the top and bottom of the stocking have varying visual textures. The accent strip between these fabrics should act as a nice contrast between the two parts of the stocking. Use the theme of the designs to help you choose fabrics. I selected a fabric that looks like falling snow to go behind the snowman. As a backdrop for the angel, I used a fabric sprinkled with stars. The red-and-white candy-cane stripe makes a cheerful setting for the Santa. Just make sure the stocking fabrics and the appliqué designs have good contrast. Have fun with them!

Cutting

Use a rotary cutter or scissors, see-through ruler, and cutting mat to cut the pieces as directed below. Measurements for all pieces include ¼-inch seam allowances.

Step 1. Trace the **Stocking Pattern** on pages 100 and 101 onto tracing paper or nonfusible interfacing to make your pattern. Place the pattern on the right side of your fabric and cut one stocking bottom. Also, cut one 1 × 5-inch strip from this fabric for a hanger.

Step 2. For the stocking top, cut one 7-inch square.

Step 3. Cut one 1 × 7-inch strip from the fabric you are using as the accent between the stocking top and bottom.

Making the Stocking

Step 1. Sew the 1 × 7-inch accent strip to the bottom of the 7-inch square stocking top. See **Diagram 1.** Press toward the accent strip.

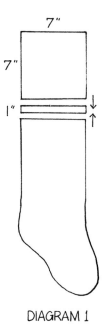

DIAGRAM 1

Step 2. Sew the Step 1 unit to the stocking bottom. See **Diagram 1.** Press toward the accent strip.

Step 3. Using the completed stocking front as a pattern, cut the stocking back. Place the stocking front and back fabrics right sides together before cutting.

Step 4. Again, using the stocking front as a pattern, cut two lining pieces. Be sure to keep the lining fabric right sides together when cutting out these pieces.

Step 5. With right sides together, sew the stocking front to the front lining at the top, as shown in **Diagram 2.** Press the seam open.

Step 6. Press the 1 × 5-inch hanger strip in half lengthwise with wrong sides together. Open the strip and press the outside edges toward the center fold. Press the strip in half lengthwise again. See **Diagram 3.** Topstitch ⅛ inch from the double-folded edge through all thicknesses. The finished strip will measure ¼ × 5 inches.

DOUBLE FOLD

FOLD

DIAGRAM 3

Step 7. Fold the hanger in half and baste it to the right side of the stocking back, with the loop pointing toward the bottom of the stocking. Position it ½ inch from the raw edge on the heel side of the stocking. See **Diagram 4.**

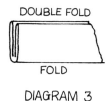

½"

STOCKING BACK
(FABRIC RIGHT SIDE)

DIAGRAM 4

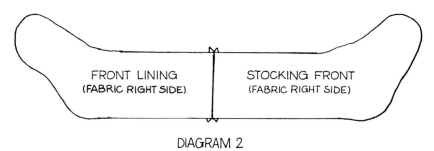

FRONT LINING
(FABRIC RIGHT SIDE)

STOCKING FRONT
(FABRIC RIGHT SIDE)

DIAGRAM 2

Step 8. Sew the stocking back to the back lining at the top, with right sides together. Press the seam open.

Step 9. Position the stocking front and lining on top of the stocking back and lining, right sides together. Pin all outside edges. Sew together, leaving a 3- to 4-inch opening in the lining section for turning the stocking right side out. See **Diagram 5.**

Step 10. Clip all curves, then turn and press. Hand stitch the opening closed.

Step 11. Push the lining down into the stocking and give it a final pressing.

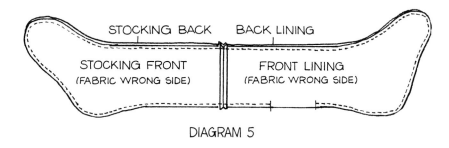

DIAGRAM 5

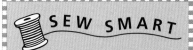

SEW SMART

To help you get nice, smooth edges when turning curved pieces, use a long-handled wooden cooking spoon with a narrow "bowl." Slide it in through the opening and push the curves with the bowl; you won't risk puncturing the fabric.

Appliqué

Step 1. Refer to "Timesaving Methods for Appliqué" on page 238 for details on the Penstitch technique. Trace and cut the appliqué designs from assorted scraps of fabric using the **Starlight Stockings Appliqué Patterns** on pages 97 through 100.

For the Angel Stocking, use the angel and the large moon with stars. For the Snowman Stocking, use the snowman and the medium and large stars. For the Santa Stocking, use Santa, the large moon, "JOY," and the small and medium stars. For the Tree Stocking, use the tree, five small trees, the small moon, and small stars.

Step 2. Center and Penstitch appliqué the designs onto the stockings and stocking tops. Refer to the **Starlight Stockings Appliqué Patterns** on pages 97 through 100, the **Appliqué Pattern Key** on page 98, and the photograph on page 92 as placement guides for designs on both stockings and stocking tops.

♥ **SEW CREATIVE** ♥

Use the black felt-tip pen to draw the snowman's mouth and eyes, and the eyes on Santa and the angel. Add an eye and a smile to the large moon, too, if you like.

Fabric Gift Bag

Finished Size: 7 × 14 inches

Materials

FABRIC BAG

½ yard
(or one 14½ × 16½-inch piece)

FABRIC BOW

⅛ yard
(or one 2 × 44-inch torn strip)

APPLIQUÉ DESIGNS

Coordinated scraps
(approximately 5 × 9-inch pieces)
or ⅛ yard *each* of several
coordinated fabrics

NOTIONS AND SUPPLIES

Appliqué film
Black, extra-fine point, permanent
felt-tip pen

Cutting, Assembly, and Appliqué

Step 1. Cut the fabric for the bag into one 14½ × 16½-inch piece.

Step 2. Turn under ¼ inch along the top (14½-inch) edge of the bag fabric and press. See **Diagram 6.** Then fold the top edge in again 2 inches and press. (This folded edge won't be stitched down until Step 4.)

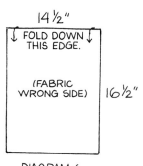

14½"

↓ FOLD DOWN ↓
THIS EDGE.

(FABRIC WRONG SIDE)

16½"

DIAGRAM 6

Step 3. Unfold the top edge. Fold the fabric in half, right sides together, so the bag measures 7¼ × 16½ inches. Pin and sew along the two raw edges using a ¼-inch seam allowance, as shown in **Diagram 7.** Turn right side out.

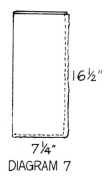

16½"

7¼"
DIAGRAM 7

Step 4. Refold and pin the top hem into position (as originally pressed in Step 2). Topstitch in place.

Step 5. Trace and cut out the appliqué design of your choice from the **Starlight Stockings Appliqué Patterns** on pages 97 through 101.

Step 6. Center and Penstitch appliqué your design to the front of the fabric bag. Refer to the photograph on page 93 as a placement guide. The seam line of the bag should be to the side.

Step 7. Put your gift in the bag and tie a 2 × 44-inch torn fabric strip into a bow around the top.

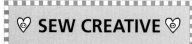

♡ SEW CREATIVE ♡

Follow these general instructions with larger pieces of fabric for larger gift bags. Add additional appliqués or fill in spaces with the stars and moons.

Appliqué Magic

These projects are all quick-and-easy ways to use Penstitch appliqué in some unexpected places. It's easy to turn ordinary brown paper into a charming country wrap, and plain paper gift bags are so simple to decorate yourself. Wooden boxes are also fun to decorate and give as gifts or fill with goodies. You can even appliqué your Christmas cards. The appliqués for these projects were designed especially for the Penstitch appliqué technique described on page 240. Follow the directions for appliquéing the designs on fabric as you branch out and try these other creative places to use appliqué.

Materials for All Appliqué Projects

APPLIQUÉ DESIGNS

Several coordinated scraps (approximately 5 × 9-inch pieces), or ⅛ yard *each* of several fabrics

NOTIONS AND SUPPLIES

Appliqué film
Black, extra-fine point, permanent felt-tip pen

Wrapping Paper

Materials: Kraft brown wrapping paper large enough for your gift; torn fabric strips for bow (½ to 1 inch wide)

What to do: Wrap a package in brown paper and fuse a design onto it. Tear strips of coordinating fabric and tie them into a bow around your package for a rustic, country look.

Paper Gift Bag

Materials: Kraft brown shopping bag, 7¾ × 9½ inches (if your favorite shop doesn't carry shopping bags, see "Quilting by Mail" on page 255 for ordering information); tissue paper; torn fabric for bow (½ to 1 inch wide)

What to do: Just appliqué your design to the front, line with tissue paper, tie on a fabric bow, and add your gift!

Christmas Card

Finished Size: 5½ × 8½ inches

Materials: Card stock, 8½ × 11 inches (stationery stores and print shops carry a variety of paper and envelopes for gift cards)

What to do: Fold 8½ × 11-inch card stock paper in half to 5½ × 8½ inches, appliqué your design, and write your Christmas greetings inside.

Shaker Box

Materials: 7 × 9-inch oval box (a variety of sizes are available at craft stores); acrylic folk art paint

What to do: If your box is unfinished, paint or stain it, let it dry, then add your design. Since it may take longer to fuse your designs onto the hard surface of a box, you may want to lay a press cloth on top of the design while pressing. See what creative ideas you can come up with!

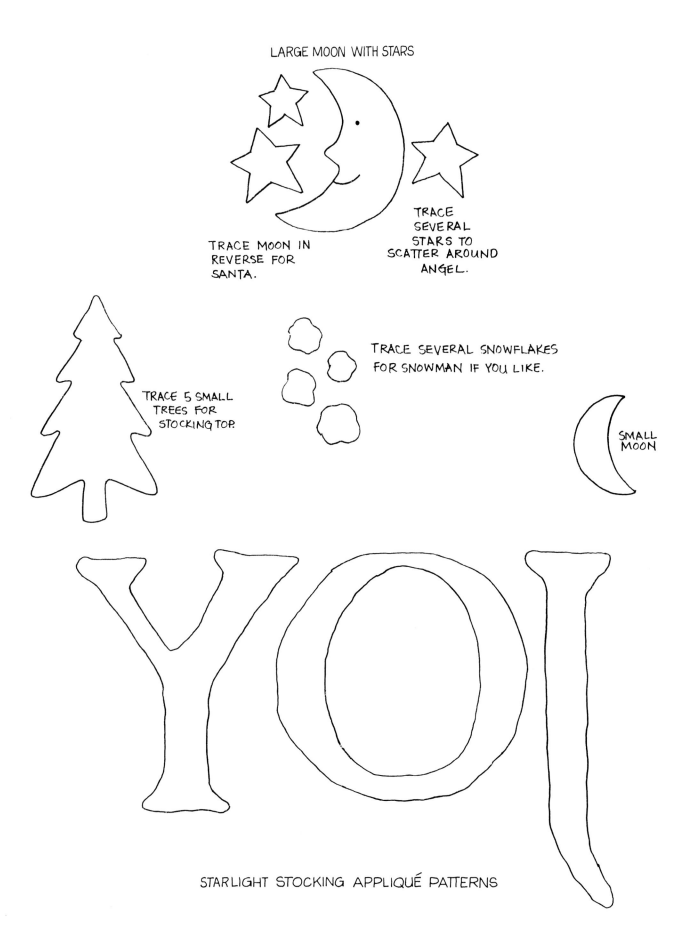

LARGE MOON WITH STARS

TRACE MOON IN REVERSE FOR SANTA.

TRACE SEVERAL STARS TO SCATTER AROUND ANGEL.

TRACE 5 SMALL TREES FOR STOCKING TOP.

TRACE SEVERAL SNOWFLAKES FOR SNOWMAN IF YOU LIKE.

SMALL MOON

STARLIGHT STOCKING APPLIQUÉ PATTERNS

Appliqué Pattern Key

——————— Tracing Line

- - - - - - Tracing Line
(will be hidden
behind other fabric)

SMALL STARS

LARGE STAR

MEDIUM
STAR

LARGE STAR

MEDIUM
STAR

STARLIGHT STOCKING APPLIQUÉ PATTERNS

CUTTING LINE

STOCKING PATTERN

SECTION A

MATCH DOTS WITH SECTION B
TO COMPLETE PATTERN.

Appliqué Pattern Key

———— Tracing Line

- - - - - Tracing Line
(will be hidden
behind other fabric)

STARLIGHT STOCKING APPLIQUÉ PATTERNS

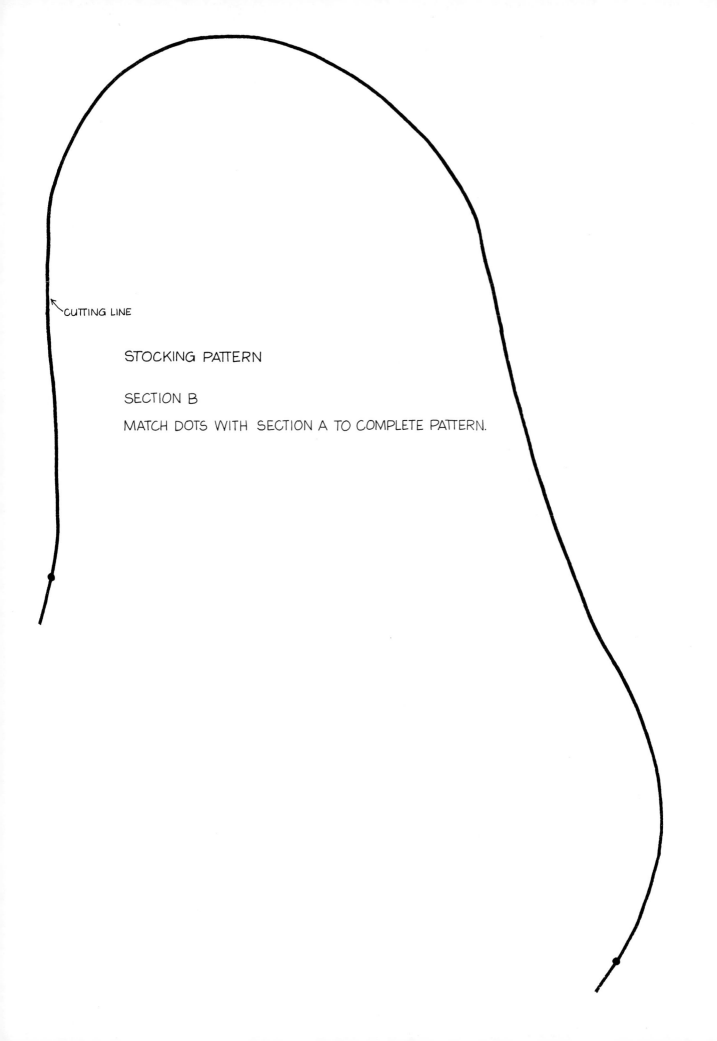

CUTTING LINE

STOCKING PATTERN

SECTION B

MATCH DOTS WITH SECTION A TO COMPLETE PATTERN.

Star-Spangled Santas

BANNER LAYOUT

Stars and Stripes Santa Banner

Finished Size: 11 × 16 inches

Put out the milk and cookies . . . wave the red, white, and blue . . . Santa's here in all his patriotic pride. Celebrate the season with a trio of star-studded Santas using quick Penstitch appliqué techniques. Choose your favorite from among the stars and stripes banner, the flag-waving Santa flanked by appliquéd stars, and the three whimsical gnome Santas with starry borders. And have yourself a merry little star-spangled season!

Materials and Cutting

Using a rotary cutter, see-through ruler, and cutting mat, prepare the pieces as directed in the chart below. Measurements for all pieces include ¼-inch seam allowances.

	YARDAGE	CUTTING	
		NO. OF PIECES	**DIMENSIONS**
Background	⅜ yard	1	8½ × 10½-inch piece
Backing		1	13 × 19-inch piece
Appliqué Pieces	⅛ yard each (or scraps) of several coordinated fabrics		
Top Border	¼ yard	1	2½ × 10½-inch piece
Triangle		1	triangle (use the **Triangle Template** on page 111)
	¼ yard	**Before You Cut:** From this strip, cut three 1 × 10½-inch strips.	
Lattice		1	1 × 44-inch strip
Binding		2	1 × 44-inch strips
Hanger		1	2 × 44-inch strip
Batting	⅜ yard	1	13 × 19-inch piece
Appliqué film Black, extra-fine point, permanent felt-tip pen			

Assembly

Press all seams toward the lattice and binding strips. Refer to the **Fabric Key** for fabric identification and to **Diagram 1** and the instructions that follow for piecing sequence.

FABRIC KEY

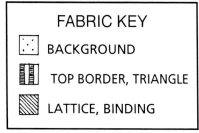

BACKGROUND

TOP BORDER, TRIANGLE

LATTICE, BINDING

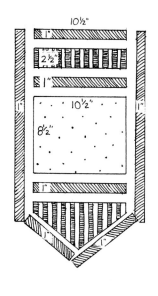

DIAGRAM 1

Step 1. Sew 1 × 10½-inch lattice strips to the top and bottom of the 2½ × 10½-inch top border piece. Press.

Step 2. Sew the Step 1 unit to the top of the 8½ × 10½-inch background piece. Press.

Step 3. Sew a 1 × 10½-inch lattice strip to the top of the triangle. Press.

Step 4. Sew a 1 × 44-inch binding strip to the bottom left side of the triangle. Press. Trim the excess, as shown in **Diagram 2.** Sew the re-

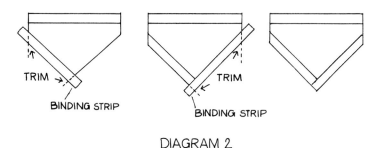

DIAGRAM 2

Step 2. Clip and trim the seam allowances in the corners. Turn right side out and hand stitch the opening closed.

Step 3. Machine or hand quilt in the ditch around the lattice and binding. Hand quilt about 1/16 inch from the edge of the Santa appliqué.

mainder of the 44-inch binding strip to the bottom right side of the triangle. Press. Trim the excess as shown.

Step 5. Sew the triangle unit to the bottom of the 8½ × 10½-inch background piece. Press.

Step 6. Cut the remaining 1 × 44-inch binding strip in half. Sew one half to each side of the wallhanging. Press. Trim the excess.

Step 7. Fold the 2 × 44-inch hanger strip in half lengthwise with right sides together. Stitch. Turn right side out. Press. Cut the hanger strip in half. Position the hangers approximately 1 inch in from the sides of the wallhanging at a 45 degree angle, as shown in **Diagram 3**. Baste into position.

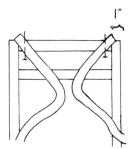

DIAGRAM 3

Appliqué

The appliqué on this wallhanging was designed especially for the Penstitch appliqué technique described on page 240.

Step 1. Cut the appliqué designs from assorted fabrics using the **Stars and Stripes Santa Appliqué Pattern** on page 109.

Step 2. Penstitch appliqué the Santa in place. Position the bottom snow piece approximately ½ inch up from the bottom edge of the background piece. Refer to the photo on page 102 and the appliqué pattern for placement. With the black pen, add a twinkling eye to Santa's profile.

SEW SMART

Refer to the appliqué patterns as you position the pieces; the dotted lines will indicate where certain pieces should be placed underneath others.

Finishing

Step 1. Position the quilt top and backing with right sides together. Lay both pieces on top of the batting and pin all three layers together. Trim the batting and backing to the same size as the top. Sew together, leaving a 3- to 4-inch opening for turning.

Flag-Waving Santa

Finished Size: 11 × 17 inches

SANTA QUILT LAYOUT

Materials and Cutting

Using a rotary cutter, see-through ruler, and cutting mat, prepare the pieces as directed in the chart below. Measurements for all pieces include ¼-inch seam allowances.

	YARDAGE	CUTTING	
		NO. OF PIECES	DIMENSIONS
Background	½ yard	1	10½ × 11½-inch piece
		2	2½ × 10½-inch pieces
Backing		1	13 × 19-inch piece
Lattice and Binding	⅛ yard	**Before You Cut:** From these strips, cut four 1 × 10½-inch strips and two 1 × 17½-inch strips.	
		2	1 × 44-inch strips
Stars		Remaining fabric	
Batting	⅜ yard	1	13 × 19-inch piece
Appliqué film			
Black, extra-fine point, permanent felt-tip pen			

Assembly

Press all seams toward the lattice and binding strips. Refer to the **Fabric Key** for fabric identification and to **Diagram 4** for piecing sequence.

```
FABRIC KEY
[ ] BACKGROUND
[/] LATTICE, BINDING
```

Step 1. Sew 1 × 10½-inch lattice strips to the top and bottom of both 2½ × 10½-inch background pieces. Press.

Step 2. Sew the Step 1 units to the top and bottom of the 10½ × 11½-inch background piece. Press.

Step 3. Sew 1 × 17½-inch binding strips to each side of the Step 2 unit to complete the wallhanging top. Press.

Appliqué

The appliqué in this wallhanging was designed especially to use the Penstitch appliqué technique described on page 240.

Step 1. Cut the appliqué designs from assorted fabrics using the **Flag-Waving Santa Appliqué Patterns** on page 110.

Step 2. Center and Penstitch appliqué the Santa, positioning him approximately ½ inch up from the bottom edge of the large background piece. Refer to the photo on page 102 and the appliqué pattern for placement guides.

Step 3. Center and Penstitch a row of five stars to the top and bottom background pieces. Position the outer stars first, then the center star, and last, the stars in between. Use your see-through ruler as a guide and refer to the photo on page 103 for placement.

Step 4. With the black pen, add Santa's twinkling eyes.

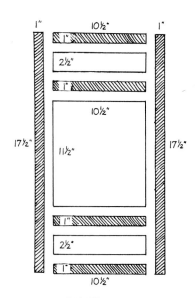

DIAGRAM 4

♥ **SEW CREATIVE** ♥

You can use any of the appliqué designs in these projects to decorate fabric gift bags or fuse them onto paper gift bags, as described in Starlight Stockings and Appliqué Magic on page 96.

Finishing

Step 1. Position the quilt top and backing with right sides together. Lay both pieces on top of the batting and pin all three layers together. Trim the batting and backing to the same size as the top. Sew together, leaving a 3- to 4-inch opening for turning.

Step 2. Clip and trim the seam allowances in the corners. Turn right side out and hand stitch the opening closed.

Step 3. Machine or hand quilt in the ditch around the lattice and binding. Hand quilt about ¹⁄₁₆ inch from the edge of the Santa and star appliqués.

Three Santa Gnomes

Finished Size: 20 × 14 inches

Materials and Cutting

Using a rotary cutter, see-through ruler, and cutting mat, prepare the pieces as described in the chart below. Measurements for all pieces include ¼-inch seam allowances.

THREE SANTA GNOMES QUILT LAYOUT

	YARDAGE	CUTTING	
		NO. OF PIECES	**DIMENSIONS**
Background	⅝ yard	3	4½ × 7½-inch pieces
Backing		1	16 × 22-inch piece
Lattice	⅛ yard	2	1 × 7½-inch strips
		2	1 × 13½-inch strips
		2	1 × 8½-inch strips
Binding		2	1 × 19½-inch strips
		2	1 × 14½-inch strips
Border	¼ yard	2	3 × 14½-inch strips
		2	3 × 13½-inch strips
Batting	½ yard	1	16 × 22-inch piece
Appliqué film Black, extra-fine point, permanent felt-tip pen			

Assembly

Press all seams toward the lattice and binding. Refer to the **Fabric Key** for fabric identification and to **Diagram 5** for piecing sequence.

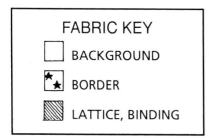

FABRIC KEY
- ☐ BACKGROUND
- ▨ BORDER
- ▨ LATTICE, BINDING

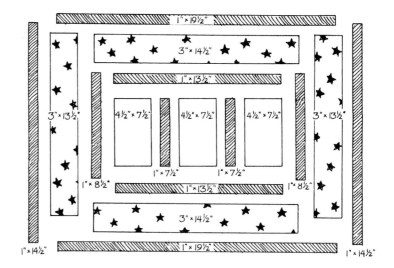

DIAGRAM 5

Step 1. Sew 1 × 7½-inch lattice strips to each side of one 4½ × 7½-inch background block. Press. This will be the center block. Sew the remaining two background blocks to each side of this center unit to make one row of three background blocks. Press.

Step 2. Sew 1 × 13½-inch lattice strips to the top and bottom of the Step 1 unit. Press. Sew 1 × 8½-inch lattice strips to the sides of this unit. Press.

Step 3. Sew 3 × 14½-inch border strips to the top and bottom of the wallhanging. Press. Sew 3 × 13½-inch border strips to the sides of the wallhanging. Press.

Step 4. Sew 1 × 19½-inch binding strips to the top and bottom of the wallhanging. Press. Sew 1 × 14½-inch binding strips to the sides of the wallhanging. Press.

Appliqué

The appliqué on this wallhanging was designed especially for the Penstitch appliqué technique described on page 240.

Step 1. Cut three Santa designs from assorted fabrics using the

Three Santa Gnomes Appliqué Pattern on this page.

Step 2. Center and Penstitch appliqué one Santa to each background block, positioning each approximately ⅝ inch up from the bottom and ¼ inch down from the top of the block.

Step 3. With the black pen, add eyes to Santa and eyes and a nose to his bear companion if you like.

Finishing

Step 1. Position the quilt top and backing with right sides together. Lay both pieces on top of the batting and pin all three layers together. Trim the batting and backing to the same size as the top. Sew them together, leaving a 3- to 4-inch opening for turning.

Step 2. Clip and trim the seam allowances in the corners. Turn right side out and hand stitch the opening closed.

Step 3. Machine or hand quilt in the ditch around the lattice and binding. Hand quilt about ⅟₁₆ inch from the edge of the Santa appliqués.

THREE SANTA GNOMES APPLIQUÉ PATTERN

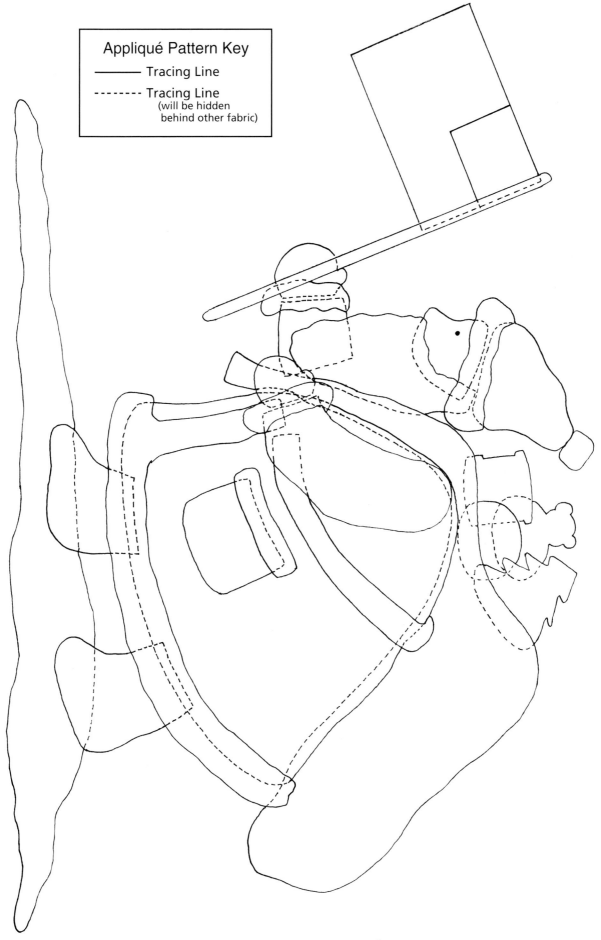

STARS AND STRIPES SANTA APPLIQUÉ PATTERN

FLAG-WAVING SANTA APPLIQUÉ PATTERNS

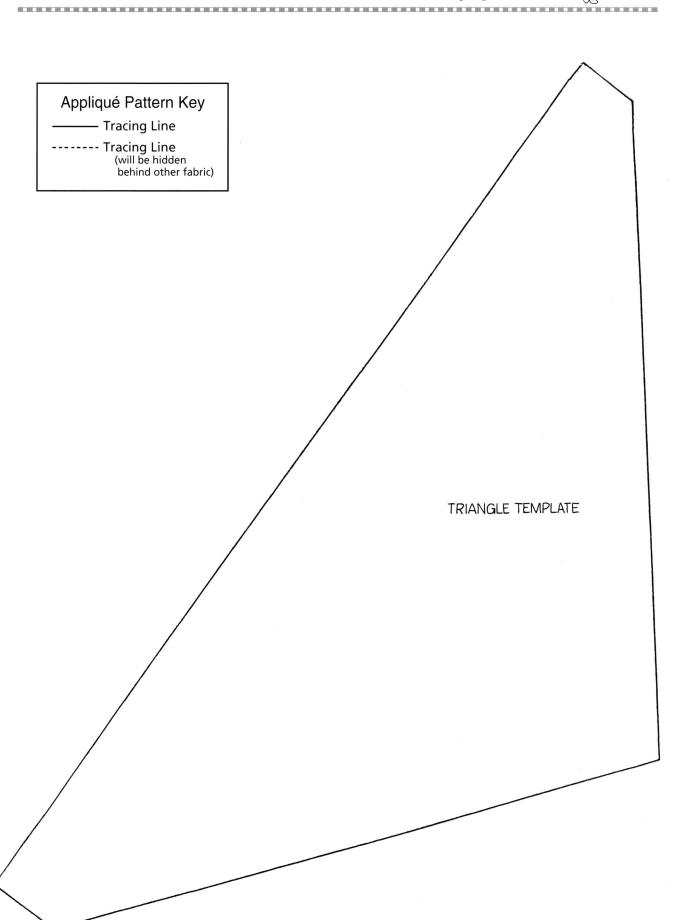

Appliqué Pattern Key
———— Tracing Line
- - - - - - - Tracing Line
(will be hidden
behind other fabric)

TRIANGLE TEMPLATE

Christmas Sampler

Capture all the warmth and charm of Christmas with these enchanting no-sew appliqué designs. Choose from two wall-hangings—one featuring a nifty collection of nine holiday designs and the other a joyful threesome of angels. You can even trim the tree with a dozen easy ornaments stitched using the featured designs. These projects go together in a twinkling with simple Penstitch appliqué techniques, leaving you lots of time to sample the joys of the season.

Ornaments

Finished Size: 3 inches square

Materials

ORNAMENT BACKGROUND

Two 3½-inch squares
   per ornament
   (⅛ yard makes six ornaments)

APPLIQUÉ DESIGNS

Coordinated scraps (or ⅛ yard
   each) of several coordinated
   fabrics

NOTIONS AND SUPPLIES

½ yard trim, braid, piping, or lace
   per ornament
½ yard ribbon per ornament
Black, extra-fine point, permanent
   felt-tip pen
Appliqué film
Smooth stuffing like FiberFil;
   shredded foam not recommended.

SEW COLORFUL

For my Christmas projects, I always prefer traditional reds and greens—the fuller and richer the color, the better. As I make new projects every year to add to my holiday decorating collection, they will all coordinate with each other. By adding a natural or tan to this color scheme, it immediately becomes "country."

Background: Use a variety of fabrics for the background. The most important consideration is whether the appliqué design will stand out against the background fabric.

Appliqué Designs: Gather all your Christmas-colored scraps together, and mix and match the print textures for an interesting combination of fabrics in your ornaments.

Appliqué

These ornaments were designed especially for the Penstitch appliqué technique described on page 240.

Step 1. Cut two 3½-inch squares for each ornament you wish to make. Cut with fabric placed right sides together.

Step 2. From the twelve **Nine-Patch Appliqué Patterns** on pages 120 and 121, choose the ones you would like to use. Trace the designs onto appliqué film and fuse the designs onto the ornament background pieces. Use the patterns and the **Appliqué Pattern Key** as guides for placing the pieces. Be sure to center the design, allowing for ¼-inch seams

all the way around. When everything is fused in place, use the black pen to draw in facial features on the cat, bear, doll, horse, goose, Santa, and angel.

♡ SEW CREATIVE ♡

In addition to being fun tree decorations, these ornaments make impressive gift package decorations. For an inspirational aroma, add Christmas-scented potpourri to your stuffing.

Making the Ornaments

Step 1. For each ornament, cut two 8- to 9-inch pieces of ribbon for a hanger. Pin and sew to the right side of the front ornament piece, as shown in **Diagram 1.** If you wish to use lace or trim on your ornaments, choose between the methods described in Steps 2 and 3. If you are not adding any trim to your ornaments, proceed to Steps 4 and 5.

DIAGRAM 1

Step 2. Pin lace or trim to the ornament front and stitch ¼ inch

from the raw edge. See **Diagram 2.** Position the ornament back and front with right sides facing and sew together, using a ¼-inch seam allowance. Leave an opening at the bottom for turning. Turn the ornament right side out, fill it with stuffing, and hand stitch the opening closed.

DIAGRAM 2

Step 3. Here's a no-sew option for attaching trim. Sew the front to the back, leaving an opening for turning. Turn, stuff, and hand stitch the opening closed. Using a hot-glue gun, glue braided trim around the edge of the ornament.

Step 4. For ornaments you wish to leave plain, with no trim, simply sew the front to the back with right sides together, leaving an opening for turning and taking a ¼-inch seam allowance. Turn the ornament right side out, fill it with stuffing, and hand stitch the opening closed.

♡ SEW CREATIVE ♡

Stitch up a dozen ornaments, tuck them into a handsome basket, and you'll have an almost-instant gift for a hostess or someone on your Christmas gift list!

Christmas Nine-Patch Wallhanging

Finished Size: 14 inches square

Materials and Cutting

Using a rotary cutter, see-through ruler, and cutting mat, prepare the pieces as directed in the chart below. Measurements for all pieces include ¼-inch seam allowances. See "Sew Colorful" on page 116 before selecting your fabric.

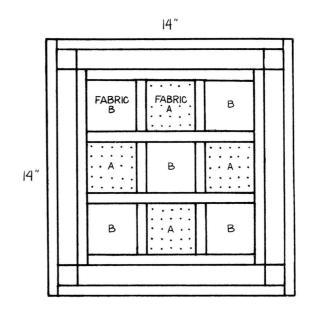

NINE-PATCH LAYOUT

	YARDAGE	CUTTING	
		NO. OF PIECES	**DIMENSIONS**
Background Fabric A	⅛ yard	4	3½-inch squares
Background Fabric B	⅛ yard	5	3½-inch squares
Appliqué Designs	⅛-yard pieces (or several coordinated scraps)		
Lattice	¼ yard	6	1 × 3½-inch strips
		4	1 × 10½-inch strips
		2	1 × 11½-inch strips
Binding		2	1 × 44-inch strips
Corner Squares		4	1½-inch squares
Border	⅛ yard	4	1½ × 11½-inch strips
Backing	½ yard	1	16-inch square
Batting	½ yard	1	16-inch square
Appliqué film Black, extra-fine point, permanent felt-tip pen			

Appliqué

The appliqué on this wallhanging was designed especially for the Penstitch appliqué technique described on page 240. Choose nine designs from the **Nine-Patch Appliqué Patterns** on pages 120 and 121. Cut the designs from the fabrics you have chosen. Fuse and Penstitch appliqué one of these designs to the center of each of the nine background squares of Fabrics A and B. Be sure to allow ¼ inch for seam allowances. Use the appliqué patterns and **Appliqué Pattern Key** as guides for placing the pieces.

Lattice

Step 1. Sew 1 × 3½-inch lattice strips to each side of the three appliquéd background squares that will be placed in the center of each row. Press all seams toward the lattice.

Step 2. Sew an appliquéd background square to each side of the three center squares to make three rows of three squares each. Remember to alternate Fabric A and B background squares, as shown in the **Nine-Patch Layout** on page 115. Press.

Step 3. Sew a 1 × 10½-inch lattice strip to the bottom of each row. Sew a lattice strip to the top edge of the top row. Stitch the three rows together, referring to the **Nine-Patch Layout** on page 115 for placement. Press.

Step 4. Sew 1 × 11½-inch lattice strips to each side. Press.

Border

Step 1. Sew 1½ × 11½-inch border strips to the wallhanging top and bottom. Press all seams toward the border.

Step 2. Sew the 1½-inch corner squares to each end of the remaining two 1½ × 11½-inch border strips. See **Diagram 3**. Pin them in position and sew them to the sides. Press.

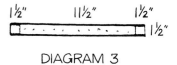

DIAGRAM 3

Binding

Step 1. Sew 1 × 44-inch binding strips to the wallhanging top and bottom. Trim the excess and press all seams toward the binding.

Step 2. Sew the excess binding strips from Step 1 to the wallhanging sides. Trim the excess and press.

Finishing

Step 1. Use the finished top as a pattern to trim the backing piece and batting to fit.

Step 2. Position the top and backing with right sides together. Lay both pieces on top of the batting and pin all three layers together. Sew together, leaving a 3- to 4-inch opening for turning.

Step 3. Turn right side out, press, and hand stitch the opening.

Step 4. Machine or hand quilt in the ditch around the background squares, border, and binding.

Joy Wallhanging

Finished Size: 13 × 16½ inches

JOY WALLHANGING
LAYOUT

Materials and Cutting

Using a rotary cutter, see-through ruler, and cutting mat, prepare the pieces as directed in the chart below. Measurements for all pieces include ¼-inch seam allowances.

SEW COLORFUL

Background: Select a light background fabric with a subtle print. The white-on-white checkerboard fabric I chose for mine adds just the right touch of sparkle to the wallhanging.

Appliqué Designs: Use a medley of cheerful red prints to create the angels' dresses, wings, and "joy." Be certain to select a variety of visual textures for these red prints, and make sure the fabrics you use for the skin tones will stand out against the background fabric.

Lattice, Binding, and Border: Use a strong green accent for the lattice and binding. A favorite red print works best for the top and bottom borders.

Appliqué

The appliqué on this wallhanging was designed especially for the Penstitch appliqué technique described on page 240.

Step 1. Using the **Angel Appliqué Patterns** on page 119, trace three angels onto appliqué film. Fuse the film onto the assorted scraps of fabric, then cut the appliqué shapes out of the fabric. Fuse and Penstitch appliqué the three angels to the 6½ × 12½-inch background piece. Be sure to allow ¼ inch for seam allowances.

Step 2. Center, fuse, and Penstitch appliqué "joy" (from the **Angel Appliqué Patterns** on page 119) to the 3½ × 12½-inch piece of background fabric. Repeat for a total of three "joy"s.

	YARDAGE	NO. OF PIECES	DIMENSIONS
		CUTTING	
Background	¼ yard	1	6½ × 12½-inch piece
		1	3½ × 12½-inch piece
Lattice	⅛ yard	5	1 × 12½-inch strips
Binding		1	1 × 44-inch strip
Top and Bottom Border	⅛ yard	2	3 × 12½-inch pieces
Appliqué Designs	⅛-yard pieces (or scraps) of several cordinated fabrics		
Backing	½ yard	1	15 × 18-inch piece
Batting	½ yard	1	15 × 18-inch piece
Appliqué film Black, extra-fine point, permanent felt-tip pen			

Lattice and Binding

Step 1. Sew 1 × 12½-inch lattice strips to the top and bottom of the 6½ × 12½-inch background piece and to the bottom of the 3½ × 12½-inch background piece. Press the seams toward the lattice. Sew the background pieces together. See **Diagram 4.** Press.

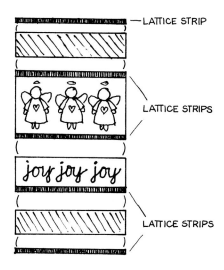

DIAGRAM 4

Step 2. Sew one 1 × 12½-inch lattice strip to each 3 × 12½-inch border piece. Press. Sew the borders to the top and bottom of the wallhanging. See **Diagram 4.** Press.

Step 3. Sew the 1 × 44-inch binding strip to the wallhanging side. Trim the excess and press. Sew the excess to the other side. Trim and press.

Finishing

Step 1. Use the finished top as a pattern to trim the backing piece and batting to fit.

Step 2. Position the top and backing with right sides together. Lay both pieces on top of the batting and pin all three layers together. Sew together, leaving a 3- to 4-inch opening for turning.

Step 3. Turn right side out, press, and hand stitch the opening.

Step 4. Machine or hand quilt in the ditch around the background pieces, border, and binding.

♡ **SEW CREATIVE** ♡

Penstitch appliqué the angel design on the opposite page to an ordinary paper bag to make a simple, inexpensive, but heavenly gift bag. Fuse the appliqué design to the bag in the same way you would fuse it to fabric.

Appliqué Pattern Key

———— Tracing Line

------- Tracing Line
(will be hidden
behind other fabric)

ANGEL APPLIQUÉ PATTERNS

USE EMBROIDERY
FLOSS TO ADD HAIR. →

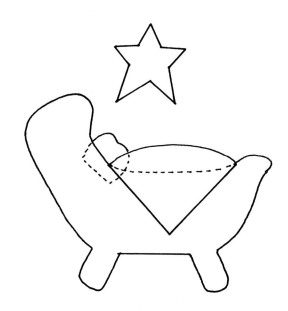

Appliqué Pattern Key

——— Tracing Line

- - - - Tracing Line
(will be hidden
behind other fabric)

NINE-PATCH APPLIQUÉ PATTERNS

DRAW IN HALO.

DRAW IN HANGER.

Gifts for Friends and Family

No one on your gift list will be left out since there's something for
everyone here. Have fun making sweatshirts, wallhangings,
banners, and fabric-covered wooden boxes. All the projects feature
no-sew appliqué, so you'll be ready with a handmade gift for any special
occasion in practically no time at all. (And don't forget that it's perfectly
all right to make a gift for yourself!)

Before you begin, take a minute to read through this checklist. These are important pointers you should keep in mind to make sure that each of your quilts is a success.

♥ Be sure you read "Techniques for More Quick Country Quilting," beginning on page 215, to familiarize yourself with fabric selection; the tools you'll need; time-saving techniques for cutting, piecing, and appliqué; as well as finishing instructions.

♥ Take advantage of the helpful hints in "Sew Colorful" at the start of each project. Here is where you'll find pointers on selecting colors and fabrics for each particular design.

♥ Prewash and press all of your fabrics.

♥ Read the step-by-step directions from start to finish, and look at all the diagrams before you cut and sew any fabric.

♥ Always use a ¼-inch seam allowance, unless there is a special note that tells you a different seam allowance is required.

♥ Refer to the **Fabric Key** for each project as a help in following the diagrams.

♥ Pay attention to the pressing directions given in the step-by-step text and to the pressing arrows shown in the diagrams.

Best Friends

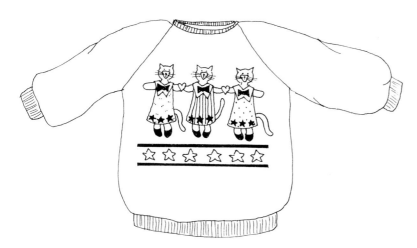

Best friend bears and cats parade three-by-three across sweatshirts and wallhangings with sentimental style. These delightful Penstitch designs are fast, fun, and easy to make. The winsome felines and chummy bears have an almost universal appeal.

Delve into your accumulated scraps to make these gifts for anyone from kids to adults. Or, indulge and make one for yourself!

Sweatshirt

Materials

SWEATSHIRT *(adult or child size)*

APPLIQUÉ PIECES

⅛ yard pieces (or several coordinated scraps)

NOTIONS AND SUPPLIES

Appliqué film
　Choose an appliqué film that doesn't need the edges sewn to remain intact and is laundry safe. Check manufacturer's instructions.

Black, extra-fine point, permanent felt-tip pen

SEW COLORFUL

The patriotic trio of red, white, and blue always works well together, and it looks great with jeans. But go with whatever three colors you like.

Sweatshirt: Choose a light-color sweatshirt if you want the design to really stand out. If you like a more subtle look, choose a medium color. You could even choose a very dark sweatshirt and keep the appliqué fabrics light.

Appliqué Designs: Gather scraps from your color scheme and vary the prints you use. The fabric for the face and head should have some contrast with each other, but should not be too dark. You want to be able to see the pen markings for the eyes and noses.

Appliqué

The appliqué on this sweatshirt was designed especially for the Penstitch appliqué technique described on page 240. The instructions are the same for both the adult- and child-size sweatshirts. However, you may opt to use fewer characters to fit on smaller sweatshirts. Use tender loving care when laundering Penstitch appliqué projects. See the tips on page 241.

Step 1. Prewash the sweatshirt and all fabrics. Press the fabrics.

Step 2. Cut appliqué designs from assorted scraps of fabric using the **Best Friends Appliqué Patterns** on page 129.

Step 3. Center and Penstitch appliqué either the bears or the cats approximately 1½ to 2 inches below the neckline rib. For the cat design, position with hands touching. Refer to the **Best Friends Appliqué Patterns** and the **Appliqué Pattern Key** for help in placing the pieces.

SEW CREATIVE

Kittens and mittens bring back memories of the childhood nursery rhyme! If you're making the cat sweatshirt, you may want to substitute the mitten designs for the stars. Just cut out three sets of mittens and six hearts. Center them between the narrow strips and fuse.

Step 4. To cut the narrow strips below the design, first cut a 1 × 13-inch strip of appliqué film and fuse it to the selected fabric. Remove the paper backing. Then, using a rotary cutter and see-through ruler, cut two ¼ × 12-inch strips.

Step 5. Fuse the first strip approximately ½ inch below the bear or cat feet. Fuse the bottom strip approximately 1¾ inches below the first strip. See the photograph on page 124 for a visual guide.

Step 6. Cut six stars and fuse them to the sweatshirt, centering the designs between the two strips.

Step 7. Use the black pen to draw eyes and balloon strings on the bears. For the cats, draw eyes and whiskers.

Wallhanging

Finished Size: 17 × 14 ½ inches

17"

14½"

WALLHANGING LAYOUT

Materials and Cutting

Using a rotary cutter, see-through ruler, and cutting mat, prepare the pieces as described in the chart on the opposite page. Measurements for all pieces include ¼-inch seam allowances. Assemble the quilt top before doing the appliqué. Press the seams after each sewing step.

SEW COLORFUL

Background: Use a light neutral for the background fabric.

Appliqué Designs: Decide on two basic colors and assemble scraps in those shades. Vary the types of prints to give your project the most sparkle. The fabric for the face and head should have some contrast with each other, but should not be too dark. You'll want to be able to see the pen markings for the eyes and noses.

Half-Inch Border, Binding, and Corner Squares: Tie the color scheme together by using one of your basic colors in the half-inch border, binding, and corner squares. Choose the stronger color of the two, and use a solid for best effect.

Border: A fabric of your other color choice will work well, in either a print, plaid, check, or stripe.

	YARDAGE	CUTTING	
		NO. OF PIECES	**DIMENSIONS**
Background	¼ yard	1	7½ × 12½-inch piece
		1	2½ × 12½-inch strip
Appliqué Pieces	⅛ yard pieces (or scraps) of several coordinated fabrics		
Lattice		3	1 × 12½-inch strips
		2	1 × 11-inch strips
Binding	¼ yard	2	1 × 16½-inch strips
		2	1 × 15-inch strips
Corner Squares		4	2-inch squares
Border	⅛ yard	2	2 × 13½-inch strips
		2	2 × 11-inch strips
Backing	½ yard	1	16 × 18-inch piece
Batting	½ yard	1	16 × 18-inch piece
Appliqué film Black, extra-fine point, permanent felt-tip pen			

Lattice

Step 1. Sew a 1 × 12½-inch lattice strip to the top and bottom of the 7½ × 12½-inch background piece. Sew a 1 × 12½-inch lattice strip to the bottom of the 2½ × 12½-inch background piece. Press the seams toward the lattice. See **Diagram 1**.

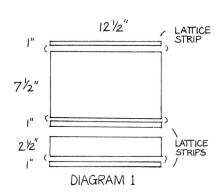

DIAGRAM 1

Step 2. Sew the top and bottom background pieces together. Press the seam toward the lattice. See **Diagram 2**.

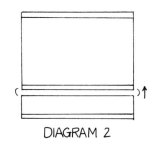

DIAGRAM 2

Step 3. Sew a 1 × 11-inch lattice strip to each side of the wallhanging. Press the seams toward the lattice. See **Diagram 3**.

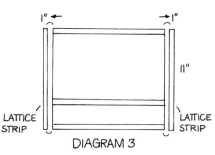

DIAGRAM 3

Border

Step 1. Sew the two 2 × 11-inch border strips to the sides of the wallhanging. Press the seams toward the lattice.

Step 2. Sew the 2-inch corner squares to each end of both 2 × 13½-inch border strips. Press the seams toward the corner squares. See **Diagram 4**.

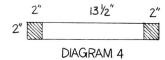

DIAGRAM 4

Step 3. Pin in position and sew the border strips with corner squares to the top and bottom of the wallhanging. Press the seams toward the lattice.

Appliqué

The appliqué on these wallhangings was designed especially for the Penstitch appliqué technique described on page 240.

Bear

Step 1. Cut appliqué designs from assorted scraps of fabric, using the bear and stars from the **Best Friends Appliqué Patterns** on the opposite page. Center and Penstitch appliqué the three bears to the 7 × 12-inch background piece. Refer to the **Best Friends Appliqué Patterns** and the **Appliqué Pattern Key** for help in placing the pieces.

Step 2. Fuse the balloon stars in place. Use the black pen to draw "strings" from the stars to the paws and mark the eyes. Penstitch around the outside of the stars on the background fabric. See the photograph on page 124 for a visual guide.

Step 3. Center and fuse five stars to the 2 × 12-inch background piece. (Again, leave space for the ¼-inch seam allowance along the edges.) Position the center star first, the outside stars next, and the in-between stars last. Penstitch around the outside of the stars.

Cat

Step 1. Cut appliqué designs from assorted scraps of fabric using the cat, mittens, and heart from the **Best Friends Appliqué Patterns** on the opposite page. Center and Penstitch appliqué the three cats to the 7 × 12-inch background piece. Refer to the **Best Friends Appliqué Patterns** and the **Appliqué Pattern Key** for help in placing the pieces.

Step 2. Fuse and Penstitch small hearts over the joined paws.

Step 3. Use the black pen to draw eyes and whiskers.

Step 4. Fuse three sets of mittens and hearts to the 2 × 12-inch background piece. Penstitch around the outside of the mittens and inside the hearts. See **Diagram 5.**

DIAGRAM 5

Binding

Step 1. Sew the two 1 × 16½-inch binding strips to the top and bottom of the wallhanging. Press the seams toward the binding.

Step 2. Sew the two 1 × 15-inch binding strips to the sides of the wallhanging. Press the seams toward the binding.

Finishing

Step 1. Use the finished top as a pattern to trim the backing and batting to fit.

Step 2. Position the top and backing with right sides together. Lay both pieces on top of the batting and pin all three layers together. Sew together, leaving a 3- to 4-inch opening for turning.

Step 3. Turn right side out, press, and hand stitch the opening.

Step 4. Machine or hand quilt on the seam line around all lattice strips, corner squares, and binding. Hand quilt ¹⁄₁₆ inch from all appliqué pieces.

Appliqué Pattern Key

——— Tracing Line

------- Tracing Line
(will be hidden
behind other fabric)

POSITION **EYES** IN EITHER SPOT.

STAR
FOR
WALL HANGINGS
(BEAR)

TAIL #2

TAIL #1 AND #3

BEST FRIENDS APPLIQUÉ PATTERNS

Noah and Friends

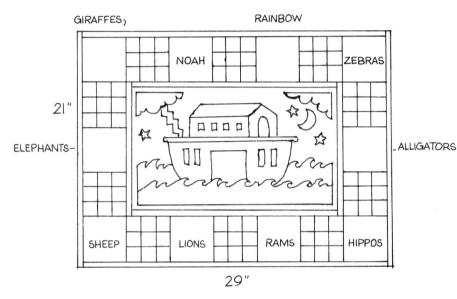

GIRAFFES
RAINBOW
NOAH
ZEBRAS
21"
ELEPHANTS
ALLIGATORS
SHEEP   LIONS   RAMS   HIPPOS
29"

QUILT LAYOUT

Embark on an age-old journey with Noah and friends! In much less than 40 days, you can create your own version of the ark surrounded by rainbows, friendly animals, and nine-patch blocks. Or, make a banner with five pairs of animal companions in a tribute to Noah's famous voyage. All aboard, everyone!

All Aboard!

Finished Quilt: 29 × 21 inches

SEW COLORFUL

The most challenging part of this project is picking the fabrics! But it's also one of the most enjoyable parts.

Appliqué Designs: The color scheme here is simple—mainly blacks and tans. There are red accents, blue water, and some cheerful, bright colors for the animals. As long as the accent colors aren't too overpowering, they will blend in nicely. Find a lively stripe for the zebras, and a swirly, curly fabric for the lion's mane.

Background: Set the scene for "40 nights" with black, starry background fabric. If you can't find a fabric with stars, appliqué a few on. Choose a light neutral for the background of the border blocks so the animals will stand out well.

Nine-Patch Blocks: Use mostly medium fabrics, but include one dark and one light in each block. That way the fabrics will blend together and won't compete with the animals.

Binding: A dark, solid binding will frame your wallhanging nicely.

	YARDAGE	CUTTING	
		NO. OF PIECES	DIMENSIONS
Center Background	⅓ yard	1	11½ × 19½-inch piece
Border Background	⅓ yard	10	4½-inch squares
Nine-Patches	⅛ yard (or one 1⅞ × 21-inch strip) *each* of *nine* fabrics	1	1⅞ × 21-inch strip *each* of *nine* fabrics
Half-Inch Border	⅛ yard	2 2	1 × 19½-inch strips 1 × 12½-inch strips
Binding	⅓ yard	4	2¾ × 44-inch strips
Backing	⅔ yard		
Batting	⅔ yard		
Appliqué Designs	⅛-yard pieces (or scraps) of several coordinated fabrics, plus one 10 × 12-inch piece for ark		
Appliqué film Black, extra-fine point, permanent felt-tip pen			

Materials and Cutting

Using a rotary cutter, see-through ruler, and cutting mat, prepare the pieces as described in the chart on this page. Measurements for all pieces include ¼-inch seam allowances.

Appliqué

The appliqué in this wallhanging was designed especially for the Penstitch appliqué technique described on page 240.

Step 1. Cut appliqué designs from assorted scraps of fabric using the **All Aboard Appliqué Patterns** starting on page 136.

Step 2. Penstitch appliqué the main center designs to the 11½ × 19½-inch background piece. Follow the numbers on the appliqué pieces for the order in which to fuse them. The water and cloud sections are positioned 1 inch from the edge of the background piece. When these pieces are fused, follow with the remaining details. Use the **All Aboard Appliqué Patterns**, the **Appliqué Pattern Key**, and the photograph on page 130 as placement guides.

Step 3. Penstitch appliqué the pairs of animals, Noah, and the rainbow to the ten 4½-inch background squares. Center the designs and be sure to allow for ¼-inch

seam allowances all the way around the squares.

Step 4. Use the black pen to draw eyes, mouths, and noses.

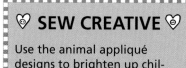

♡ **SEW CREATIVE** ♡

Use the animal appliqué designs to brighten up children's sweatshirts (see page 125), backpacks, or canvas tote bags.

Nine-Patch Blocks

Step 1. Arrange the nine 1⅞ × 21-inch nine-patch strips into three sets of three strips each. Sew them together into three 4⅝ × 21-inch strip sets. See **Diagram 1.** Press all seams in each strip set in one direction.

Step 2. Cut each strip set into ten 1⅞ × 4⅝-inch sections. See **Diagram 2.**

Step 3. Re-sew the sections together into nine-patch blocks, as shown in **Diagram 3.** Alternate arrangements of sections to make random patterns. You may need to flip-flop or re-press the seam allowances so they fall in opposite directions for easier sewing. Sew ten nine-patch blocks. Press.

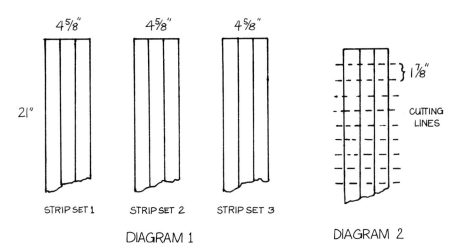

4⅝"   4⅝"   4⅝"

21"

} 1⅞"

CUTTING LINES

STRIP SET 1   STRIP SET 2   STRIP SET 3

DIAGRAM 1   DIAGRAM 2

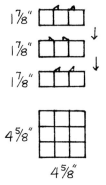

1⅞"
1⅞"
1⅞"

4⅝"

4⅝"

DIAGRAM 3

Step 4. Measure the nine-patch blocks. Because the nine-patches will be sewn to the 4½-inch appliqué squares, it is essential that the two kinds of blocks match exactly. You may need to do some trimming to make up for some slight deviations due to stitching the seams in the nine-patch blocks. If the nine-patch blocks are larger than the appliqué blocks, trim the nine-patch blocks down to 4½ inches square. Use a see-through ruler or make a 4½-inch square template and trim an even amount off all four sides of the nine-patch blocks.

Attaching the Borders

Step 1. Sew the 1 × 19½-inch border strips to the top and bottom of the center panel. Press all seams toward the half-inch border. Sew the 1 × 12½-inch border strips to the sides of the center panel. Press.

Step 2. Lay out the wallhanging using the **Quilt Layout** on page 131 and the photograph on page 130 as guides. The top and bottom border rows will alternate three nine-patches and two appliqué squares. The side borders will alternate two nine-patches and three appliqué squares.

Step 3. Keeping track of your layout, sew together the nine-patches and appliqué squares for the top and bottom borders. Press all seams toward the appliqué squares. Pin the borders in position and sew them to the top and bottom of the wallhanging. Press all seams toward the half-inch border.

Step 4. Sew together the nine-patches and appliqué squares for the side borders. Press. Pin the borders in position and sew them to the sides of the wallhanging. Press.

Layering the Quilt

Arrange and baste the backing, batting, and quilt top together, as described in "Layering the Quilt" on page 249. Trim the batting and backing to ¾ inch from the raw edge of the quilt top.

SEW SMART

Your basting needle will not glide easily through the heavier appliqué pieces. You'll need to baste around the appliqués.

Binding the Quilt

Using the four 2¾ × 44-inch binding strips, follow the directions for "Binding the Quilt" on page 249.

Finishing Stitches

In the seam line, outline the half-inch border and the nine-patches with machine or hand quilting. Quilt in the background, ¹⁄₁₆ inch away from all appliqué designs.

Two by Two Banner

Finished Size: 9½ × 26 inches

Materials and Cutting

Using a rotary cutter, see-through ruler, and cutting mat, prepare the pieces as described in the chart below. Measurements for all pieces include ¼-inch seam allowances.

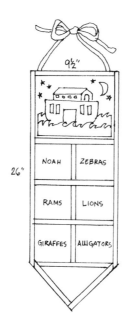

BANNER LAYOUT

	YARDAGE	CUTTING	
		NO. OF PIECES	**DIMENSIONS**
Background	⅓ yard	1	7 × 9-inch piece
		6	4½-inch squares
Large Triangle	¼ yard	1	triangle (use the **Triangle Template** on page 136)
Hanger		1	2 × 44-inch strip
Lattice	⅙ yard (6 inches)	3	1 × 4½-inch pieces
		5	1 × 9-inch strips
Binding		1	1 × 44-inch strip
		2	1 × 24-inch strips
Backing	⅓ yard	1	12 × 28-inch piece
Batting	⅓ yard	1	12 × 28-inch piece
Appliqué Designs	⅛-yard pieces (or scraps) of several coordinated fabrics, plus one 6 × 8-inch piece for ark		
Appliqué film Black, extra-fine point, permanent felt-tip pen			

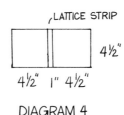

Appliqué

The appliqué in this wallhanging was designed especially for the Penstitch appliqué technique described on page 240.

Step 1. Cut appliqué designs from assorted scraps of fabric using the **Two by Two Appliqué Patterns** on page 142.

Step 2. Penstitch appliqué the ark designs in the center of the 7 × 9-inch background piece. The water, main ark piece, and larger door need to be positioned and fused first. The water is positioned ½ inch from the raw edges. Use the photograph on page 130, the **Two by Two Appliqué Patterns,** and the **Appliqué Pattern Key** as placement guides. When these pieces are fused, follow with the remaining details.

Step 3. Select six designs from the **All Aboard Appliqué Patterns** starting on page 136 and Penstitch them onto the six 4½-inch background squares. Center the designs and be sure to allow for ¼-inch seam allowances all the way around each square.

Step 4. Use the black pen to draw eyes, noses, and mouths.

Making the Banner

Press all seams toward the lattice or binding.

Step 1. Lay out the banner using the **Banner Layout** on the opposite page as a guide.

Step 2. Keeping track of your layout, sew 1 × 4½-inch lattice strips between the two 4½-inch background squares from each of the three rows. See **Diagram 4.** Press.

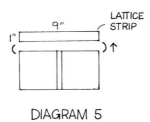

DIAGRAM 4

Step 3. Sew 1 × 9-inch lattice strips to the top of each of the three rows of two squares. See **Diagram 5.** Sew a 1 × 9-inch lattice strip to the bottom of the bottom row of two squares. Press.

DIAGRAM 5

Step 4. Sew a 1 × 9-inch lattice strip to the top of the 7 × 9-inch background piece.

Step 5. Sew together the three rows of two squares. Press. Sew the 7 × 9-inch background piece to the top of this unit. See **Diagram 6.** Press.

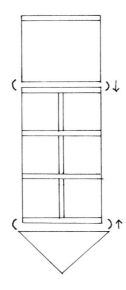

DIAGRAM 6

Step 6. Sew the triangle to the bottom of the banner, as shown in **Diagram 6.** Press. Sew the 1 × 44-inch binding strip to the bottom left of the triangle. Press. Trim the excess. Sew the remainder to the bottom right of the triangle. Press. Trim the excess. See **Diagram 7.**

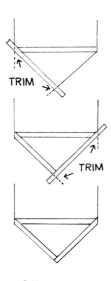

DIAGRAM 7

Step 7. Sew 1 × 24-inch binding strips to the sides of the wallhanging. Trim the excess and press. See **Diagram 8.**

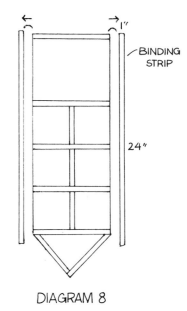

DIAGRAM 8

Hangers

Step 1. Fold the 2 × 44-inch hanger strip in half lengthwise with right sides together. Stitch. Cut the strip in half and turn the two strips right side out. Press.

Step 2. Pin each strip in place approximately 1 inch from the sides of the wallhanging, positioning them at a 45 degree angle. See **Diagram 9.** Baste in position.

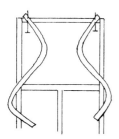

DIAGRAM 9

Finishing

Step 1. Position the top and backing with right sides together. Lay both pieces on top of the batting and pin all three layers together. Trim the batting and backing to the same size as the top. Sew them together, leaving a 3- to 4-inch opening in the side for turning.

Step 2. Turn right side out, press, and hand stitch the opening.

Step 3. In the seam line, outline all lattice and binding with machine or hand quilting. Quilt the background pieces ¹⁄₁₆ inch away from all appliqué designs.

Appliqué Pattern Key

——— Tracing Line

- - - - - Tracing Line
(will be hidden
behind other fabric)

TRIANGLE TEMPLATE

ALL ABOARD APPLIQUÉ PATTERNS

ALL ABOARD APPLIQUÉ PATTERNS

ALL ABOARD
APPLIQUÉ PATTERNS

RAINBOW- LAY DOWN BIGGEST PIECE FIRST.
OVERLAP PIECES IN SEQUENCE.
SMALLEST PIECE IS LAID DOWN LAST.

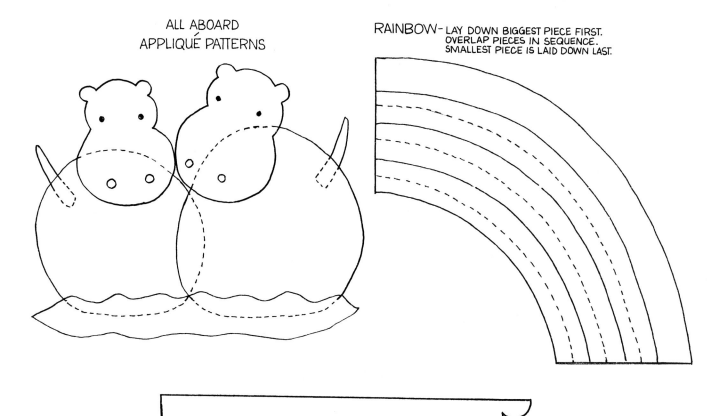

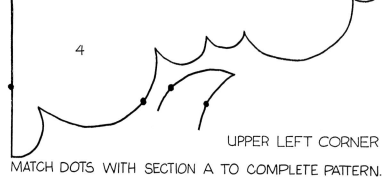

4

UPPER LEFT CORNER

MATCH DOTS WITH SECTION A TO COMPLETE PATTERN.

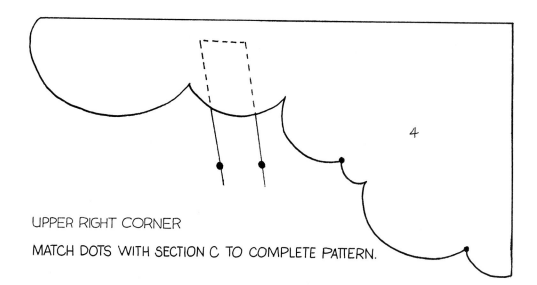

4

UPPER RIGHT CORNER

MATCH DOTS WITH SECTION C TO COMPLETE PATTERN.

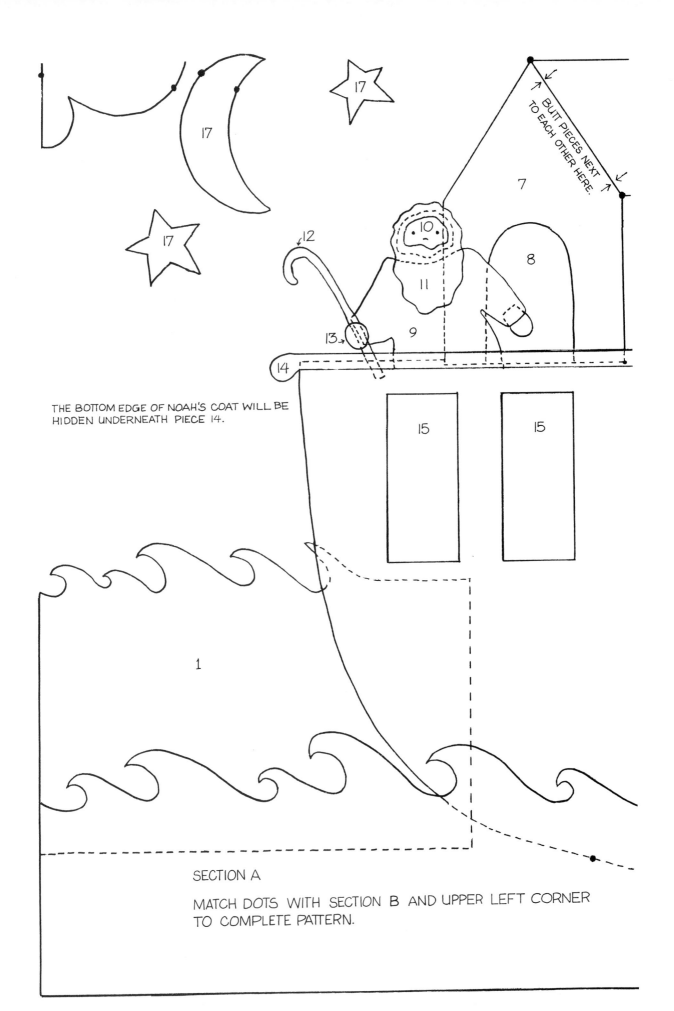

BUTT PIECES NEXT
TO EACH OTHER HERE.

7

8

17

17

17

12

10

11

9

13

14

THE BOTTOM EDGE OF NOAH'S COAT WILL BE
HIDDEN UNDERNEATH PIECE 14.

15

15

1

SECTION A

MATCH DOTS WITH SECTION B AND UPPER LEFT CORNER
TO COMPLETE PATTERN.

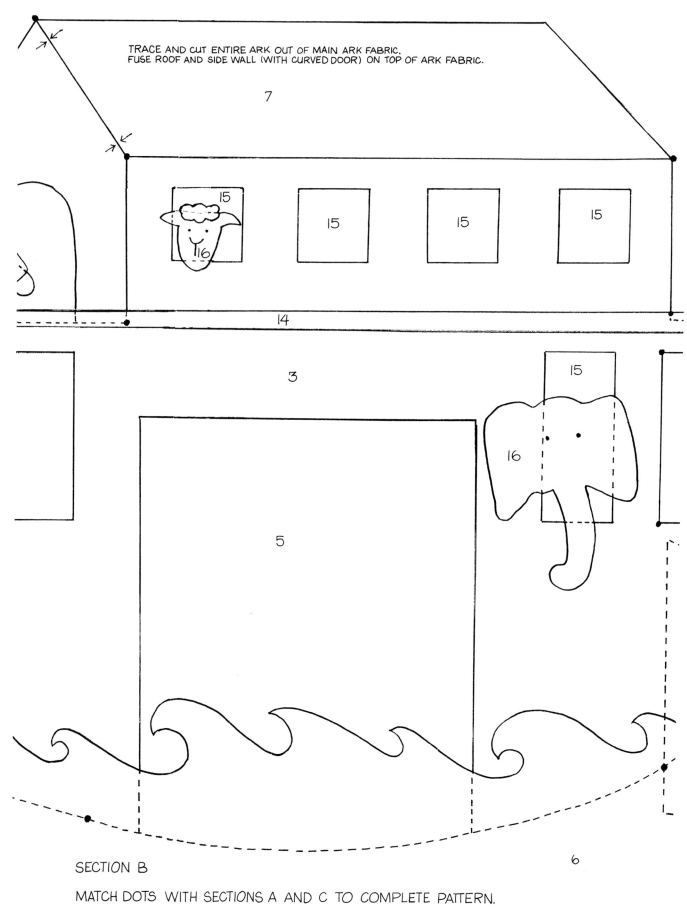

TRACE AND CUT ENTIRE ARK OUT OF MAIN ARK FABRIC.
FUSE ROOF AND SIDE WALL (WITH CURVED DOOR) ON TOP OF ARK FABRIC.

7

15

15

15

15

16

14

3

5

15

16

SECTION B

MATCH DOTS WITH SECTIONS A AND C TO COMPLETE PATTERN.

ALL ABOARD APPLIQUÉ PATTERNS

6

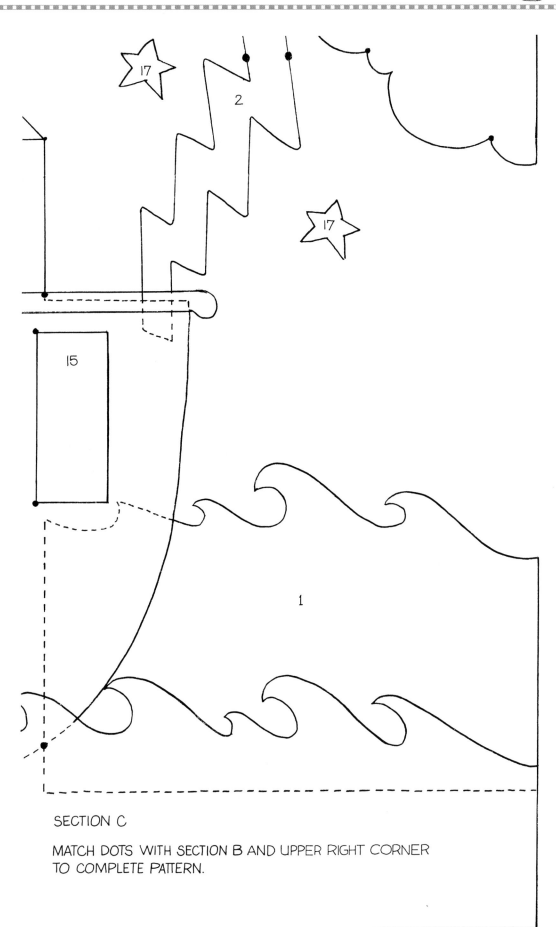

SECTION C

MATCH DOTS WITH SECTION B AND UPPER RIGHT CORNER
TO COMPLETE PATTERN.

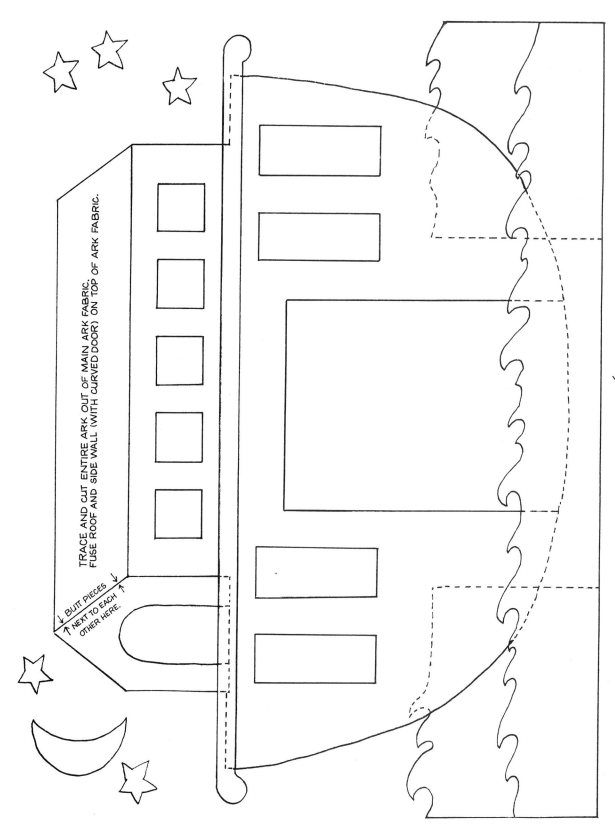

TRACE AND CUT ENTIRE ARK OUT OF MAIN ARK FABRIC.
FUSE ROOF AND SIDE WALL (WITH CURVED DOOR) ON TOP OF ARK FABRIC.

↓ BUTT PIECES ↓
↑ NEXT TO EACH ↑
OTHER HERE.

TWO BY TWO APPLIQUÉ PATTERNS

Basket Bouquets

This interpretation of an old favorite block has
baskets set around center diamonds with appliquéd hearts. Stitch a large or small version
and make a plump pillow to coordinate.

Basket Bouquets

41"

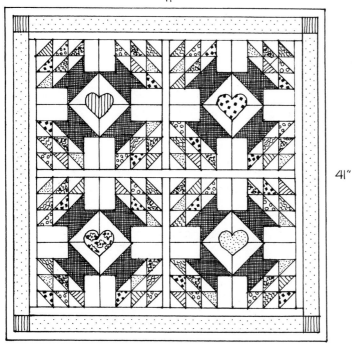

41"

BLOOMING BASKETS QUILT LAYOUT

Blooming Baskets

Finished Quilt: 41 inches square
Finished Block: 8 inches square

Materials

Obvious directional prints are not recommended.

FABRIC A

Use six fabrics.

Basket Tops, Corner Squares, and
Hearts   ¼ yard
each of *six* fabrics

FABRIC B

Block Background   1⅝ yards

FABRIC C

Use four fabrics.

Basket Bottoms   ¼ yard
each of *four* fabrics

FABRIC D

Lattice   ⅓ yard
Binding   ⅔ yard
  TOTAL   1 yard

FABRIC E

Two-Inch Border   ⅓ yard

BACKING   1¼ yards

BATTING   1¼ yards

SEW COLORFUL

The color scheme is basically two colors plus a background fabric.

Baskets: Choose four fabrics for the basket bottoms. This color should be a little stronger than the one in the basket tops. For the tops, choose one light, three mediums, and two darks, and vary the print textures. Choose four of the triangle fabrics for the hearts.

Background: Look for a light neutral with a subtle pattern.

Lattice and Binding: Choose a solid that coordinates with the color of the basket bottoms.

Two-Inch Border and Corner Squares: To pull your quilt together, look for a border fabric that combines both of your chosen colors. Pick one of the triangle fabrics for the corner squares.

Cutting Directions

Prewash and press all of your fabrics. Using a rotary cutter, see-through ruler, and cutting mat, prepare the strips as described in the first column in the chart below. Then from those strips, cut the pieces listed in the second column. Some portions of the quilt need to be cut only once, so no additional cutting information will appear in the second column. Measurements for all pieces include ¼-inch seam allowances.

	FIRST CUT		SECOND CUT	
	NO. OF STRIPS	DIMENSIONS	NO. OF PIECES	DIMENSIONS
FABRIC A	**Basket Tops:** from *each* of the *six* fabrics, cut the following			
	1	5 × 44-inch piece	2	5 × 14-inch pieces
	Corner Squares (choose *one* Fabric A)			
	4	2½-inch squares		
FABRIC B	**Background**			
	2	7 × 44-inch strips	4	7 × 12-inch pieces
			1	5 × 14-inch piece
	6	5 × 44-inch strips	16	5 × 14-inch pieces
	2	4½ × 44-inch strips	32	4½ × 2½-inch pieces
FABRIC C	**Basket Bottoms:** from *each* of the *four* fabrics, cut the following			
	1	7 × 12-inch piece		
	1	5 × 14-inch piece		
FABRIC D	**Lattice**			
	6	1½ × 44-inch strips		
	Binding			
	4	5½ × 44-inch strips		
FABRIC E	**Border**			
	4	2½ × 44-inch strips		

Making Triangle Sets

Step 1. Refer to "Speedy Triangles" on page 231 for how to mark, sew, and cut.

Step 2. Position the 5 × 14-inch Fabric A and B pieces with right sides together. You will have twelve sets. On each set draw a grid of four 2⅞-inch squares. See **Diagram 1.**

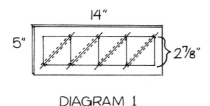

DIAGRAM 1

Step 3. After sewing and cutting are complete, press the seams toward Fabric A. You will have made a total of ninety-six 2½-inch triangle sets, sixteen of each Fabric A.

Step 4. Position four 5 × 14-inch Fabric B and C pieces with right sides together. On each of the four sets, draw a grid of four 2⅞-inch squares. See **Diagram 2.**

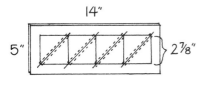

DIAGRAM 2

Step 5. After sewing and cutting are complete, press the seams toward Fabric C. You will have made a total of thirty-two 2½-inch triangle sets, eight of each Fabric C.

Step 6. Position four 7 × 12-inch Fabric B and C pieces with right sides together. On each of the four sets, draw a grid of two 4⅞-inch squares. See **Diagram 3.**

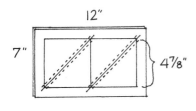

DIAGRAM 3

Step 7. After sewing and cutting are complete, press the seams toward Fabric C. You will have made a total of sixteen 4½-inch triangle sets, four of each Fabric C.

Making the Blocks

Throughout this section, refer to the **Fabric Key** to identify the fabric placements in the diagrams. Also, it's a good idea to review "Assembly Line Piecing" on page 233 before you get started. Because this project has so many different fabrics in the basket tops, I suggest assembling two blocks at a time. Be sure to press as you go and follow the arrows for pressing direction.

For each block, select one triangle set of each Fabric A (six total), and two small and one large triangle set of Fabric C for the basket base. (I didn't mix colors for the basket bases.) Lay out the pieces for two blocks next to your sewing machine.

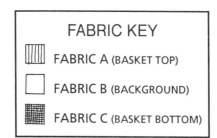

FABRIC KEY

▥ FABRIC A (BASKET TOP)

☐ FABRIC B (BACKGROUND)

▦ FABRIC C (BASKET BOTTOM)

Section One

Step 1. Sew two 2½-inch Fabric A/B triangle sets to two additional 2½-inch Fabric A/B triangle sets. Position them with right sides together, as shown in **Diagram 4.** Use the continuous-seam technique described on page 234 to join both sets together. Press the seams and cut the joining threads. Pay close attention so that the triangle sets are positioned as shown in **Diagram 4.**

DIAGRAM 4

Step 2. Sew two additional 2½-inch Fabric A/B triangle sets to the right ends of the Step 1 units. Press. See **Diagram 5.**

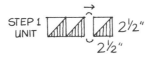

DIAGRAM 5

Step 3. Sew two 2½-inch Fabric A/B triangle sets to two additional 2½-inch Fabric A/B triangle sets, as shown in **Diagram 6.** Press the seams in the opposite direction as in Step 1.

DIAGRAM 6

Step 4. Sew two 2½-inch Fabric B/C triangle sets to the ends of the Step 3 units. See **Diagram 7.** Press.

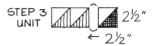

DIAGRAM 7

Step 5. Sew the two Step 2 units to the two Step 4 units. See **Diagram 8.** Press.

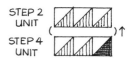

DIAGRAM 8

Step 6. Sew one 2½ × 4½-inch Fabric B piece to each of the Step 5 units, as shown in **Diagram 9.** Press.

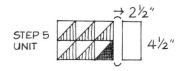

DIAGRAM 9

Section Two

Step 1. Sew two 2½-inch Fabric A/B triangle sets to two 2½-inch Fabric B/C triangle sets. See **Diagram 10.** Press.

DIAGRAM 10

Step 2. Sew two Step 1 units to two 2½ × 4½-inch Fabric B pieces. See **Diagram 11.** Press.

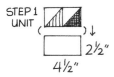

DIAGRAM 11

Step 3. Sew two Step 2 units to two 4½-inch Fabric B/C triangle sets, as shown in **Diagram 12.** Press.

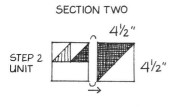

DIAGRAM 12

Section Assembly

Sew Section One to Section Two, as shown in **Diagram 13.** *Press the seam open for this step.*

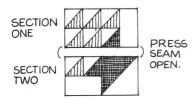

DIAGRAM 13

Repeat the steps from "Making the Blocks" through "Section Assembly," working on two blocks at a time, to complete a total of sixteen blocks.

Sewing the Blocks and Lattice

Step 1. Use the photograph on page 143 and **Diagram 14** as a guide to sew the quilt top to-

gether. Position and then sew the blocks together in sets of four.

Step 2. Cut one 1½ × 44-inch Fabric D lattice strip in half. Sew one half between each pair of blocks. Trim the excess and press all seams toward the lattice. Refer to **Diagram 14.**

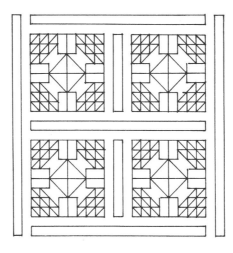

DIAGRAM 14

Step 3. Sew one lattice strip between the two rows. Trim the excess and press.

Step 4. Sew lattice strips to the quilt top and bottom. Trim the excess and press. Sew lattice strips to the quilt sides. Trim the excess and press.

Hearts

Step 1. Using leftover scraps of four Fabric As, cut out a heart front and back from each of the four fabrics for the center of each block. Use the **Large Heart Appliqué Pattern** on page 151.

Step 2. Position the heart fronts and backs right sides together and sew. Clip the curves and trim the seam allowance to ⅛ inch. Slit the back of the hearts and turn. Press.

Step 3. Pin the hearts in position in the center of each block and

hand appliqué in place. After the hearts are appliquéd to the quilt top, you may want to cut the fabric out from behind the appliqué to eliminate bulk.

Two-Inch Border

Step 1. Sew 2½ × 44-inch Fabric E border strips to the quilt top and bottom. Trim the excess and press all seams toward the border.

Step 2. Measure the sides of the quilt up to, but not including, the top and bottom borders that were just added. Allow ¼ inch on the ends of each strip so they will fit correctly after the corner squares are added. Sew the 2½-inch corner squares to each end of the border strips. Press the seams toward the border.

Step 3. Pin the border strips with attached corner squares to the sides of the quilt. Sew and press.

Layering the Quilt

Arrange and baste the backing, batting, and quilt top together, following the directions for "Layering the Quilt" on page 249. Trim the batting and backing to ¾ inch from the raw edge of the quilt top.

Binding the Quilt

Using the strips cut from Fabric D, follow the directions in "Binding the Quilt" on page 249.

♡ **SEW CREATIVE** ♡

This quilt could make a nice friendship quilt since there are lots of open, light-colored spaces where people could sign their names.

Finishing Stitches

Quilt in the ditch around the baskets, and quilt diamonds in the background squares, as shown in **Diagram 15.**

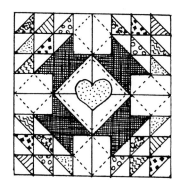

DIAGRAM 15

Little Baskets Wallhanging

Finished Quilt: 17 inches square
Finished Block: 6 inches square

LITTLE BASKETS
WALLHANGING LAYOUT

Materials

Obvious directional prints are not recommended. See "Sew Colorful" on page 144.

FABRIC A

Use four fabrics.
Basket Tops and Heart   ⅛ yard
each of *four* fabrics

FABRIC B

Block Background   ½ yard

FABRIC C

Use four fabrics.
Basket Bottoms   ¼ yard

FABRIC D

Half-Inch Border and
    Binding   ¼ yard

FABRIC E

One-and-a-Half-Inch Border   ⅛ yard

BACKING

⅝ yard, cut into 22-inch square

BATTING

⅝ yard, cut into 22-inch square

Cutting Directions

Prewash and press all of your fabrics. Using a rotary cutter, see-through ruler, and cutting mat, prepare the strips as described in the first column in the chart below. Then from those strips, cut the pieces listed in the second column. Some portions of the quilt need to be cut only once, so no additional cutting information will appear in the second column. Measurements for all pieces include ¼-inch seam allowances.

	FIRST CUT		SECOND CUT	
	NO. OF STRIPS	DIMENSIONS	NO. OF PIECES	DIMENSIONS
FABRIC A	**Basket Tops:** from *each* of the *four* fabrics, cut the following			
	1	4½ × 9½-inch piece		
FABRIC B	**Background**			
	1	2 × 44-inch strip	8	2 × 3½-inch pieces
			6	2-inch squares
	2	4½ × 44-inch strips	4	4½ × 9½-inch pieces
			4	4½-inch squares
			2	2-inch squares
	4	6-inch squares		

FIRST CUT		SECOND CUT	
NO. OF STRIPS	DIMENSIONS	NO. OF PIECES	DIMENSIONS
FABRIC C — Basket Bottoms: from *each* of the *four* fabrics, cut the following			
1	4½-inch square		
1	6-inch square		
FABRIC D — Half-Inch Border			
2	1 × 44-inch strips	4	1 × 22-inch strips
Binding			
2	2¾ × 44-inch strips	4	2¾ × 22-inch strips
FABRIC E — One-and-a-Half-Inch Border			
2	2 × 44-inch strips	4	2 × 22-inch strips

Making Triangle Sets

Step 1. Refer to "Speedy Triangles" on page 231 for how to mark, sew, and cut.

Step 2. Position the 4½ × 9½-inch Fabric A and B pieces with right sides together. You will have four sets. On each set draw a grid of three 2⅜-inch squares. See **Diagram 16.**

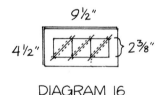

DIAGRAM 16

Step 3. After sewing and cutting are complete, press the seams toward Fabric A. You will have made a total of 24 Fabric A/B 2-inch triangle sets, 6 of each Fabric A. You will use only 20 of the triangle sets in the quilt.

Step 4. Position the 4½-inch Fabric B and C squares with right sides together. You will have four sets. On each set draw a grid of one 2⅜-inch square. See **Diagram 17.**

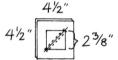

DIAGRAM 17

Step 5. After sewing and cutting are complete, press the seams toward Fabric C. You will have made a total of eight Fabric B/C 2-inch triangle sets, two of each Fabric C.

Step 6. Position the 6-inch Fabric B and C squares with right sides together. You will have four sets. On each set draw a grid of one 3⅞-inch square. See **Diagram 18.**

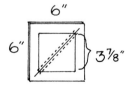

DIAGRAM 18

Step 7. After sewing and cutting are complete, press the seams toward Fabric C. You will have made a total of eight 3½-inch Fabric B/C triangle sets, two of each Fabric C. You will use only four of the triangle sets in the quilt.

Making the Blocks

Throughout this section, refer to the **Fabric Key** to identify the fabric placements in the diagrams. Be sure to press as you go, and follow the arrows for pressing direction. You will be making four basket blocks.

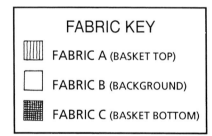

FABRIC KEY

▥ FABRIC A (BASKET TOP)

□ FABRIC B (BACKGROUND)

▦ FABRIC C (BASKET BOTTOM)

Section One

Step 1. Using the continuous-seam technique, sew four 2-inch Fabric A/B triangle sets to four 2-inch Fabric B squares. Position the triangles as shown in **Diagram 19.** Press toward the triangle set.

DIAGRAM 19

Step 2. Sew four more 2-inch Fabric A/B triangle sets to four more 2-inch Fabric B squares, as shown in **Diagram 20** on page 150. Press.

DIAGRAM 20

Step 3. Sew four 2-inch Fabric A/B triangle sets to the four Step 1 units. See **Diagram 21.** Press.

DIAGRAM 21

Step 4. Sew four 2-inch Fabric B/C triangle sets to the four Step 2 units. See **Diagram 22.** Press.

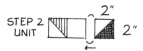

DIAGRAM 22

Step 5. Sew the four Step 3 units to the four Step 4 units. See **Diagram 23.** Press.

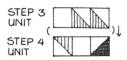

DIAGRAM 23

Step 6. Sew four 2 × 3½-inch Fabric B pieces to the four Step 5 units. See **Diagram 24.** Press.

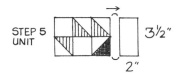

DIAGRAM 24

Section Two

Step 1. Sew four 2-inch Fabric A/B triangle sets to four 2-inch Fabric B/C triangle sets. See **Diagram 25.** Press.

DIAGRAM 25

Step 2. Sew the Step 1 units to four 2 × 3½-inch Fabric B pieces. See **Diagram 26.** Press.

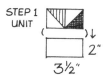

DIAGRAM 26

Step 3. Sew the Step 2 units to four 3½-inch Fabric B/C triangle sets. See **Diagram 27.** Press.

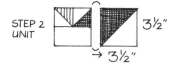

DIAGRAM 27

Basket and Block Assembly

Step 1. Sew Section One to Section Two, making sure the units are positioned as shown in **Diagram 28.** *Press the seams open for this step.*

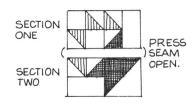

DIAGRAM 28

Step 2. Use the photograph on page 143 and the **Little Baskets**

Wallhanging Layout on page 148 as guides to position and sew the four blocks together.

Half-Inch Border

Step 1. Sew 1 × 22-inch Fabric D border strips to the top and bottom of the quilt. Trim the excess and press the seams toward the border.

Step 2. Sew the two remaining strips to the sides of the quilt. Trim the excess and press.

One-and-a-Half-Inch Border

Step 1. Sew 2 × 22-inch Fabric E border strips to the top and bottom of the quilt. Trim the excess and press the seams toward the one-and-a-half-inch border.

Step 2. Compare and fit the remaining 2-inch border strips to the sides of the quilt. Measure up to, but do not include, the top and bottom borders you just added. Allow an extra ¼ inch on the ends of each strip so they will fit correctly after the corner triangle sets are added. Sew one 2-inch Fabric A/B triangle set to each end of the side border strips, as shown in **Diagram 29.** Press.

DIAGRAM 29

Step 3. Pin in position and sew the 2-inch border strips with attached corner squares to the quilt sides. Press.

Heart

Using a leftover scrap of one Fabric A, cut out two hearts using the **Small Heart Appliqué**

Pattern on this page. Machine or hand appliqué the heart to the center of the block. Follow Steps 2 and 3 under "Hearts" for Blooming Baskets on page 147.

Layering the Quilt

Arrange and baste the backing, batting, and quilt top together, following the directions for "Layering the Quilt" on page 249. Trim the batting and backing to ¼ inch from the raw edge of the quilt top.

Binding the Quilt

Using the four 2¾ × 22-inch binding strips, follow the directions for "Binding the Quilt" on page 249.

Finishing Stitches

Quilt in the ditch around the baskets and heart. Stitch a diamond in each of the background squares.

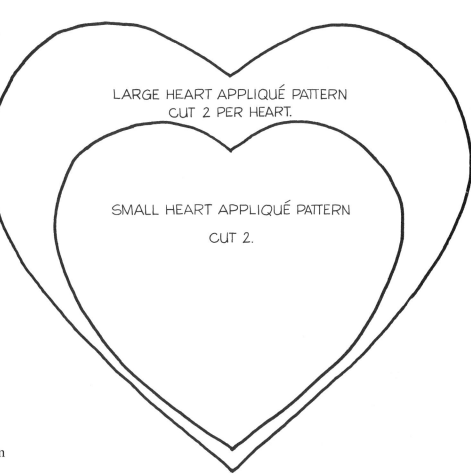

LARGE HEART APPLIQUÉ PATTERN
CUT 2 PER HEART.

SMALL HEART APPLIQUÉ PATTERN
CUT 2.

Little Baskets Pillow

Finished Pillow: 17 inches square

Materials

Use the Materials list for the wallhanging on page 148. The yardage requirements are the same. Fabric D will be the half-inch and third border of the pillow. Do not cut the backing and batting. You will also need a 1–pound bag of smooth stuffing like FiberFil for the pillow form.

Cutting Directions

Cutting directions for the pillow are the same as for the Little Baskets Wallhanging, except for the binding. Instead of binding, you will be cutting third border strips from Fabric D. You will need to cut two 1¼ × 44-inch strips. From these strips, cut four 1¼ × 22-inch strips.

Assembly

Construction for the pillow is exactly the same as for the Little Baskets Wallhanging. Follow all the steps from "Making Triangle Sets" through "Layering the Quilt," beginning on page 149.

Third Border

Sew 1¼ × 22-inch Fabric D border strips to the top and bottom of the pillow. Trim the excess and press the seams toward the third border. Sew the remaining two border strips to the sides of the pillow. Trim the excess and press.

Finishing

Step 1. Using the pillow front as a pattern, trim the backing piece to fit. With right sides together, sew the pillow front to the back, *using a ½-inch seam allowance.* Leave a 10-inch opening at the bottom of the pillow for turning and inserting the pillow form.

Step 2. Make a custom-fit pillow form from the batting and stuffing. See the directions on page 253. Turn the pillow right side out, insert the pillow form, and hand stitch the opening.

Countryside Samplers

17"

2½"
2½"
2½"
3"
3½"
3½"
5"
4"
2"
3½"
2½"
2½"
2½"
6"
3½"
2½"
3½"
3½"
3"
3½"
3½"
3"

14½"

WALLHANGING LAYOUT

Enjoy a fresh slice of Americana! Capture the simple pleasures of a day in the country with a Penstitch appliqué (no-sew!) sampler. A contented cat, a slice of watermelon, a red ripe apple, a frolicking lamb, and a country cottage mingle with Uncle Sam and Old Glory in the Patriotic Sampler. The designs switch to favorite holiday themes like a rocking horse, a gingerbread man, and an angel in Santa's Sampler. Use any of these designs to create ornaments or decorate wooden boxes that will add just the right touch of relaxed countryside charm to your home.

Patriotic Sampler

Finished Size: $17 \times 14\frac{1}{2}$ inches

SEW COLORFUL

The look here is Americana country, so red, tan, and blue are perfect.

Appliqué Designs: Look for stripes to use for the flag and Uncle Sam's trousers. Add accent colors in blues and greens for the roof, cat, hearts, apple leaf, star (with the moon), and quilt block.

Background: Choose a variety of neutrals. Vary them from a light muslin color to a medium tan. You can incorporate some subtle prints, checks, or stripes for a nice variety of textures. Just make sure the appliqué design will stand out on the selected background. Tea-dyed fabrics are perfect here.

Borders and Binding: The first border should be an accent color that brightens your sampler. The second border should be a shade similar to the background fabrics, and the wide third border should tie everything together. For this wider border, don't be afraid to go with a large-scale plaid or check. Use a darker solid for the binding.

Materials and Cutting

Using a rotary cutter, see-through ruler, and cutting mat, prepare the pieces as directed in the chart below. Measurements for all pieces include ¼-inch seam allowances.

Background Assembly

Press the seams after each step, following the direction of the arrows in the diagrams.

Step 1. Sew one 2½-inch square to one 2½ × 3-inch piece. See **Diagram 1.** Press.

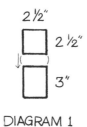

DIAGRAM 1

Step 2. Sew the Step 1 unit to one 3½ × 5-inch piece. See **Diagram 2.** Press.

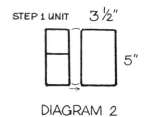

DIAGRAM 2

	YARDAGE	CUTTING	
		NO. OF PIECES	**DIMENSIONS**
Appliqué Background	⅛ yard (or scraps) of several coordinated fabrics	2	2½-inch squares
		1	2½ × 3-inch piece
		1	3½ × 5-inch piece
		1	3½ × 4-inch piece
		1	2 × 3½-inch piece
		1	2½ × 6-inch piece
		1	3½-inch square
		1	2½ × 3½-inch piece
		1	3 × 3½-inch piece
Appliqué Designs	⅛-yard pieces (or scraps) of several coordinated fabrics		
First Border		2	1 × 10½-inch strips
		2	1 × 9-inch strips
Binding	⅛ yard (Cut three 1 × 44-inch strips.)	2	1 × 16½-inch strips
		2	1 × 15-inch strips
Second Border	⅛ yard (or one 1 × 44-inch strip)	2	1 × 11½-inch strips
		2	1 × 10-inch strips
Third Border	⅙ yard (6 inches) (Cut two 2½ × 44-inch strips.)	2	2½ × 12½-inch strips
		2	2½ × 14-inch strips
Backing	½ yard	1	16 × 18-inch piece
Batting	½ yard	1	16 × 18-inch piece
Appliqué film Black, extra-fine point, permanent felt-tip pen			

Step 3. Sew one 3½ × 4-inch piece to one 2 × 3½-inch piece, as shown in **Diagram 3.** Press.

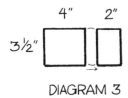

DIAGRAM 3

Step 4. Sew the Step 2 unit to the Step 3 unit. See **Diagram 4.** Press.

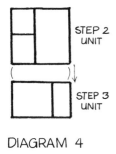

DIAGRAM 4

Step 5. Sew one 2½-inch square to one 2½ × 6-inch piece. See **Diagram 5.** Press.

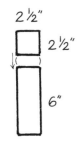

DIAGRAM 5

Step 6. Sew one 3½-inch square to one 2½ × 3½-inch piece, as shown in **Diagram 6.** Press.

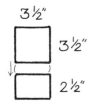

DIAGRAM 6

Step 7. Sew the Step 6 unit to one 3 × 3½-inch piece. See **Diagram 7.** Press.

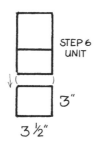

DIAGRAM 7

Step 8. Sew the Step 5 unit to the Step 7 unit. See **Diagram 8.** Press.

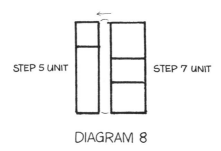

DIAGRAM 8

Step 9. Sew the Step 4 unit to the Step 8 unit, as shown in **Diagram 9.** Press. The background section will measure 8 × 10½ inches.

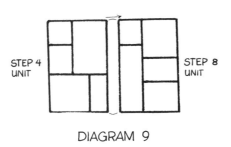

DIAGRAM 9

Borders

Press all border seams away from the center background section. Refer to the **Wallhanging Layout** on page 153 for placement guidance.

First Border

Sew 1 × 10½-inch first border strips to the wallhanging top and bottom. Press. Sew 1 × 9-inch strips to the wallhanging sides. Press.

Second Border

Sew 1 × 11½-inch second border strips to the wallhanging top and bottom. Press. Sew 1 × 10-inch strips to the wallhanging sides. Press.

Third Border

Sew 2½ × 12½-inch third border strips to the wallhanging top and bottom. Press. Sew 2½ × 14-inch strips to the wallhanging sides. Press.

Binding

Sew 1 × 16½-inch binding strips to the wallhanging top and bottom. Press all seams toward the binding. Sew 1 × 15-inch strips to the wallhanging sides. Press. (Wait for "Finishing" on page 156 to complete the edges of this binding.)

Appliqué

These wallhangings were designed especially for the Penstitch appliqué technique described on page 240.

Step 1. Cut appliqué designs from assorted scraps of fabric using the **Patriotic Sampler Appliqué Patterns** on page 158.

Step 2. Penstitch appliqué designs in the center of each background piece. Position and fuse one design at a time. Use the photograph on page 152 as a placement guide.

Step 3. Use the black pen to draw eyes where needed.

Step 4. For the cat design, use two strands of embroidery floss to make French knots for the eyes; use the stem stitch to make the nose and mouth. See "Stitches for Special Touches" on page 248 for instructions on these details.

♥ SEW CREATIVE ♥

Instead of quilting a diagonal grid in the third border, use the appliqué pattern outlines as quilting templates. You could hand or machine quilt the star, moon, apple, house, and hearts in this border area.

Finishing

Step 1. Use the finished top as a pattern to trim the backing piece and batting to fit.

Step 2. Position the top and backing with right sides together. Lay both pieces on top of the batting and pin all three layers together. Sew together, leaving a 3- to 4-inch opening for turning.

Step 3. Turn right side out, press, and hand stitch the opening.

Step 4. Machine or hand quilt in the ditch around all the background pieces. Quilt in the ditch around the first and second borders and binding. Quilt a 1-inch diagonal grid in the third border. You may also quilt on the background pieces, 1/16 inch away from the appliqué designs, if you like.

Santa's Sampler

Finished Size: 17 × 14½ inches

This project uses the same basic materials, cutting information, and step-by-step directions as appear above for the Patriotic Sampler. For the appliqué, use the **Santa's Sampler Appliqué Patterns** on page 159. Use the black pen to draw the angel's wand and halo.

SEW COLORFUL

Appliqué Designs: It's country Christmas, so use a lot of tan and black to accompany the traditional red and green. Including these two colors gives your wallhanging a warmer, well-aged look.

Background: Choose a variety of light neutrals, from light muslin to tan with subtle patterns. Just make sure the appliqué design stands out on the selected background piece. The background fabrics could be tea-dyed for a homespun look.

Borders and Binding: Use a strong solid for your first accent border and binding. Coordinate the second narrow border with the background fabrics. The wide third border should be your favorite Christmas fabric. A red plaid like the one I chose says country and Christmas loud and clear!

Ornaments

You can make an endless combination of ornaments from these designs. I've made up a calico cat ornament (shown in the photograph on page 152), but you could opt for any of the patterns—a rocking horse, a lamb, Santa Claus, or even Uncle Sam! Just use the background units from the samplers as "building blocks." Select one of the background pieces as your ornament shape and apply the corresponding appliqué design.

Materials

ORNAMENT BACKGROUND

Two pieces of scrap fabric for front and back (See Cutting Requirements for each design to determine size.)

RIBBON HANGER

½ yard per ornament (⅛ to ½ inch wide)

APPLIQUÉ DESIGNS

Coordinated fabric scraps

NOTIONS AND SUPPLIES

Appliqué film
Black, extra-fine point, permanent felt-tip pen
Smooth stuffing like FiberFil

Appliqué

Step 1. Choose an appliqué design. Cut two background pieces the same dimensions as used for that design on the sampler. (See the **Wallhanging Layout** on page 153 for measurements.)

Step 2. Penstitch appliqué the design to the front of the background piece. Be sure to center the design, allowing for ¼-inch seams all the way around.

Making the Ornament

Step 1. Cut two 9-inch pieces of ribbon for hangers. Pin and sew them to the right side of the front piece, as shown in **Diagram 10.**

DIAGRAM 10

Step 2. Pin the ornament front and back with right sides together. Sew, leaving an opening for turning. (Be careful to keep the ribbon ends from getting caught in the seam allowances.) Trim the corners and turn the ornament right side out. Press.

Step 3. Stuff the ornament. Hand stitch the opening.

Shaker Box

These cheery boxes can be purchased unfinished in a craft shop and decorated in a flash to fill with homemade goodies. Or make a nesting set to hold those odds and ends from buttons to bows that always seem to collect on the dresser.

Materials

Small, unfinished round or oval
Shaker box
Several coordinated fabric scraps
for appliqué designs

NOTIONS AND SUPPLIES

Appliqué film
Acrylic folk-art paint
Black, extra-fine point, permanent
felt-tip pen

Decorating the Box

Choose a small Shaker box suitable for the size of the design you have chosen from the appliqué patterns. The boxes shown in the photograph on page 152 range in size from a 3 × 5-inch oval to a 5½-inch-diameter round box.

Step 1. Paint the boxes to coordinate with the fabrics you will use. Let the paint dry thoroughly.

SEW SMART

Thin the paint with a little water, as I did, for a less opaque look.

Step 2. Penstitch appliqué your favorite design to the box lid. Use stars, hearts, or moons to decorate the box sides. (Use the star patterns from the angel's wand and the moon/star design.) The appliqué film doesn't fuse quite as easily to the box as it does to fabric. But be careful not to use too hot an iron or you'll melt the fusing film. Since it may take longer to fuse your designs onto the hard surface of a box, you may want to lay a press cloth on top of the design while pressing.

Appliqué Pattern Key

———— Tracing Line

-------- Tracing Line
(will be hidden
behind other fabric)

*Note: Patterns appear on pages
158 and 159.*

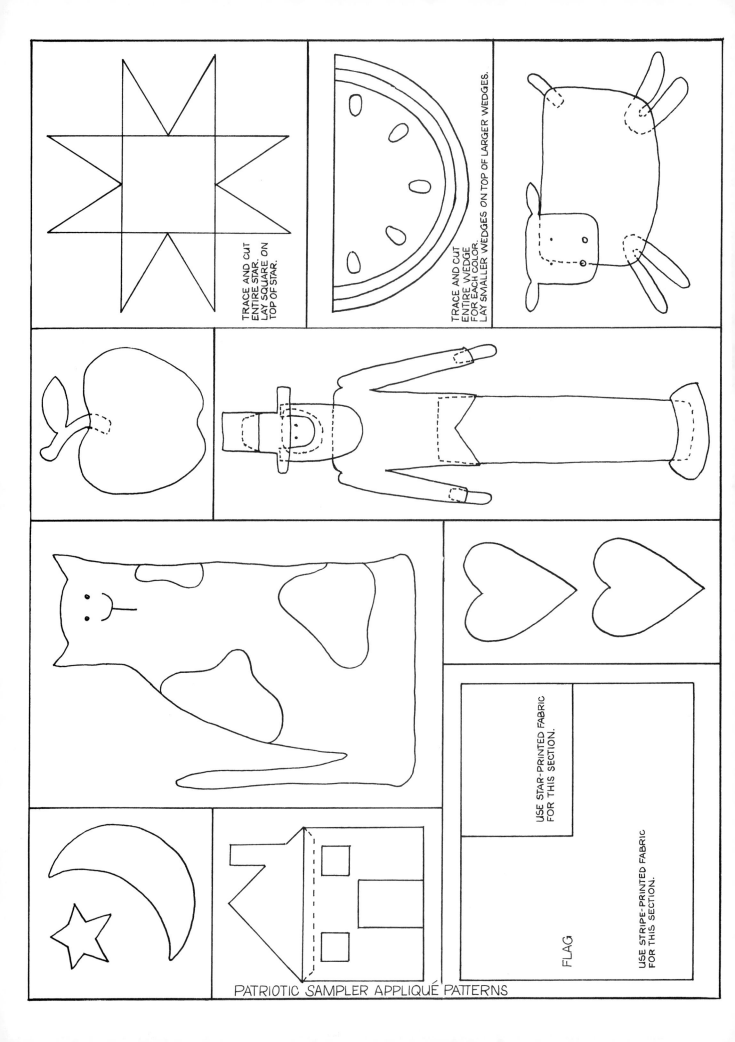

TRACE AND CUT
ENTIRE STAR.
LAY SQUARE ON
TOP OF STAR.

TRACE AND CUT
ENTIRE WEDGE
FOR EACH COLOR.
LAY SMALLER WEDGES ON TOP OF LARGER WEDGES.

USE STAR-PRINTED FABRIC
FOR THIS SECTION.

USE STRIPE-PRINTED FABRIC
FOR THIS SECTION.

FLAG

PATRIOTIC SAMPLER APPLIQUÉ PATTERNS

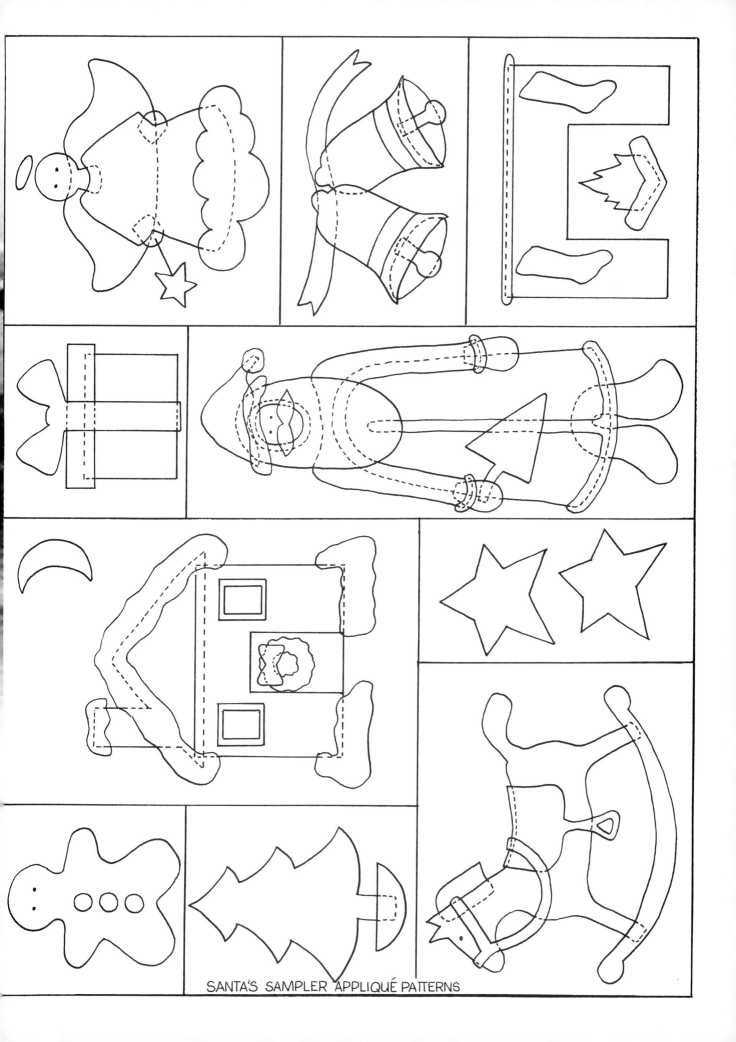

SANTA'S SAMPLER APPLIQUÉ PATTERNS

©1988 Debbie Mumm

KIDS AND CRIBS

Is there anything sweeter than seeing a baby napping under a quilt
you've made? Or anything more satisfying than having a little boy
or girl point with pride to a quilt you made just for them? You'll easily
find something to please your favorite kids, whether they're into
ducks, dinosaurs, kites, or tic-tac-toe. To make the project even more
special, you might want to take them along to help choose the
fabrics. Who knows, you might uncover a budding quilter!

Before you begin, take a minute to read through this checklist. These are important pointers you should keep in mind to make sure that each of your quilts is a success.

♥ Be sure you read "Techniques for More Quick Country Quilting," beginning on page 215, to familiarize yourself with fabric selection; the tools you'll need; time-saving techniques for cutting, piecing, and appliqué; as well as finishing instructions.

♥ Take advantage of the helpful hints in "Sew Colorful" at the start of each project. Here is where you'll find pointers on selecting colors and fabrics for each particular design.

♥ Prewash and press all of your fabrics.

♥ Read the step-by-step directions from start to finish, and look at all the diagrams before you cut and sew any fabric.

♥ Always use a ¼-inch seam allowance, unless there is a special note that tells you a different seam allowance is required.

♥ Refer to the **Fabric Key** for each project as a help in following the diagrams.

♥ Pay attention to the pressing directions given in the step-by-step text and to the pressing arrows shown in the diagrams.

Game Quilts

34"

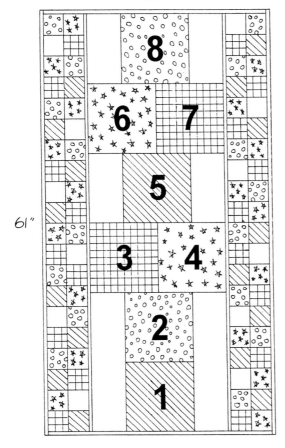

61"

HOPSCOTCH QUILT LAYOUT

Here's a terrific gift idea for slightly older kids. These quilts are fun from beginning to end. Let your fabric cravings run wild and go for those dazzling and daring new fabrics that you've had your eye on! Youngsters will love the bright colors and can amuse themselves playing tic-tac-toe or keep warm by snuggling under the hopscotch quilt while watching a favorite show. Remember, these quilts are made to be used!

Hopscotch and Television Floor Quilt

Finished Quilt: 34 × 61 inches

Materials

Directional prints are okay to use for this project. Just be sure to watch the placement so the design of the print is going in the right direction on your quilt.

FABRIC A

Hopscotch Squares, Squares
Border, and Markers   ⅝ yard
each of *four* fabrics

FABRIC B

Background   ⅝ yard

FABRIC C

Half-Inch Border
and Binding   ⅝ yard

SCRAPS

Coordinated scraps
for appliqué numbers

BACKING   1⅞ yards

BATTING   1⅞ yards

Use a thick batting for this quilt.

NOTIONS AND SUPPPLIES

Sewable appliqué film
Tear-away paper
Nontoxic plastic pellets
for filling markers

SEW COLORFUL

Bright and bold was the direction I took here. Kids are more attracted to fun, bright colors and fabrics. You might even get them involved in picking colors for this one! Just about anything goes, as long as the numbers show up.

Hopscotch Squares: I started with a multicolor print in a kid-appealing design. From that, I chose the other three hopscotch squares colors. Make sure that the black numbers will stand out on each.

Background: I looked for a white that included some of my hopscotch colors. A solid white would show dirt and be a little dull here.

Cutting Directions

Prewash and press all of your fabrics. Using a rotary cutter, see-through ruler, and cutting mat, prepare the strips as described in the first column in the chart below. Then from those strips, cut the pieces listed in the second column. Some portions of the quilt need to be cut only once, so no additional cutting information will appear in the second column. Measurements for all pieces include ¼-inch seam allowances.

	FIRST CUT		SECOND CUT	
	NO. OF STRIPS	DIMENSIONS	NO. OF PIECES	DIMENSIONS
FABRIC A	Hopscotch Squares: from *each* of the *four* fabrics, cut the following			
	1	10½ × 44-inch strip	2	10½-inch squares
	Small Squares Border: from *each* of the *four* fabrics, cut the following			
	2	3½ × 44-inch strips	17	3½-inch squares
	Play Markers: from *each* of the *four* fabrics, cut the following			
	Before You Cut: Use the remainder of the 10½ × 44-inch strip to cut these squares.			
	2	3½-inch squares		
FABRIC B	Background			
	3	5½ × 44-inch strips	2	5½ × 20½-inch pieces
			4	5½ × 10½-inch pieces
	1	3½ × 44-inch strip	12	3½-inch squares
FABRIC C	Half-Inch Border			
	3	1 × 44-inch strips		
	Binding			
	6	2¾ × 44-inch strips		

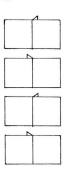

Appliqué Numbers

Step 1. Refer to "Machine Appliqué" on page 240 for details on this technique. Using the **Number Appliqué Patterns** on page 169, trace and cut appliqué numbers 1 through 8. Numbers must be traced in reverse, as drawn.

Step 2. Lay out the hopscotch squares in a pleasing arrangement. See the **Hopscotch Quilt Layout** on page 163 and the photograph on page 162 for a placement guide. Keep track of your layout while appliquéing the numbers. Machine appliqué one number to the center of each of the eight 10½-inch Fabric A squares.

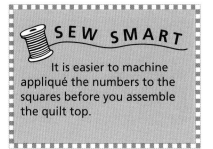

SEW SMART

It is easier to machine appliqué the numbers to the squares before you assemble the quilt top.

Making the Hopscotch Center

Use the **Hopscotch Quilt Layout** on page 163 as a guide for assembling the center of the quilt. Hopscotch squares with numbers will be referred to by their appliqué number; the square with the number 1 on it is "square one."

Step 1. Sew square one to square two. Position the pieces with right sides together and sew using a ¼-inch seam allowance. Make sure the numbers will be in the correct position after stitching. Press the seam toward square one.

Step 2. Sew one 5½ × 20½-inch background piece to each side of the Step 1 unit. Press the seams toward squares one and two.

Step 3. Sew square three to the left side of square four. Press the seam toward square four. Sew this unit to the top of the Step 2 unit. Press the seam toward squares three and four.

Step 4. Sew one 5½ × 10½-inch background piece to each side of square five. Press seams toward square five. Sew this unit to the top of the Step 3 unit. Press seam toward squares three and four.

Step 5. Sew square six to the left side of square seven. Press the seam toward square six. Sew this unit to the top of the Step 4 unit. Press the seam toward squares six and seven.

Step 6. Sew one 5½ × 10½-inch background piece to each side of square eight. Press seams toward square eight. Sew this unit to the top of the Step 5 unit. Press seam toward squares six and seven.

Half-Inch Border

Step 1. Cut one 1 × 44-inch Fabric C strip in half to make two 1 × 22-inch strips. Sew one of these strips to each of the remaining two 1 × 44-inch strips to make two 1 × 66-inch strips.

Step 2. Sew one 1 × 66-inch strip to each side of the hopscotch center. Trim the excess and press the seams toward the half-inch border.

Small Squares Border

Before starting to sew, lay out the eighty 3½-inch squares (seventeen of each hopscotch square fabric and twelve of the background fabric) in pairs along the sides of the quilt top. Each side has forty squares. For balance, try to put six background squares on each side and an equal number of the other colors. Keep track of this layout when you start to sew.

Step 1. Sew the squares together into pairs. Press the seams in opposite directions in each row. See **Diagram 1.**

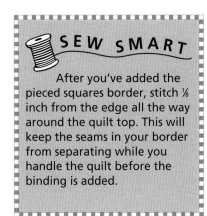

DIAGRAM 1

Step 2. Sew the pairs together to make two squares border strips.

Step 3. Fit the squares border strips to the sides of the quilt. If adjustments are necessary, make them by taking in or letting out a few of the seam allowances no more than ¹⁄₁₆ inch. Pin them in position and sew. Press the seams toward the half-inch border.

SEW SMART

After you've added the pieced squares border, stitch ⅛ inch from the edge all the way around the quilt top. This will keep the seams in your border from separating while you handle the quilt before the binding is added.

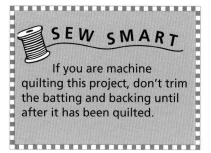
Layering the Quilt

Arrange and baste the backing, batting, and quilt top together, following the directions for "Layering the Quilt" on page 249.

> **SEW SMART**
>
> If you are machine quilting this project, don't trim the batting and backing until after it has been quilted.

Machine Quilting

Machine quilt in the seam line around all hopscotch squares and half-inch borders. Refer to "Quilting by Machine" on page 253 for details on this technique. Quilt a square 1 inch inside each hopscotch square. Repeat the quilting to make a second and third square, each time quilting 1 inch inside the previous line. In the background pieces, quilt 1½-inch squares that are randomly placed and overlapping in places. Quilt diagonal lines from corner to corner in the border squares.

    Since I was using a variety of colors, I chose clear nylon thread for machine quilting. This type of thread can put some stress on your machine, so be sure everything is in tip-top shape before you begin quilting with it. You'll probably need to adjust the tension to accommodate the nylon thread.

Binding the Quilt

Step 1. Trim the backing and batting to ¼ inch from the raw edge of the quilt top.

Step 2. Sew four 2¾ × 44-inch binding strips together into pairs to make two 2¾ × 87½-inch binding strips. Using the 2¾ × 44-inch strips for the top and bottom binding and the 2¾ × 87½-inch strips for the sides, follow the directions on page 249 for "Binding the Quilt."

> ♡ **SEW CREATIVE** ♡
>
> Purchase extra fabric or piece together leftover scraps from the hopscotch quilt to make a coordinating pillow. Or sew four 10½-inch squares together and add a binding to make an oversized floor pillow.

Play Markers

With right sides together, match up four sets of 3½-inch squares. Sew the sets together on all four sides, leaving a 1½-inch opening for turning and stuffing. Clip the corners and turn. Fill each marker with plastic pellets and slip stitch the opening closed.

Tic-Tac-Toe Game Board

Finished Quilt: 20 inches square

> ## SEW COLORFUL
>
> You'll combine five fabrics to make this little game board. Directional prints are not recommended for the borders.
>
> **Wide Border and Squares:** First, pick out a lively, fun multicolor print for this wide border. From the colors in this print, choose your two favorites for the tic-tac-toe squares. These two colors should have good contrast to each other.
>
> **Lattice and Binding:** For the tic-tac-toe bars (lattice), black stood out well against both of the squares fabrics. Whatever color you choose, repeat it in the binding.
>
> **Half-Inch Borders:** The first half-inch border needs to be different from the lattice fabric but also needs to have good contrast to the squares. Repeat a square fabric for the second half-inch accent border.
>
> **Markers:** The markers should also show contrast to the squares. Make one set out of one of your multicolor prints.

Materials and Cutting

Prewash and press all of your fabrics. Using a rotary cutter, see-through ruler, and cutting mat, prepare the strips as described in the chart below. Measurements for all pieces include ¼-inch seam allowances.

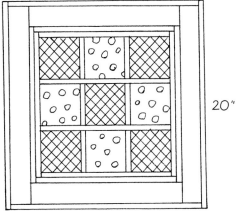

20"

20"

TIC-TAC-TOE QUILT LAYOUT

	YARDAGE	CUTTING	
		NO. OF PIECES	DIMENSIONS
		Before You Cut: From one fabric cut four squares and from the other cut five squares.	
Gameboard Squares	⅙ yard (6 inches) *each* of *two* fabrics	5	4½-inch squares
		4	4½-inch squares
Lattice	⅛ yard	6	1 × 4½-inch strips
		2	1 × 13½-inch strips
Binding		2	1 × 19½-inch strips
		2	1 × 20½-inch strips
First Half-Inch Border	⅛ yard	2	1 × 13½-inch strips
		2	1 × 14½-inch strips
Second Half-Inch Border	⅛ yard	2	1 × 14½-inch strips
		2	1 × 15½-inch strips
Wide Border	⅙ yard (6 inches)	2	2½ × 15½-inch strips
		2	2½ × 19½-inch strips
Backing	⅔ yard	1	23-inch square
Batting	⅔ yard	1	23-inch square
X and O Markers	⅛ yard *each* of *two* fabrics	10	3½-inch squares from *each* of *two* fabrics
Appliqué Xs and Os	Coordinated scraps		

Appliqué film (sewable)
Tear-away paper
Nontoxic plastic pellets for filling markers

Lattice

Referring to the **Tic-Tac-Toe Quilt Layout** on page 167 and the photograph on page 162, lay out the nine 4½-inch game board squares. Keep track of the layout as you sew.

Step 1. Sew 1 × 4½-inch lattice strips to each side of the three game board squares that will be placed in the center of each row. See **Diagram 2.** Press all seams toward the lattice.

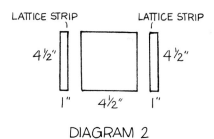

DIAGRAM 2

Step 2. Sew a game board square to each side of the three center squares to make three rows of three squares each. See **Diagram 3.** Press.

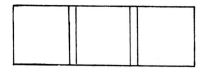

DIAGRAM 3

Step 3. Sew a 1 × 13½-inch lattice strip to each side of the *center* row only. Press the seams toward the lattice. Sew the three rows together. Press.

Borders and Binding

First Half-Inch Border

Step 1. Sew the 1 × 13½-inch border strips to the quilt top and bottom. Press all seams toward the border.

Step 2. Sew the 1 × 14½-inch border strips to the sides. Press.

Second Half-Inch Border

Step 1. Sew the 1 × 14½-inch border strips to the quilt top and bottom. Press all seams toward the second half-inch border.

Step 2. Sew the 1 × 15½-inch border strips to the sides. Press.

Wide Border

Step 1. Sew the 2½ × 15½-inch border strips to the quilt top and bottom. Press all seams toward the wide border.

Step 2. Sew the 2½ × 19½-inch border strips to the quilt sides. Press.

Binding

Step 1. Sew the 1 × 19½-inch binding strips to the quilt top and bottom. Press all seams toward the binding.

Step 2. Sew the 1 × 20½-inch binding strips to the sides. Press.

Finishing

Step 1. Position the top and backing with right sides together. Lay both pieces on top of the batting and pin all three layers together. Sew together, leaving a 3- to 4-inch opening for turning. Trim the backing and batting to the same size as the top.

Step 2. Turn the game board right side out, press, and hand stitch the opening.

Step 3. Machine quilt in the seam line around all lattice, borders, and binding. Quilt a 1½-inch diagonal grid in the wide border. Refer to "Quilting by Machine" on page 253 for details on this technique.

X and O Markers

Appliqué

Step 1. Refer to "Machine Appliqué" on page 240 for details on this technique. Using the **X and O Appliqué Patterns** on this page and the opposite page, trace and cut five Xs and five Os.

Step 2. Use five 3½-inch squares of the first color and machine appliqué one X to the center of each square. Machine appliqué one O to the center of five 3½-inch squares of the second color.

Making the Markers

With right sides together, match up ten sets of 3½-inch squares. For each set, use one appliquéd square and a plain square of the same fabric for the back. Sew the sets together on all four sides, leaving a 1½-inch opening in the bottom for turning and stuffing. Clip the corners and turn the markers right side out. Fill each marker with plastic pellets and slip stitch the opening closed. Now start playing!

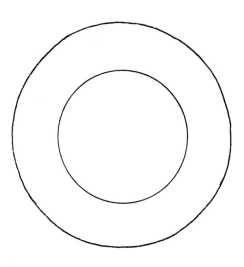

APPLIQUÉ PATTERNS

Rub-a-Dub Ducks

34"

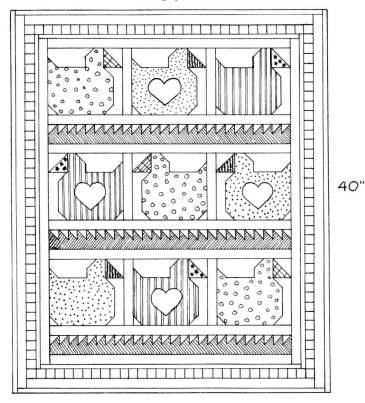

40"

QUILT LAYOUT

It's naptime with a flock of web-footed friends! Surround a special infant with pastel ducks floating serenely on the water. Any baby will grow fond of this crib set that includes a quilt, bumper pads, and pillows. The cheerful quilt and accessories sew up surprisingly quickly with this easy-to-piece duckling. (When you attach the bumpers for your little one, tie the bows on the *outside* of the crib.)

Baby Ducks Quilt

Finished Quilt: 34 × 40 inches
Finished Block: 8 × 7 inches

Materials

Obvious directional prints are not recommended.

FABRIC A

Use three fabrics.
Ducks and Squares Border   ⅓ yard
each of *three* fabrics

FABRIC B

Block Background	⅔ yard
Lattice	½ yard
Outside Border	¼ yard
TOTAL	1⅓ yards

FABRIC C

Use three fabrics.
Beaks and Squares Border   ¼ yard
each of *three* fabrics

FABRIC D

Water and Squares Border	⅝ yard
Half-Inch Border	⅛ yard
Binding	⅓ yard
TOTAL	1 yard

BACKING   1⅛ yards

BATTING   1⅛ yards

Note: Use total yardage for Fabrics B and D. Use individual yardages if you want to use multiple fabrics for blocks, lattice, borders, or binding.

SEW COLORFUL

Pastels are perfect for the nursery. I chose colors appropriate for both girls and boys.

Ducks: First, select three fabrics for your ducks. Since the duck is a fairly simple block with few pieces, you should choose more active prints for the duck bodies. Remember to look for different visual textures in these prints. Pull complementary accent colors out of the

duck body prints to choose three fabrics for the beaks.

Background: I broke away from a tan background here and used a fresh, crisp white. White has a soft, clean look that just seems appropriate for a baby project.

Water: I used a medium blue that complemented my other pastels. I wouldn't suggest

using a blue any darker than the one in my quilt.

Borders and Binding: Since the blue is a little deeper color, it works very well for the half-inch border and the binding. You could also use a deeper shade of one of the duck colors. Using all the duck, beak, and water fabrics in the scrap squares border ties all the fun colors together.

Cutting Directions

Prewash and press all of your fabrics. Using a rotary cutter, see-through ruler, and cutting mat, prepare the strips as described in the first column in the chart that follows. Then from those strips,

cut the pieces listed in the second column. Some portions of the quilt need to be cut only once, so no additional cutting information will appear in the second column. Measurements for all pieces include ¼-inch seam allowances.

	FIRST CUT		SECOND CUT	
	NO. OF STRIPS	**DIMENSIONS**	**NO. OF PIECES**	**DIMENSIONS**
FABRIC A	**Ducks:** from *each* of the *three* fabrics, cut the following			
	1	6 × 44-inch strip	1	6 × 10-inch piece
			3	5½-inch squares
	1	1½ × 44-inch strip	3	1½ × 4½-inch pieces
			3	1½ × 3½-inch pieces
			3	1½ × 2½-inch pieces
			3	1½-inch squares
	Squares Border: from *each* of the *three* fabrics, cut the following			
	1	1½ × 40-inch strip		

	FIRST CUT		SECOND CUT	
	NO. OF STRIPS	DIMENSIONS	NO. OF PIECES	DIMENSIONS
FABRIC B	**Duck Blocks**			
	1	6 × 44-inch strip	2	6 × 16-inch pieces
			1	6 × 10-inch piece
	1	6 × 44-inch strip	1	6 × 16-inch piece
			2	6 × 10-inch pieces
	1	5 × 44-inch strip	3	5 × 8-inch pieces
	1	2½ × 44-inch strip	9	2½ × 3½-inch pieces
	2	1½ × 44 strips	9	1½ × 5½-inch pieces
			9	1½-inch squares
	Lattice			
	Before You Cut: From *two* of the 44-inch strips, cut the pieces listed in the second column. The remaining nine strips require no further cutting.			
	11	1½ × 44-inch strips	6	1½ × 7½-inch strips
	Outside Border			
	4	1½ × 44-inch strips		
FABRIC C	**Squares Border:** from *each* of the *three* fabrics, cut the following			
	Before You Cut: Cut the strips for the squares border before cutting the pieces for the blocks.			
	1	1½ × 40-inch strip		
	Blocks: from *each* of the *three* fabrics, cut the following			
	1	5 × 8-inch piece		
FABRIC D	**Water**			
	3	1½ × 44-inch strips	3	1½ × 26½-inch strips
	2	6 × 44-inch strips	3	6 × 16-inch pieces
	Squares Border			
	1	1½ × 40-inch strip		
	Half-Inch Border			
	4	1 × 44-inch strips		
	Binding			
	4	2¾ × 44-inch strips		

Making Triangle Sets

Step 1. Refer to "Speedy Triangles" on page 231 for how to mark, sew, and cut.

Step 2. Position the 6 × 10-inch Fabric A and B pieces with right sides together. You will have three sets. On each set draw a grid of eight 1⅞-inch squares. See **Diagram 1.**

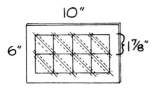

DIAGRAM 1

Step 3. After sewing and cutting are complete, press the seams toward Fabric A. You will have made a total of forty-eight 1½-inch Fabric A/B triangle sets, sixteen of each duck and background fabric. You will use only fifteen of each of these triangle sets.

Step 4. Position the 5 × 8-inch Fabric B and C pieces with right sides together. You will have three sets. On each set draw a grid of two 2⅞-inch squares. See **Diagram 2.**

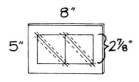

DIAGRAM 2

Step 5. After sewing and cutting are complete, press the seams toward Fabric C. You will have made a total of twelve 2½-inch Fabric B/C triangle sets, four of each beak and background fabric. You will use only three of each of these triangle sets.

Step 6. Position the 6 × 16-inch Fabric B and D pieces with right sides together. You will have three sets. On each set draw a grid of fourteen 1⅞-inch squares. See **Diagram 3.**

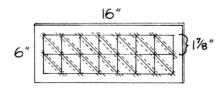

DIAGRAM 3

Step 7. After sewing and cutting are complete, press the seams toward Fabric D. You will have made a total of eighty-four 1½-inch Fabric B/D triangle sets. You will use only seventy-eight of these triangle sets.

Making the Blocks

Throughout this section, refer to the **Fabric Key** to identify the fabric placements in the diagrams. Also, it's a good idea to review "Assembly-Line Piecing" on page 233 before you get started. It is more efficient to do the same step for each block at the same time than to piece one entire block together at a time. Be sure to press as you go and follow the arrows for pressing direction.

You will be making a total of nine duck blocks, three each of three fabric combinations. Before you start sewing, coordinate duck and beak fabrics for each of the three combinations. Keep track of the combinations as you sew. First, you will make six blocks that face right. The three blocks that face left will be made last.

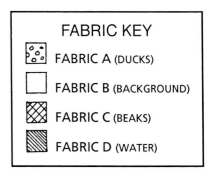

FABRIC KEY
FABRIC A (DUCKS)
FABRIC B (BACKGROUND)
FABRIC C (BEAKS)
FABRIC D (WATER)

Section One (Facing Right)

Step 1. Sew six 1½-inch Fabric A/B triangle sets to six 1½-inch Fabric B squares. Position them right sides together and line them up next to your sewing machine. Stitch the first set together, then butt the next set directly behind and continue sewing without breaking your thread. Press toward Fabric B and cut the joining threads. Pay close attention so that the triangle sets are positioned as shown in **Diagram 4.**

DIAGRAM 4

In each of the remaining steps, use the same continuous-seam method.

Step 2. Sew the six Step 1 units to six 2½ × 3½-inch Fabric B pieces. See **Diagram 5.** Press.

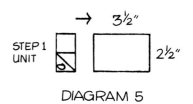

DIAGRAM 5

Step 3. Sew six 1½-inch Fabric A/B triangle sets to six 1½-inch Fabric A squares. See **Diagram 6.** Press.

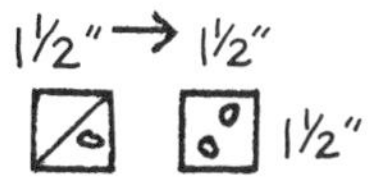

DIAGRAM 6

Step 4. Sew the six Step 3 units to six 1½ × 2½-inch Fabric A pieces. See **Diagram 7.** Press.

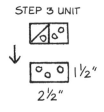

DIAGRAM 7

Step 5. Sew the six Step 4 units to the six Step 2 units, as shown in **Diagram 8.** Press.

Step 6. Sew the six Step 5 units to six 2½-inch Fabric B/C triangle sets. See **Diagram 9.** Press.

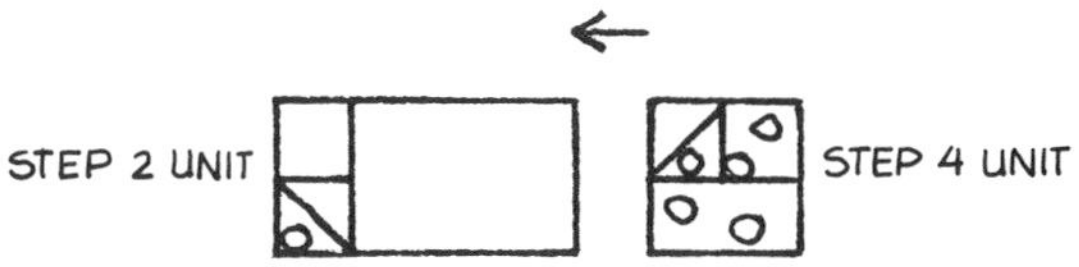

STEP 2 UNIT   STEP 4 UNIT

DIAGRAM 8

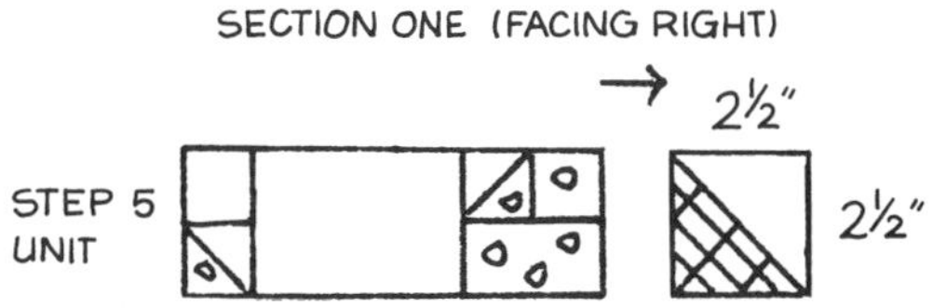

SECTION ONE (FACING RIGHT)

STEP 5 UNIT   2½″   2½″

DIAGRAM 9

Section Two (Facing Right)

Step 1. Sew six 1½-inch Fabric A/B triangle sets to six 1½ × 4½-inch Fabric A pieces. See **Diagram 10.** Press.

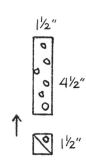

DIAGRAM 10

Step 2. Sew the six Step 1 units to six 5½-inch Fabric A squares. See **Diagram 11.** Press.

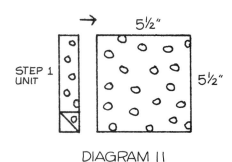

5½″

STEP 1 UNIT   5½″

DIAGRAM 11

Step 3. Sew six 1½-inch Fabric A/B triangle sets to six 1½ × 3½-inch Fabric A pieces. See **Diagram 12.** Press.

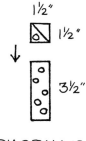

1½″
1½″
3½″

DIAGRAM 12

Step 4. Sew the six Step 3 units to six additional 1½-inch Fabric A/B triangle sets. See **Diagram 13.** Press.

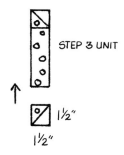

STEP 3 UNIT

1½″
1½″

DIAGRAM 13

Step 5. Sew the six Step 4 units to six 1½ × 5½-inch Fabric B pieces, as shown in **Diagram 14.** Press.

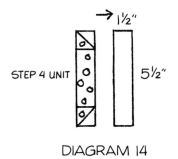

STEP 4 UNIT   1½″   5½″

DIAGRAM 14

Step 6. Sew the six Step 5 units to the six Step 2 units. See **Diagram 15.** Press.

Section Assembly
(Facing Right)

Sew Section One to Section Two, as shown in **Diagram 16.** Press toward Section Two.

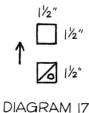

SEW SMART

For an accurate fit to the water strips, double-check to make certain your blocks measure 7½ × 8½ inches.

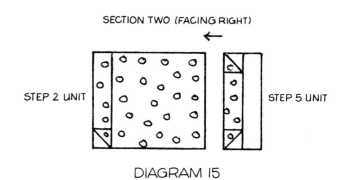

DIAGRAM 15

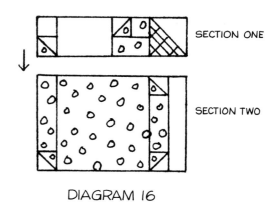

DIAGRAM 16

Section One (Facing Left)

Step 1. Sew three 1½-inch Fabric A/B triangle sets to three 1½-inch Fabric B squares. See **Diagram 17.** Press.

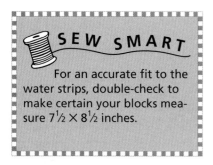

DIAGRAM 17

Step 2. Sew the three Step 1 units to three 2½ × 3½-inch Fabric B pieces. See **Diagram 18.** Press.

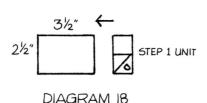

DIAGRAM 18

Step 3. Sew three 1½-inch Fabric A/B triangle sets to three 1½-inch Fabric A squares. See **Diagram 19.** Press.

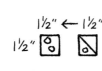

DIAGRAM 19

Step 4. Sew the three Step 3 units to three 1½ × 2½-inch Fabric A pieces. See **Diagram 20.** Press.

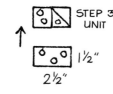

DIAGRAM 20

Step 5. Sew the three Step 4 units to the three Step 2 units. See **Diagram 21.** Press.

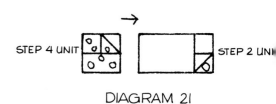

DIAGRAM 21

Step 6. Sew the three Step 5 units to three 2½-inch Fabric B/C triangle sets. See **Diagram 22.** Press.

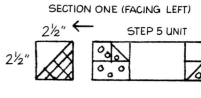

DIAGRAM 22

Section Two (Facing Left)

Step 1. Sew three 1½-inch Fabric A/B triangle sets to three 1½ × 4½-inch Fabric A pieces. See **Diagram 23.** Press.

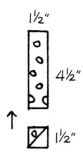

DIAGRAM 23

Step 2. Sew the three Step 1 units to three 5½-inch Fabric A squares. See **Diagram 24.** Press.

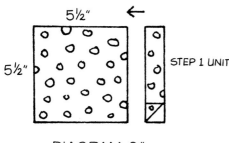

DIAGRAM 24

Step 3. Sew three 1½-inch Fabric A/B triangle sets to three 1½ × 3½-inch Fabric A pieces. See **Diagram 25.** Press.

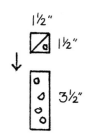

DIAGRAM 25

Step 4. Sew the three Step 3 units to three additional 1½-inch Fabric A/B triangle sets, as shown in **Diagram 26.** Press.

Step 5. Sew the three Step 4 units to three 1½ × 5½-inch Fabric B pieces. See **Diagram 27.** Press.

Step 6. Sew the three Step 5 units to the three Step 2 units. See **Diagram 28.** Press.

Section Assembly
(Facing Left)

Sew Section One to Section Two, as shown in **Diagram 29.** Press toward Section Two. For an accurate fit, make sure the completed blocks measure 7½ × 8½ inches.

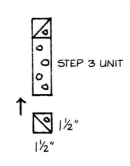

STEP 3 UNIT

DIAGRAM 26

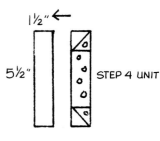

STEP 4 UNIT

DIAGRAM 27

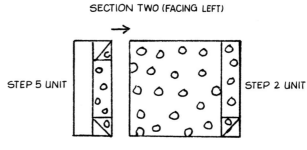

SECTION TWO (FACING LEFT)

STEP 5 UNIT   STEP 2 UNIT

DIAGRAM 28

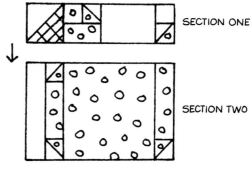

SECTION ONE

SECTION TWO

DIAGRAM 29

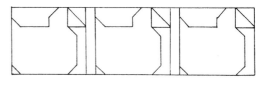

DIAGRAM 31

Hearts

Step 1. Lay out the duck blocks in a pleasing arrangement, with three rows of three blocks each. Place the three ducks that face left in the center row. Keep track of your layout while appliquéing the hearts. See the **Quilt Layout** on page 171 for a guide to placing your hearts.

Step 2. Cut out the hearts from leftover scraps of Fabrics A and C using the **Heart Appliqué Pattern** on page 185. Machine or hand appliqué hearts to the body of the center duck in the top and bottom row and to the first and third ducks in the center row. See "Machine Appliqué" on page 240 or "Hand Appliqué" on page 241 for appliqué techniques.

Lattice

Step 1. Sew the 1½ × 7½-inch Fabric B lattice strips to each side of the center blocks from each of the three rows. See **Diagram 30.** Press all seams toward the lattice.

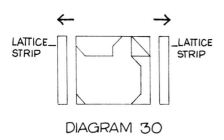

DIAGRAM 30

Step 2. Sew a block to each side of those lattice strips to make the three rows of three blocks. See **Diagram 31.** Press. Make sure that your rows are 26½ inches long. Double-check your seam allowances and take in or let out ⅟₁₆ inch if necessary.

Step 3. Sew 1½ × 44-inch lattice strips to *both the top and the bot-*

tom of all three rows. Trim the excess and press. You will have three remaining 1½ × 44-inch lattice strips. Set those three strips and the three rows of blocks aside until the water strips are assembled.

Making the Water Strips

Each water strip is made up of twenty-six 1½-inch Fabric B/D triangle sets. Use the **Quilt Layout** on page 171 and the photograph on page 170 as a guide for positioning the triangle sets.

Step 1. Sew together three rows of twenty-six triangle sets each. Press all seams in one direction in each strip.

Step 2. Fit and sew 1½ × 26½-inch Fabric D strips to the bottom of each row of triangles. Press the seams toward Fabric D.

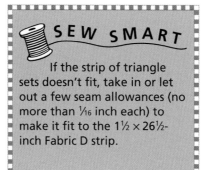

SEW SMART

If the strip of triangle sets doesn't fit, take in or let out a few seam allowances (no more than ⅟₁₆ inch each) to make it fit to the 1½ × 26½-inch Fabric D strip.

Making the Quilt Top

Step 1. Fit and sew the water strips to the bottom of each of the three rows of duck blocks. Press all seams toward the lattice.

Step 2. Stitch together the three rows of ducks floating on the water. Press.

Step 3. Sew one 1½ × 44-inch lattice strip to the bottom of the quilt. Trim the excess and press.

Step 4. Sew the remaining 1½ × 44-inch lattice strips to the quilt sides. Trim the excess and press.

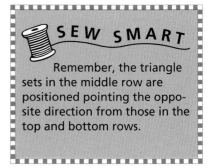

SEW SMART

Remember, the triangle sets in the middle row are positioned pointing the opposite direction from those in the top and bottom rows.

Borders

Half-Inch Border

Step 1. Sew 1 × 44-inch Fabric D border strips to the quilt top and bottom. Trim the excess and press all seams toward the border.

Step 2. Sew 1 × 44-inch border strips to the quilt sides. Trim the excess and press.

Scrap Squares Border

Step 1. Take the seven $1\frac{1}{2} \times 40$-inch squares border strips (one each of Fabrics A and C, and one Fabric D). Arrange them in a pleasing order. Sew the seven strips together, alternating sewing direction with each strip sewn. Press the seams all in one direction. Make a $7\frac{1}{2} \times 40$-inch strip set. See **Diagram 32.**

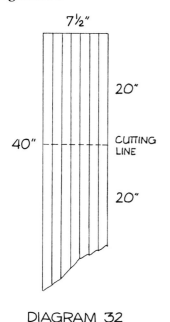

DIAGRAM 32

Step 2. Cut this strip set in half. Resew the halves together to make a $14\frac{1}{2} \times 20$-inch strip set. See **Diagram 33.**

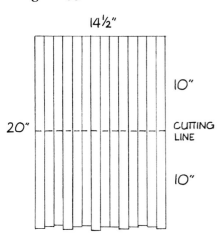

DIAGRAM 33

Step 3. Cut this strip set in half again. Resew the halves together to make a $10 \times 28\frac{1}{2}$-inch strip set. From this, cut five $1\frac{1}{2} \times 28\frac{1}{2}$-inch strips, as shown in **Diagram 34.**

Step 4. With a seam ripper, remove two individual squares from one of the $1\frac{1}{2} \times 28\frac{1}{2}$-inch strips. Add one square to each of two other strips to make two strips with twenty-nine squares each. Fit and sew these two border strips to the top and bottom of the quilt. If the border doesn't fit the quilt top, see "Hints on Fitting a Scrap Border" on page 244 to make the necessary adjustments. Press all seams toward the half-inch border.

Step 5. With a seam ripper, remove two sets of nine squares each from the strip that you took the two individual squares from. Add one set of nine squares to each of the two remaining strips to make two strips with thirty-seven squares each. Fit and sew these border strips to the sides of the quilt. Press.

Outside Border

Step 1. Sew $1\frac{1}{2} \times 44$-inch Fabric B border strips to the quilt top and bottom. Trim the excess and press all seams toward the border.

Step 2. Sew $1\frac{1}{2} \times 44$-inch border strips to the quilt sides. Trim the excess and press.

Layering the Quilt

Arrange and baste the backing, batting, and quilt top together, following the directions in "Layering the Quilt" on page 249. Trim the batting and backing to $\frac{1}{4}$ inch from the raw edge of the quilt top.

Binding the Quilt

Using the four $2\frac{3}{4} \times 44$-inch binding strips, follow the directions in "Binding the Quilt" on page 249.

Finishing Stitches

Outline each duck by quilting in the ditch or $\frac{1}{4}$ inch from the seam lines. Outline the appliqué hearts and quilt a heart in the body of the ducks without appliqué hearts using the **Heart Appliqué Pattern** on page 185 as a template. Outline the water, half-inch border, and squares border. Quilt a $1\frac{1}{2}$-inch diagonal grid in the background.

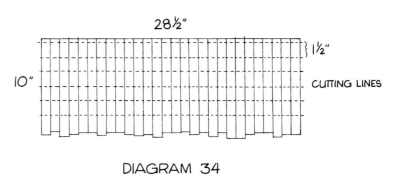

DIAGRAM 34

Baby Ducks Crib Bumpers

Finished Size of Head and Foot
 Bumpers: 28 × 9 inches
Finished Size of Side Bumpers:
 53 × 9 inches
Finished Block: 8 × 7 inches

Materials

Obvious directional prints are not recommended.

FABRIC A

Use three fabrics.
Ducks   ½ yard
                    each of *three* fabrics

FABRIC B

Block Background   ¾ yard
Lattice and Border   ½ yard
   TOTAL   1¼ yards

FABRIC C

Use three fabrics.
Beaks   ⅛ yard (6 inches)
                    each of *three* fabrics

FABRIC D

Water Border   ⅓ yard

FABRIC E

Fabric Ties   1 yard

BACKING   1⅔ yards

BATTING   40 × 55-inch piece

Note: Use a loftier (6-ounce) batting
 for the bumpers.

Before You Begin

Many of the assembly techniques
for the Baby Ducks Crib Bumpers
are the same as for those given earlier for the Baby Ducks Quilt.
Throughout these directions, you
will be referred back to the Baby
Ducks Quilt for steps that are identical. Specific assembly directions
needed for the crib bumpers are
given in detail here.

Cutting Directions

Prewash and press all of your fabrics. Using a rotary cutter, see-
through ruler, and cutting mat,
prepare the strips as described in
the first column in the chart on
the opposite page. Then from
those strips, cut the pieces listed
in the second column. Some portions of the quilt need to be cut
only once, so no additional cutting
information will appear in the second column. Measurements for all
pieces include ¼-inch seam
allowances.

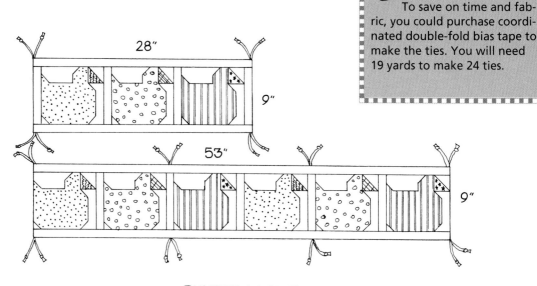

BUMPER LAYOUT

	FIRST CUT		SECOND CUT	
	NO. OF STRIPS	DIMENSIONS	NO. OF PIECES	DIMENSIONS
FABRIC A	Duck Blocks: from *each* of the *three* fabrics, cut the following			
	1	8 × 12-inch piece		
	1	5½ × 44-inch strip	6	5½-inch squares
	2	1½ × 44-inch strips	6	1½ × 4½-inch pieces
			6	1½ × 3½-inch pieces
			6	1½ × 2½-inch pieces
			6	1½-inch squares
FABRIC B	Blocks			
	1	8 × 44-inch strip	3	8 × 12-inch pieces
	1	5 × 44-inch strip	3	5 × 11-inch pieces
	2	2½ × 44-inch strips	18	2½ × 3½-inch pieces
	4	1½ × 44-inch strips	18	1½ × 5½-inch pieces
			18	1½-inch squares
	Lattice and Border (above Blocks)			
	4	1½ × 44-inch strips	4	1½ × 27-inch strips
			4	1½ × 7½-inch strips
	2	1½ × 44-inch strips	2	1½ × 28½-inch strips
	3	1½ × 44-inch strips	14	1½ × 7½-inch strips
FABRIC C	Beaks: from *each* of the *three* fabrics, cut the following			
	1	5 × 11-inch piece		
FABRIC D	Water Border (below Blocks)			
	6	1½ × 44-inch strips	4	1½ × 27-inch strips
			2	1½ × 28½-inch strips
FABRIC E	Fabric Ties			
	24	1½ × 44-inch strips	24	1½ × 28-inch strips
	BACKING			
	Before You Cut: Fold the 1⅔-yard piece of backing fabric in half, cut edge to cut edge. Fold in half again so the piece is approximately 15 × 44 inches. Rotary cut three 10-inch strips, making the cuts parallel to the selvage edges of the fabric.			
	3	10 × 60-inch strips	2	10 × 55-inch pieces
			2	10 × 30-inch pieces
	BATTING			
	2	10 × 55-inch pieces		
	2	10 × 30-inch pieces		

Making Triangle Sets

Step 1. Refer to "Speedy Triangles" on page 231 for how to mark, sew, and cut.

Step 2. Position the 8 × 12-inch Fabric A and B pieces with right sides together. You will have three sets. On each of the three sets, mark a grid of fifteen 1⅞-inch squares. See **Diagram 35.**

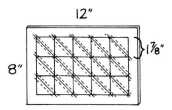

DIAGRAM 35

Step 3. After sewing and cutting are complete, press the seams toward Fabric A. You will have made a total of ninety 1½-inch Fabric A/B triangle sets, thirty of each Fabric A.

Step 4. Position the 5 × 11-inch Fabric B and C pieces with right sides together. You will have three sets. On each of the three sets, mark a grid of three 2⅞-inch squares. See **Diagram 36.**

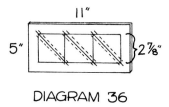

DIAGRAM 36

Step 5. After sewing and cutting are complete, press the seams toward Fabric C. You will have

made a total of eighteen 2½-inch Fabric B/C triangle sets, six of each Fabric C.

Making the Blocks

Follow all steps for Section One, Section Two, and Section Assembly (Facing Right) for the Baby Ducks Quilt, beginning on page 174. You will be making a total of 18 blocks facing right (six of each of the three different duck/beak color combinations) instead of six as in the directions.

Lattice and Water Border

Step 1. Lay out the duck blocks in two rows of three blocks each for the head and foot bumpers and two rows of six blocks each for the side bumpers. Keep track of your layout while sewing on the lattice.

Step 2. For the head and foot bumpers, sew 1½ × 7½-inch lattice strips to each side of the center blocks from each of the two rows. See **Diagram 37.** Press all seams toward the lattice. Sew a block to each side of those lattice strips to make two rows of three blocks. See the **Bumper Layout** on page 180. Sew a 1½ × 7½-inch lattice strip to each end of both rows. Press.

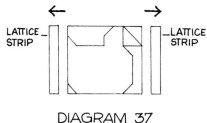

DIAGRAM 37

Step 3. Sew 1½ × 28½-inch lattice strips to the top of both rows of blocks. Press the seams toward the lattice. Sew 1½ × 28½-inch Fabric D border strips to the bottom of both rows of blocks. Press the seams toward Fabric D.

Step 4. For the side bumpers, sew 1½ × 7½-inch lattice strips to the right side of all blocks *except* the last block in each row. Press all seams toward the lattice. Sew the blocks together to make two rows of six blocks each. See the **Bumper Layout** on page 180. Press.

Step 5. Sew two pairs of 1½ × 27-inch lattice strips together to make two 1½ × 53½-inch strips. Press. Sew these 1½ × 53½-inch lattice strips to the top of both rows of blocks. Press the seams toward the lattice.

Step 6. Sew two pairs of 1½ × 27-inch Fabric D border strips together to make two 1½ × 53½-inch strips. Press. Sew these 1½ × 53½-inch Fabric D border strips to the bottom of both rows of blocks. Press the seams toward Fabric D.

Fabric Ties

Step 1. Fold each tie strip in half lengthwise with wrong sides together and press. Reopen and then fold each long edge in to the center, fold, and press again. Topstitch along the double-folded edge of the ties. Tie a knot in each end of each tie. Fold each tie in half.

Step 2. Pin the ties to the right side of the upper and lower edges of each bumper, with the tie folds even with the bumper raw edges. For the head and foot bumpers, place one tie ¼ inch in from raw edge at each corner. For the side bumpers, place one tie at each corner and ties at the second and fourth lattice strips. The folded edges of the ties will be sewn into the seam allowances when the top is sewn to the backing and batting. See the **Bumper Layout** on page 180 for placement.

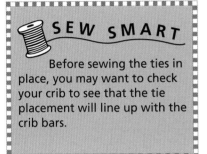

SEW SMART

Before sewing the ties in place, you may want to check your crib to see that the tie placement will line up with the crib bars.

Bumper Assembly

Step 1. For the head and foot bumpers, position the top and the 10 × 30-inch backing piece with right sides together. Lay both pieces on top of the 10 × 30-inch batting piece and pin all three layers together.

SEW SMART

When sewing the top and back together, be careful not to get the loose ends of the ties caught in your seam allowances.

Step 2. Using a ¼-inch seam allowance, sew the layers together, leaving a 3- to 4-inch opening for turning. Trim the backing and batting to the same size as the top. Turn right side out and hand stitch the opening.

Step 3. Repeat Steps 1 and 2, using the 10 × 55-inch backing and batting pieces for the side bumpers.

Finishing Stitches

Machine quilt in the seam lines around the lattice and border strips.

Just Ducky Pillow

Finished Pillow: 10 × 9 inches

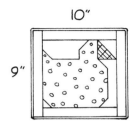

PILLOW LAYOUT

SEW COLORFUL

See "Sew Colorful" for the Baby Ducks Quilt on page 172. I chose the medium blue for the water to use as the border fabric around the duck. This coordinates with all three duck fabrics and ties all the colors together with the bumpers and the quilt. For a crisp, finished look, I repeated the white background color in the piping.

Materials and Cutting (for one pillow)

Prewash and press all of your fabrics. Using a rotary cutter, seethrough ruler, and cutting mat, prepare the pieces as directed in the chart below. Measurements for all pieces include ¼-inch seam allowances.

	YARDAGE	CUTTING	
		NO. OF PIECES	DIMENSIONS
Fabric A	¼ yard	1	5½-inch square
		1	4 × 8-inch piece
		1	1½ × 4½-inch piece
		1	1½ × 3½-inch piece
		1	1½ × 2½-inch piece
		1	1½-inch square
Fabric B Backing	⅓ yard	**Before You Cut:** Cut the backing piece first.	
		1	9½ × 10½-inch piece
Background		1	4 × 8-inch piece
		1	5-inch square
		1	2½ × 3½-inch piece
		1	1½ × 5½-inch piece
		1	1½-inch square
Fabric C Beak	⅙ yard (6 inches)	1	5-inch square
Fabric D Border	⅛ yard	2	1½ × 8½-inch strips
		2	1½ × 9½-inch strips
Batting (for pillow form)	⅜ yard	2	11 × 12-inch pieces
Purchased Piping	1¼ yards		
Stuffing (for pillow form): One 1-pound bag of smooth stuffing like FiberFil; shredded foam is not recommended.			

Before You Begin

Many of the assembly techniques for the Just Ducky Pillow are the same as for those given earlier for the Baby Ducks Quilt. Throughout these directions, you will be referred back to the quilt for steps that are identical. Specific assembly directions needed for the pillow are given in detail here.

Making Triangle Sets

Step 1. Refer to "Speedy Triangles" on page 231 for how to mark, sew, and cut.

Step 2. Position the 4 × 8-inch Fabric A and B pieces with right sides together. You will have one set. Mark a grid of three 1⅞-inch squares. See **Diagram 38.**

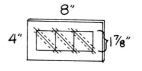

DIAGRAM 38

Step 3. After sewing and cutting are complete, press the seams toward Fabric A. You will have made a total of six 1½-inch Fabric A/B triangle sets. You will use only five of the triangle sets.

Step 4. Position the 5-inch Fabric B and C squares with right sides together. You will have 1 set. Mark a grid of one 2⅞-inch square. See **Diagram 39.**

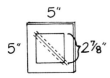

DIAGRAM 39

Step 5. After sewing and cutting are complete, press the seams toward Fabric C. You will have made a total of two 2½-inch Fabric B/C triangle sets, but will use only one triangle set.

Making the Block

Follow all steps for Section One, Section Two, and Section Assembly (Facing Right) for the Baby Ducks Quilt, beginning on page 174. You will be making only one block instead of the six in the directions.

Border

Sew the 1½ × 8½-inch border strips to the top and bottom of the duck block. Press toward the borders. Sew the 1½ × 9½-inch border strips to the sides. Press.

♡ **SEW CREATIVE** ♡

If you'd like, appliqué a heart onto your duck pillow before finishing.

Piping

Step 1. Using a zipper foot on your sewing machine, sew the purchased piping to the right side of the pillow front. Starting at the center bottom edge, place the corded edge toward the center of the pillow front and sew along the ¼-inch seam line. Start sewing 1 inch in from the piping end, leaving this end free for finishing later.

Step 2. As you approach each corner, make a clip in the piping seam allowance, which will allow you to turn the corner. Stop sewing approximately 1 inch from the point where you started sewing.

Step 3. Leaving an overlap of 1¼ inch, trim the excess piping. On one of the loose ends, remove the stitching on the piping to expose the cord. Trim only the cord even with the cord in the other end. Fold over ¼ inch on the end of the fabric, and slip the other loose end in, butting the ends of the cord up against each other.

Step 4. Finish by continuing to sew the piping into position along the edge of the pillow front. This gives a nice finish to the piping without overlapping the cording.

Finishing

Step 1. With right sides together, sew the pillow front to the 9½ × 10½-inch backing piece, using a ¼-inch seam allowance. Leave a 5- to 6-inch opening at the bottom for turning and inserting the pillow form.

Step 2. Make a pillow form from the batting and stuffing, referring to "Making Custom-Fit Pillow Forms" on page 253.

Step 3. Insert the pillow form and hand stitch the opening.

HEART APPLIQUÉ PATTERN

Dinosaur Fever

28″

22″

QUILT LAYOUT

Catch dinosaur fever and let your imagination run wild with these bright, bold projects. Dinosaurs fascinate many of today's youngsters, as they have since they were first discovered. You can match any color scheme when you stitch up the eye-catching wallhanging or the fun holder for books or art projects. Quick appliqué allows you to make these for a budding paleontologist almost faster than you can say "stegosaurus."

Dino-Rific Quilt

Finished Quilt: 28 × 22 inches

SEW COLORFUL

I took a departure from my country colors for this one. Bright and bold primaries are terrific for decorating a child's bedroom.

Dinosaurs: Choose a complementary pair of bright colors for each dinosaur. Then try to vary the textures within each block.

Background: With these bright colors, I chose a white-on-muslin for the background. It has some texture and gives a bolder look than if you used a tan or other background color.

Squares Lattice: Using all the dinosaur fabrics allows you to tie all the various colors together.

Binding: Select one of your strong dinosaur fabrics for the binding. I used a fun black-and-red stripe.

Materials and Cutting

Using a rotary cutter, see-through ruler, and cutting mat, prepare the pieces as directed in the chart below. Measurements for all pieces include ¼-inch seam allowances.

	YARDAGE	CUTTING	
		NO. OF PIECES	**DIMENSIONS**
Fabric A Background	⅞ yard	4	7½ × 10½-inch pieces
Squares Lattice		10	1½ × 12-inch strips
Border		4	2½ × 44-inch strips
Fabric B* Dinosaurs and Squares Lattice	¼ yard *each* of *six* different fabrics and ⅛ yard *each* of *four* different fabrics	1	1½ × 12-inch strip *each* of the *ten* fabrics
Binding	⅓ yard	4	2¾ × 44-inch strips
Backing	¾ yard	1	27 × 33-inch piece
Batting	¾ yard	1	27 × 33-inch piece
Appliqué film Black, extra-fine point, permanent felt-tip pen Four ⅛-inch black buttons for eyes			

*For the dinosaurs and squares lattice, you will need a total of ten different fabrics.
 If you are using scraps, make sure that you have six larger pieces for the dinosaur bodies.

Making the Quilt

Assemble the quilt top before doing the appliqué. Press the seams after each sewing step.

Squares Lattice

Step 1. Sew the twenty 1½ × 12-inch lattice strips together. Alternate ten Fabric A background fabric strips with ten different Fabric B appliqué fabric strips. See **Diagram 1.** Sew the twenty strips together, alternating sewing direction with each strip sewn. Press the seams toward the darker fabric as you go. Make a 12 × 20½-inch strip set.

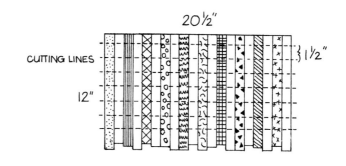

DIAGRAM 1

Step 2. Cut this strip set into six 1½ × 20½-inch strip sets. See **Diagram 1.**

Step 3. Using a seam ripper, separate one of the strips into two strip sets with seven squares each. Using the **Quilt Layout** on page 187 as a guide for placement, sew one squares lattice strip between two 7½ × 10½-inch background pieces. See **Diagram 2.** Take in or let out a few seam allowances 1/16 inch if necessary. Press all seams toward the background pieces. Sew the remaining strip between the two remaining background pieces. Press.

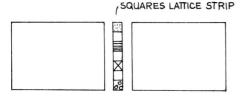

SQUARES LATTICE STRIP

DIAGRAM 2

Step 4. Using a seam ripper, remove three individual squares from the six leftover squares from Step 3. Add 1 square to each of three lattice strips to make three strips with 21 squares each. Fit and sew lattice strips to the bottom of both rows, and to the top of the top row. Press. Sew together the two rows. Press.

Step 5. With a seam ripper, remove 3 squares from each of the two remaining strips to make two strips with 17 squares each. Fit and sew these squares lattice strips to the sides of the quilt.

Border

Step 1. Sew 2½ × 44-inch border strips to the quilt top and bottom. Trim the excess and press all seams toward the border.

Step 2. Sew 2½ × 44-inch border strips to the quilt sides. Trim the excess and press.

Appliqué

This quilt was designed especially for the Penstitch appliqué technique described on page 240. If you have chosen bright colors, you may choose to simply fuse the designs into place and skip marking the Penstitch, as it may not show up well on your fabrics.

Step 1. Cut appliqué designs from selected fabrics using the **Dinosaur Appliqué Patterns** starting on page 193.

Step 2. Penstitch appliqué the designs in the center of each background piece. Position and fuse one design at a time. Use the photograph on page 186 and the **Quilt Layout** on page 187 as placement guides.

Step 3. Sew 1/8-inch black buttons to each dinosaur as indicated on the pattern for eyes.

Layering the Quilt

Arrange and baste the backing, batting, and quilt top together following the directions for "Layering the Quilt" on page 249. Trim the batting and backing to ¼ inch from the raw edge of the quilt top.

Binding the Quilt

Using the four 2¾ × 44-inch binding strips, follow the directions on page 249 for "Binding the Quilt."

Finishing Stitches

Machine or hand quilt in the ditch around all background pieces. Outline the dinosaurs by quilting 1/16 inch away from the edge of the appliqué design. Quilt in the ditch around the border. Quilt a 1½-inch diagonal grid in the background and border, using four different coordinating thread colors and alternating colors with each diagonal line.

Quilt-O-Saurus Art Holder

Finished Quilt: 15 × 17½ inches

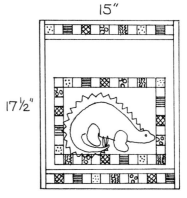

15"

17½"

QUILT LAYOUT

SEW COLORFUL

Refer to "Sew Colorful" for the Dino-Rific Quilt on page 187. If you make both the wallhanging and the art holder, use some of your leftover pieces from the wallhanging to add colors to the squares lattice in the art holder.

However, if you're making the art holder only, you will be using just two or three fabrics for your dinosaur. For the squares lattice, you'll need to supplement with two to three complementary colors.

Materials and Cutting

Using a rotary cutter, see-through ruler, and cutting mat, prepare the pieces as directed in the chart below. Measurements for all pieces include ¼-inch seam allowances.

	YARDAGE	CUTTING	
		NO. OF PIECES	**DIMENSIONS**
Background	½ yard	1	14 × 14½-inch piece
		1	7½ × 10½-inch piece
		1	9½ × 12½-inch piece (for pocket lining)
Squares Lattice		5	1½ × 12-inch strips
Half-Inch Border	⅛ yard	2	1 × 14½-inch strips
Binding		2	1 × 14½-inch strips
		2	1 × 18-inch strips
Squares Lattice	⅛ yard (or scraps) *each* of *five* coordinated fabrics	1	1½ × 12-inch strip *each* of the *five* fabrics
Hanging Tabs	⅛ yard	1	2 × 20-inch strip
Backing	⅝ yard	1	20 × 23-inch piece
Batting	⅝ yard	1	20 × 23-inch piece
Appliqué Designs	⅛-yard pieces (or scraps) of two or three coordinated fabrics		

Appliqué film
Black, extra-fine point, permanent felt-tip pen
One ½-inch-diameter × 17-inch-long wooden dowel
Two dowel ends or wooden beads
Acrylic paint
One ⅛-inch black button for eye
(Wooden dowels can be purchased at hardware stores, and dowel ends can be found at craft stores.)

Making the Quilt

Assemble the quilt top before doing the appliqué. Press the seams as you go.

Half-Inch Border

Sew 1 × 14½-inch border strips to the top and the bottom of the 14 × 14½-inch background piece. (The top and bottom are the sides that measure 14½ inches.) Press the seams toward the border. Set this piece aside until later.

Squares Lattice

Step 1. Sew the ten 1½ × 12-inch squares lattice strips together. Alternate the five background fabric strips with the five different fabric strips. See **Diagram 3.** Sew the ten strips together, alternating sewing direction with each strip sewn. Press the seams toward the darker fabric as you go. Make a 10½ × 12-inch strip set.

Step 2. Cut this strip set into seven 1½ × 10½-inch strip sets. See **Diagram 3.**

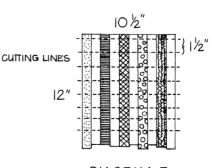

DIAGRAM 3

Step 3. Using the **Quilt Layout** on page 189 and **Diagram 4** as guides for placement, fit and sew lattice strips to the top and the bottom of the 7½ × 10½-inch background piece. Take in or let out a few seam allowances ⅟₁₆ inch if necessary. Press the seams toward the background piece.

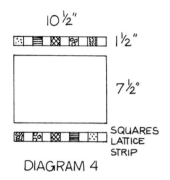

DIAGRAM 4

Step 4. With a seam ripper, remove one square from each of two lattice strips to make two strips with nine squares each. Sew one lattice strip to each side of the same background piece. See **Diagram 5.** Press. Set this pocket piece aside until later.

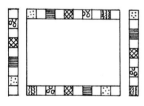

DIAGRAM 5

Step 5. Using a seam ripper, remove two sets of 4 squares from one lattice strip. Sew one set of 4 squares to each of the two remaining lattice strips to make two strips with 14 squares each. Fit and sew these lattice strips to the top and the bottom of the larger

background piece with the half-inch border strips sewn on. Press the seams toward the half-inch border.

Binding

Step 1. Sew 1 × 14½-inch binding strips to the top and bottom of the wallhanging. Press all seams toward the binding.

Step 2. Sew 1 × 18-inch binding strips to the sides of the wallhanging. Press.

Pocket Assembly

Step 1. With right sides together, position the pocket from Step 4 above to the 9½ × 12½-inch background piece (pocket lining). Sew them together, leaving a 3- to 4-inch opening for turning along the bottom edge.

Step 2. Trim the corners and turn the pocket right side out and press, pressing the opening closed.

Step 3. On the top edge of the pocket only, topstitch ⅟₁₆ inch from the top edge and in the seam line between the squares lattice and the background piece.

Step 4. Position the pocket on the front of the large background piece. The pocket should be ½ inch above the bottom half-inch border strip seam and 1 inch in from each binding seam on the sides. Refer to the **Quilt Layout** on page 189 for placement guidance. Pin in position and topstitch along the bottom and sides of the pocket edge. Leave the top open so you can insert coloring books

or artwork. Sew a second row of topstitching in the seam line between the squares lattice and the background piece.

Appliqué

This project was designed especially for the Penstitch appliqué technique described on page 240. If you have chosen bright colors, you may choose to simply fuse the designs into place and skip marking the Penstitch, as it will not show up well on dark fabrics.

Step 1. Cut appliqué designs from selected fabrics using your favorite creature from the **Dinosaur Appliqué Patterns** starting on page 193.

Step 2. Penstitch appliqué the design in the center of the pocket. Use the photograph on page 186 as a placement guide.

Step 3. Sew a ⅛-inch black button to the dinosaur as indicated on the pattern for an eye.

Hanging Tabs

Step 1. Use the 2 × 20-inch strip of fabric you cut for the hanging tabs. Fold it in half lengthwise with wrong sides together and press. Reopen and then fold each long edge in to the center; fold and press again. Topstitch along both edges of the fabric strip.

Step 2. Using a ruler and a rotary cutter, cut four 4-inch pieces from the strip. Fold each piece in half so the cut ends meet; press.

Step 3. On the right side of the wallhanging top, space the tabs evenly across the top of the wallhanging and pin them in position. Position the tabs with the raw edges even with the raw edge of the binding. See **Diagram 6.** Baste the tabs into position. They will be sewn into the seam when the wallhanging is finished.

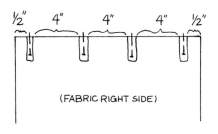

½"   4"   4"   4"   ½"

(FABRIC RIGHT SIDE)

DIAGRAM 6

Finishing

Step 1. Use the finished top as a pattern to trim the backing piece and batting to fit.

Step 2. Position the top and backing with right sides together. Lay both pieces on top of the batting and pin all three layers together. Sew together, leaving a 3- to 4-inch opening for turning.

Step 3. Turn right side out, press, and hand stitch the opening.

Step 4. Machine or hand quilt in the ditch around the binding and half-inch border strips. Quilt along the sides and bottom edge of the pocket.

Step 5. Cut a ½-inch dowel to the width of the quilt, plus 2 inches. Stain or paint the dowel and wooden dowel ends to coordinate with your wallhanging. Run the dowel through the hanging tabs, and glue on the dowel ends.

♡ **SEW CREATIVE** ♡

Create a fun, washable sweatshirt or art apron by fusing on your favorite dinosaur, and then finishing the edges with colorful fabric paint so the edges stay intact and don't fray. (Be sure to prewash any fabrics you plan to launder.)

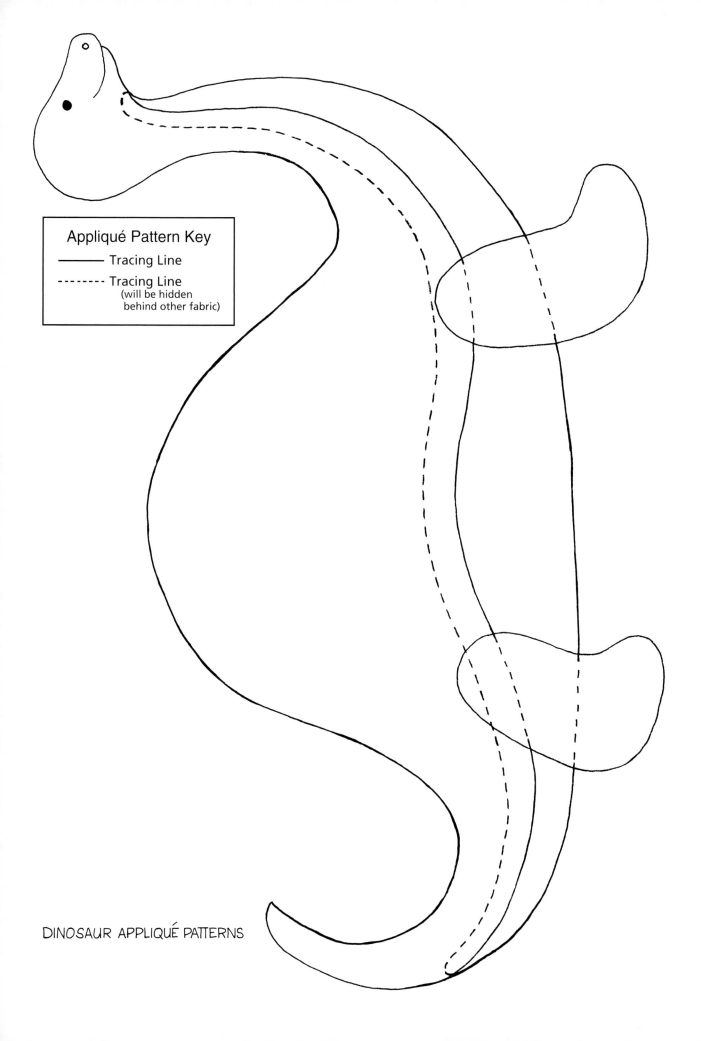

Appliqué Pattern Key

——— Tracing Line

- - - - Tracing Line
(will be hidden
behind other fabric)

DINOSAUR APPLIQUÉ PATTERNS

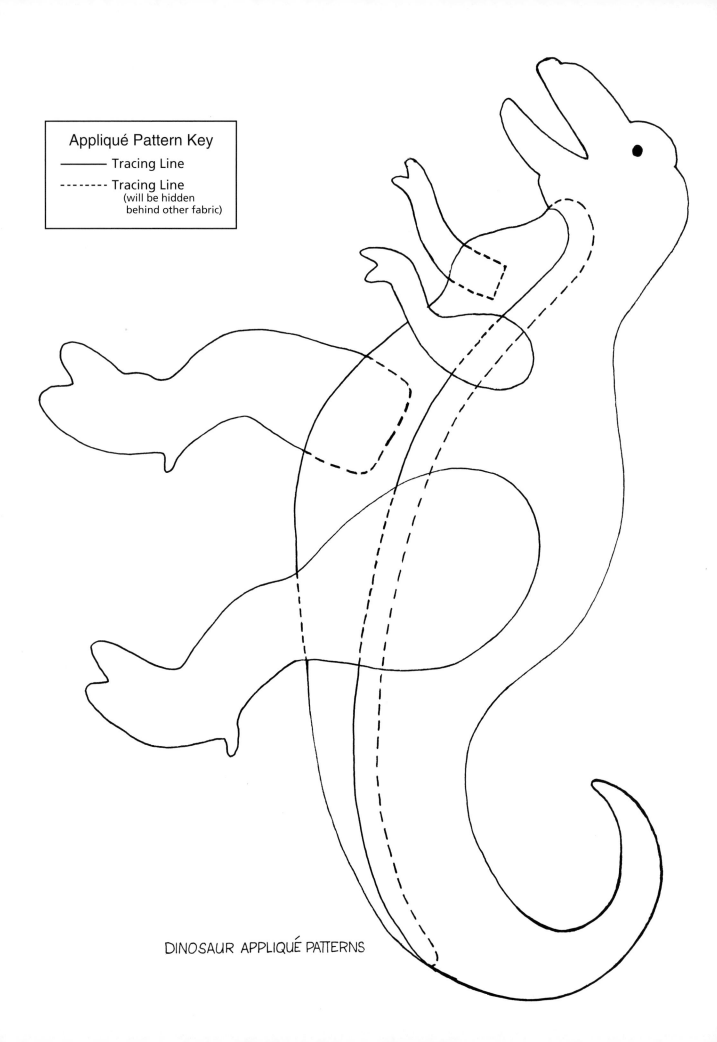

Appliqué Pattern Key

———— Tracing Line

- - - - - Tracing Line
(will be hidden
behind other fabric)

DINOSAUR APPLIQUÉ PATTERNS

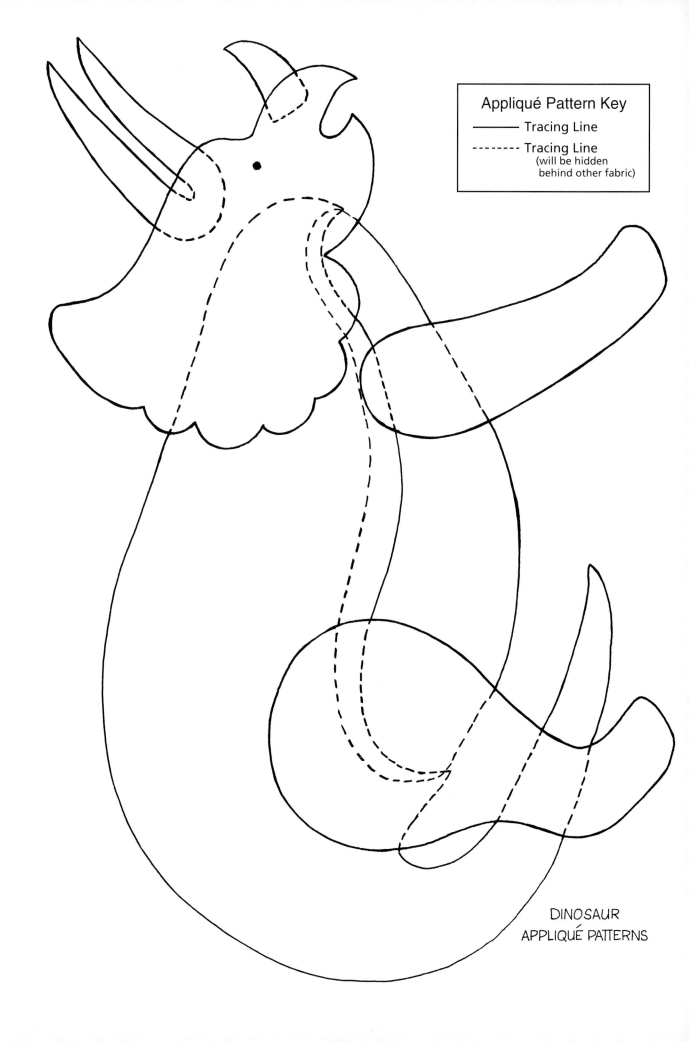

Appliqué Pattern Key
——— Tracing Line
------- Tracing Line
(will be hidden
behind other fabric)

DINOSAUR
APPLIQUÉ PATTERNS

High-Flying Kites

High-Flying Kites

Catch a case of spring fever at the sight of these kites soaring through the air. Create this breezy wallhanging in vibrant springtime pastels. You're bound to have as much fun making your own kites with fabric and thread as you did with paper and string when you were a child. Best of all, no kite-eating trees will get in your way!

Finished Quilt: 22½ × 21½ inches
Finished Block: 4 × 8 inches

Materials

FABRIC

Use four fabrics.	
Kites, Kite Tails, and	
Scrap Border	⅛ yard
	each of *four* fabrics

FABRIC B

Block Background	½ yard

FABRIC C

Lattice, Binding, and	
Kite Tails	½ yard

BACKING   ¾ yard

BATTING   ¾ yard

NOTIONS AND SUPPLIES

Pearl cotton

22½"

21½"

QUILT LAYOUT

SEW COLORFUL

Fresh country pastels were my choice for these harbingers of spring. For a totally different look, you could use bright primary colors. Either of these color palettes would make this project a delightful addition to a young child's room.

Kites: Look for a multicolored print and use that as a guide to pick fabrics for the other kites. My fabrics included pink, green, yellow, and blue. If you use pastels, choose vibrant pastels over light pastels so that your design will stand out.

Background: To simulate the sky, I looked for a light blue fabric. Be certain that there is good contrast between all your kite fabrics and the background.

Lattice and Binding: A medium blue was a good choice for the lattice. You want this fabric to tie in well with the color scheme, but not overpower the kite colors.

Border: The multicolor border uses all the kite fabrics and creates a colorful finish to the edges of the quilt.

Cutting Directions

Prewash and press all of your fabrics. Using a rotary cutter, see-through ruler, and cutting mat, prepare the strips as described in the first column of the chart below. Then from those strips, cut the pieces listed in the second column. Some portions of the quilt need to be cut only once, so no additional cutting information will appear in the second column. Measurements for all pieces include ¼-inch seam allowances.

	FIRST CUT		SECOND CUT	
	NO. OF STRIPS	**DIMENSIONS**	**NO. OF PIECES**	**DIMENSIONS**
FABRIC A	Kites: from *each* of the *four* fabrics, cut the following			
	Before You Cut: The strip below does not need to be exactly 4½ inches wide. Use the width of your ⅛-yard piece.			
	1	4½ × 14-inch piece		
	Kite Tails: from *each* of the *four* fabrics, cut the following			
	6	1 × 1½-inch pieces		
FABRIC B	Background			
	3	4½ × 44-inch strips	4	4½ × 14-inch pieces
			8	4½-inch squares
FABRIC C	Lattice			
	4	1 × 44-inch strips	6	1 × 8½-inch strips
			5	1 × 18-inch strips
	Binding			
	4	2¾ × 44-inch strips		
	Kite Tails			
	8	1 × 1½-inch pieces		

Making Triangle Sets

Step 1. Refer to "Speedy Triangles" on page 231 for how to mark, sew, and cut.

Step 2. Position the 4½ × 14-inch Fabric A and B pieces with right sides together. You will have four sets, one of each Fabric A. On each set, draw a grid of four 2⅞-inch squares. See **Diagram 1.**

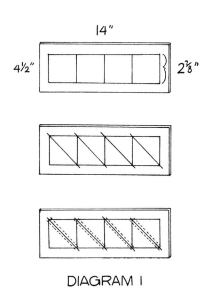

DIAGRAM 1

Step 3. After sewing and cutting are complete, press the seams toward Fabric A on four triangle sets and toward Fabric B on the remaining four triangle sets for each of the four Fabric As. You will have made a total of thirty-two 2½-inch Fabric A/B triangle sets, eight of each Fabric A.

Making the Blocks

Throughout this section, refer to the **Fabric Key** to identify the fabric placement in the diagrams. Also, it's a good idea to review "Assembly-Line Piecing" on page 233 before you get started. It is more efficient to do the same step for each block at the same time than to piece one entire block together at a time. Be sure to press as you go, and follow the arrows for pressing direction. You will be making a total of eight blocks.

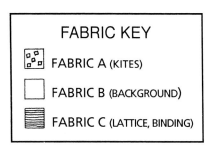

FABRIC KEY
- FABRIC A (KITES)
- FABRIC B (BACKGROUND)
- FABRIC C (LATTICE, BINDING)

Step 1. Before you start sewing, match up the Fabric A/B triangle sets into pairs. Use the same Fabric A in each block, and the pairs should have one triangle set with the seam pressed toward Fabric B and one triangle set with the seam pressed toward Fabric A. You will have a total of 16 pairs. Position them with right sides together, as shown in **Diagram 2.** Use the continuous-seam technique described on page 234 to sew all 16 sets together. Press the seams in the same direction on all 16 sets and cut the joining threads.

DIAGRAM 2

Step 2. Match up the Step 1 units into pairs, using the same Fabric A in each block. You will have a total of eight pairs. Position them with right sides together, as shown in **Diagram 3.** Sew all eight sets together. Press the seams in the same direction on all the units.

Step 3. Sew eight Step 2 units to eight 4½-inch Fabric B squares. See **Diagram 4.** Press.

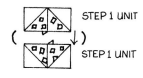

DIAGRAM 3

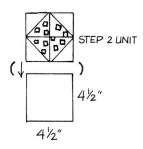

DIAGRAM 4

Lattice

Step 1. Lay out the kite blocks in a pleasing arrangement with two rows of four blocks each. Keep track of your layout while sewing on the lattice.

Step 2. Sew the 1 × 8½-inch Fabric C lattice strips to the right side of six kite blocks. The block on the right end of each row will not get a lattice strip. See **Diagram 5.** Press all seams toward the lattice. Sew three of these blocks, plus one block without lattice, together to make a row of four kites. See **Diagram 6.** Press toward the lattice. Repeat for the second row.

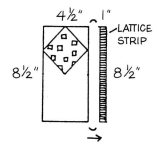

DIAGRAM 5

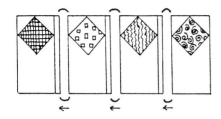

DIAGRAM 6

Step 3. Sew a 1 × 18-inch lattice strip between the rows of kites to join the rows together.

Step 4. Add 1 × 18-inch lattice strips to the top and bottom of the quilt. Press toward the lattice. Sew the remaining two lattice strips to the quilt sides. Press toward the lattice.

Scrap Border

Step 1. Using scraps from the four Fabric As, cut several 11-inch-long strips. The strips should vary in width from 1½ to 4 inches. Sew them together to make an 11 × 21-inch strip set. See **Diagram 7.** Change sewing direction with each strip sewn and press all seams in one direction.

Step 2. From that strip set, cut four 2 × 21-inch strips. See **Diagram 7.**

Step 3. Trim two of these strips down to 2 × 19 inches. Fit, pin, and sew a 2 × 19-inch border strip to the top and the bottom of the quilt. Press the seams toward the lattice.

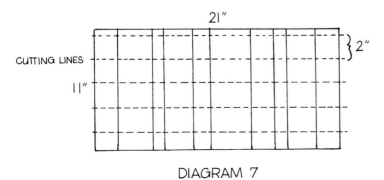

DIAGRAM 7

♡ **SEW CREATIVE** ♡

Make extra scrap borders to trim the edges of curtains, and create a coordinated look for a child's room.

Step 4. Fit, pin, and sew the 2 × 21-inch border strips to the quilt sides. Press.

Kite Tails

Step 1. You should have a total of thirty-two 1 × 1½-inch pieces, twenty-four of Fabric A and eight of Fabric C. Use pinking shears to trim about ⅛ inch on all four sides of each fabric rectangle.

Step 2. Thread a "sharp" needle and tie a knot at the end of the thread. On each of the fabric rectangles, hand stitch short running stitches through the center, as shown in **Diagram 8.** Pull the thread to gather the fabric. Wrap the thread around the center of each bow and tie a knot on the back. See **Diagram 8.** Each kite uses four bows, one of Fabric C and one of each Fabric A that is different from the kite.

Step 3. Thread a needle with an 8-inch piece of pearl cotton and tie a knot at one end of the thread. From the back of the quilt top, bring the needle up through the

fabric at the bottom corner of the kite at the seam line. Run the needle through the center of each of the four bows, spacing the first one approximately ½ to ¾ inch from the edge of the kite and spacing the bows approximately ¾ inch apart. Tie a knot on the back of the fourth bow. Trim the ends of the thread.

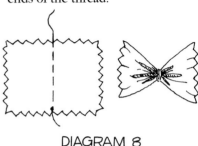

DIAGRAM 8

SEW SMART

If you wish to keep the tails in position, hand tack each bow into place from the back of the quilt top.

Layering the Quilt

Arrange and baste the backing, batting, and quilt top together, following the directions in "Layering the Quilt" on page 249. Trim the batting and backing to ¼ inch from the raw edge of the quilt top.

Binding the Quilt

Using the 2¾ × 44-inch Fabric C strips, follow the directions on page 249 for "Binding the Quilt."

Finishing Stitches

Outline your kites by quilting in the ditch or ¼ inch away from the seam lines. Outline the lattice and quilt in the ditch between the strips in the scrap border.

Raggedy Rag Dolls

15"

17"

RAG DOLL WALLHANGING LAYOUT

Rag dolls were once the cherished possessions of little pioneers crossing the prairie. Dolls were made from a favorite outgrown dress or scraps from Mother's sewing basket. This wallhanging, doll, and doll's quilt pay tribute to little girls and their dolls from every generation. They're all quick and easy to sew, so it won't take long to stitch one of these for your favorite little girl—or for yourself if you haven't outgrown your love of dolls!

Rag Doll Wallhanging

Finished Size: 15 × 17 inches

Materials

FABRIC A
Background $\frac{1}{3}$ yard

FABRIC B
Half-Inch Border
   and Binding $\frac{1}{6}$ yard (6 inches)
Hanging Tabs $\frac{1}{8}$ yard
   (or one 2 × 20-inch strip)

SCRAP BORDER
Several coordinated fabric scraps

BACKING $\frac{1}{2}$ yard

BATTING $\frac{1}{2}$ yard

APPLIQUÉ PIECES
Doll Jumper $\frac{1}{4}$ yard
Doll and Hearts
   in Border $\frac{1}{8}$ yard pieces
   (or several coordinated scraps)
Doll Hair   3 × 6-inch piece
Teddy Bear   3 × 6-inch piece
Cotton Batting
   for Teddy Bear   3 × 3-inch piece

NOTIONS AND SUPPLIES
Two $\frac{3}{8}$-inch buttons for eyes
Two $\frac{3}{16}$-inch black buttons
   for teddy bear
Assorted buttons for border,
   ranging in size from $\frac{3}{8}$ to
   $1\frac{1}{16}$ inch (I used 14)
Sewable appliqué film
Embroidery floss to match
   appliqué fabrics
Black, extra-fine point,
   permanent felt-tip pen
Black pearl cotton
Black quilting thread
Wooden dowel, $\frac{1}{2}$-inch
   diameter × 17 inches long
Two dowel ends or wooden beads
Acrylic paint

SEW COLORFUL

Old, antique, and country are the images we conjure up when we think of rag dolls. Take these images with you when you choose your fabrics for these projects. I combined rich reds and blues with tans and browns to get an Early American look. You can substitute two other colors for the red and blue and still have a similar look.

Applique Designs: Choose the appliqué fabrics first. Look for old-fashioned prints and plaids for the clothes. Rag dolls traditionally have red-striped socks with black shoes. For the face and hands, look for a tea-dyed–look fabric.

Background: By using a very warm and a little darker background fabric as I have, the whole project will take on a more "antiquey" look.

Borders and Binding: If you have enough fabric scraps to use all different fabrics in the border, it will enhance the old-fashioned "scrappy" look of your project. Coordinate these fabrics with your appliqué fabrics. For the light tan hearts, I suggest using as many different fabrics as you can, but it's fine to repeat a few of them because the same tan will look a little different on different fabric squares. Use different shapes and sizes of buttons to finish your border. Solid black is effective in the half-inch border and binding, as long as there is some black in your prints, the shoes, and the embroidery thread.

Cutting Directions

Using a rotary cutter, see-through ruler, and cutting mat, prepare the strips as described in the first column in the chart below. Then from those strips, cut the pieces listed in the second column. Some portions of the wallhanging need to be cut only once, so no additional cutting information will appear in the second column. Measurements for all pieces include ¼-inch seam allowances.

	FIRST CUT		SECOND CUT	
	NO. OF STRIPS	DIMENSIONS	NO. OF PIECES	DIMENSIONS
FABRIC A	Background			
	1	9½ × 11½-inch piece		
	Half-Inch Border			
	2	1 × 44-inch strips	2	1 × 9½-inch strips
			2	1 × 12½-inch strips
	Binding			
	2	1 × 44-inch strips	2	1 × 14½-inch strips
			2	1 × 17½-inch strips
SCRAPS	Scrap Border			
	26	2½-inch squares		
BACKING				
	1	17 × 19-inch piece		
BATTING				
	1	17 × 19-inch piece		

Appliqué

The appliqué in this wallhanging was designed especially to use the buttonhole embroidery technique described on page 241. However, you may use Penstitch or machine appliqué if you prefer. For the buttonhole embroidery or machine appliqué, be sure to use a sewable appliqué film.

Step 1. Cut the appliqué designs from assorted fabrics using the **Rag Doll Appliqué Pattern** on pages 210 and 211. Cut 26 appliqué hearts from assorted scraps of fabric using the **Small Heart Appliqué Pattern** on page 210.

Step 2. Position the doll face piece over the appliqué pattern. With a pencil, lightly trace the mouth, hearts, and eyelashes. Make a mark for the position of the button eyes and fused nose.

> **SEW SMART**
>
> The eyes will be sewn on and the face will be completed after the wallhanging top is assembled. It's hard to press effectively if you have already sewn buttons to your wallhanging.

Step 3. Appliqué all the pieces of the doll design onto the 9½ × 11½-inch background piece. Use the **Rag Doll Appliqué Pattern** and the **Appliqué Pattern Key** as guides to position and fuse the design. Use the buttonhole embroidery technique described on page 241 to finish the edges of the appliquéd doll.

Step 4. Center and appliqué the hearts that you cut in Step 1 to the

twenty-six 2½-inch scrap border squares. After fusing, hand stitch the hearts to the background squares using one strand of black quilting thread. Make the stitches ¼ inch apart and approximately ¼ inch in length, as shown in **Diagram 1.**

DIAGRAM 1

Half-Inch Border

Step 1. Sew the 1 × 9½-inch Fabric B border strips to the top and bottom of the wallhanging. Press all seams toward the border.

Step 2. Sew one 1 × 12½-inch border strip to each side. Press.

Scrap Border

Step 1. Lay out the border squares with appliquéd hearts around the wallhanging top in a pleasing arrangement. Sew together two strips of five squares each for the top and bottom and two strips of eight squares each for the sides. Press all seams in one direction.

Step 2. Sew the five-square strips to the top and bottom of the wallhanging. Press all seams toward the half-inch border.

Step 3. Sew the eight-square strips to the wallhanging sides. Press.

Binding

Step 1. Sew the 1 × 14½-inch binding strips to the top and

bottom of the wallhanging. Press all seams toward the binding.

Step 2. Sew the 1 × 17½-inch binding strips to the sides. Press.

Hanging Tabs

Step 1. Cut one 2 × 20-inch strip of Fabric B. Fold it in half with wrong sides together. Press. Reopen and then fold each long edge in to the center, fold, and press again. Topstitch along the edge of both sides of the fabric strip.

Step 2. Using the ruler and rotary cutter, cut four 4-inch pieces from the strip. Fold each piece in half so the cut ends meet. Press.

Step 3. On the right side of the quilt top, space the tabs evenly across the top of the quilt and pin them in position. Position the tabs with the raw edges even with the raw edge of the binding. See **Diagram 2.** Baste the tabs into place. They will be sewn into the seam when the wallhanging is finished.

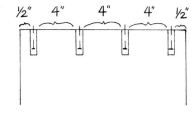

DIAGRAM 2

Finishing the Doll Face

Use the felt-tip pen to draw the mouth, hearts, and eyelashes. Color in the hearts with a red colored pencil. Fuse the nose into position. Sew two ⅜-inch buttons into place for the eyes.

Doll Hair

Step 1. Using the 3 × 6-inch fabric scrap, cut twenty ¼ × 3-inch strips.

Step 2. Put two ¼-inch strips together and tie a knot in the center. See **Diagram 3.** Repeat with the remaining 18 strips. You will have a total of ten knots.

DIAGRAM 3

Step 3. Hand stitch each knot to the doll's head where indicated on the pattern. Sew the knot down and let the four ends of each knot stand up like hair. Trim the ends to approximately ½ to ¾ inch long.

Doll's Teddy Bear

Step 1. Make a template by tracing the **Teddy Bear Pattern** on page 210 onto template plastic, posterboard, or lightweight cardboard.

Step 2. Cut the 3 × 6-inch piece of teddy bear fabric in half to make two 3-inch squares. Position them *wrong sides together,* sandwiching the 3-inch square batting scrap in the middle. Trace one teddy bear onto the *right side* of the top fabric scrap. This tracing line is your sewing line.

Step 3. Sew on the tracing line through all three layers, all the way around the teddy bear. Trim ⅛ inch away from your stitching line. Sew two ³⁄₁₆-inch buttons to the body of the teddy bear as indicated on the pattern.

Step 4. Hand tack the bear into position on the doll's arm. See the photograph on page 202 as a guide for placement.

Finishing

Step 1. Position the top and backing with right sides together. Lay both pieces on top of the batting and pin all three layers together. Trim the batting and backing to the same size as the top. Sew together, leaving a 3- to 4-inch opening for turning.

Step 2. Turn the wallhanging right side out and hand stitch the opening.

Step 3. Machine or hand quilt in the ditch around the borders and the binding, and between the squares in the border. Outline the doll by quilting ¹⁄₁₆ inch away from the edge of the design. Quilt a 1½-inch diagonal grid in the background behind the doll.

> ♥ **SEW CREATIVE** ♥
>
> Here's how to make a wooden dowel hanger with heart-shaped ends as shown in the photograph on page 202. Use the **Small Heart Appliqué Pattern** on page 210 to cut out dowel ends from ¾- to 1-inch-thick wood. Drill ½-inch holes on the sides of the hearts, and paint them with red acrylic paint. For a more primitive or country look, carve or sand down the sharp edges of your hearts before you paint them.

Step 4. Sew assorted buttons to the center of some hearts in the border squares. Use black pearl cotton or crochet thread to sew the buttons into place. Tie the knot on the top for some buttons and on the back of the quilt for other buttons.

Step 5. Stain or paint the wooden dowel and dowel ends to coordinate with your wallhanging. Run the dowel through the hanging tabs and glue on the dowel ends.

Rag Doll

Finished Size: Approximately 16 inches tall

Materials

DOLL   ⅓ yard muslin (or two 12 × 18-inch pieces)

SHOES   One 6 × 7-inch piece

DRESS   ⅓ yard (or two 12 × 18-inch pieces)

HAIR   ⅛ yard

NOTIONS AND SUPPLIES

⅓ yard nonfusible interfacing
Smooth stuffing like FiberFil; shredded foam is not recommended.
Two ⅜-inch buttons for eyes
Assorted buttons, ribbons, and spools for finishing touches on dresses (See page 255 for a mail-order source of bulk buttons and small wooden spools.)
Black, extra-fine point, permanent felt-tip pen

SEW COLORFUL

For the Rag Dolls, I used the same color scheme as described in "Sew Colorful" for the Rag Doll Wallhanging on page 204. You need to select just three fabrics for the doll.

Body: Look for a fabric with a tea-dyed look for a time-worn appearance.

Dress: Use a print with an old-fashioned look, or a plaid. If you're making the quilt, you'll want to coordinate the two to go together. Choose your favorite fabric for her dress and use that in the quilt as well.

Hair: Traditionally, most Raggedy Ann dolls have red hair. You may want to follow tradition or have fun experimenting. Anything from muslin to brown, red, or navy will work.

Assembly

Use ¼-inch seam allowances.

Step 1. Use the **Rag Doll Patterns** on pages 212 and 213. Trace the doll and shoe onto nonfusible interfacing to make the patterns.

Step 2. With fabric right sides together, cut the doll body (cut two per doll) out of muslin, and the shoes (cut 4 per doll) out of black fabric.

Step 3. With right sides together, pin and sew a shoe piece to the bottom of each of the four legs. Press the seams toward the shoe.

Step 4. With right sides together, pin and sew the doll front and back together. Leave a 3- to 4-inch opening in the side for turning. Clip and trim the curves, turn, and press.

SEW SMART

For smoother curves, trim the seam allowances with pinking shears.

Step 5. Stuff the doll and hand stitch the opening. Use a knitting needle to help push stuffing into the arms and legs.

Step 6. To make the dress, use the **Dress Pattern** on page 214. Trace the dress onto nonfusible interfacing to make a pattern. Place the pattern piece on the fold of your fabric. Cut two dress pieces for each doll.

Step 7. With right sides together, pin and sew the side and sleeve seams in the dress. Leave the neck open. Clip the curves. Press.

Step 8. Put the dress on the doll body. Turn under a ¼-inch seam allowance on the neck edge. With a needle and thread, hand sew a running stitch approximately ⅛ inch from the folded edge. Pull on the thread to gather the neck edge and tie a knot. Turn under approximately 1 inch on each sleeve. Sew a running stitch approximately ¾ inch from the folded edge and pull the thread to gather each sleeve opening. Turn under a ¼-inch seam allowance on the bottom edge and hand sew a running stitch ⅛ inch from the folded edge for the hem.

Step 9. For the hair, cut two 1½ × 44-inch strips of fabric. Fold each strip in half lengthwise with wrong sides together and press. Using a rotary cutter, cut sixteen 4½-inch pieces. Tie a knot in the center of each of the sixteen pieces. With a needle and thread, hand sew the pieces of hair into position on the doll's head along the seam line. Start at the top center and work down each side, positioning each knot approximately ½ inch apart. You may choose to trim the hair to approximately 1 to 1¼ inches in length.

Step 10. Sew two ⅜-inch buttons to the doll's face for eyes. Using the **Rag Doll Patterns** on page 212, cut and fuse a nose and heart-shape cheeks to the doll's face. If you prefer, two ¹¹⁄₁₆-inch buttons can be used for the cheeks. Draw the doll's mouth with the black felt-tip pen.

Finishing Touches

Have fun personalizing your doll with buttons, trims, and embellishments.

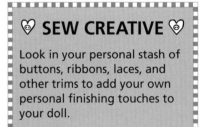

♡ **SEW CREATIVE** ♡

Look in your personal stash of buttons, ribbons, laces, and other trims to add your own personal finishing touches to your doll.

Necklace

The necklace I made has 12 small buttons and three ⅝-inch unfinished wooden spools.

Step 1. Wrap the spools with a coordinating color of embroidery thread. Use a dot of tacky glue to hold the thread end in place.

Step 2. Starting with three buttons, string the buttons and spools onto a 10-inch piece of embroidery thread. Position the necklace around the doll's neck and tie a knot in the thread. Trim the ends.

Dress

Buttons: Sew four small buttons to the dress with black embroidery thread. Position the buttons approximately 1 inch apart.

Bow : Cut an 18-inch piece of ⅛-inch ribbon. Tie a bow in the center and hand stitch the bow to the front of the dress at the neckline. Sew an ¹¹⁄₁₆-inch button to the center of the bow.

Doll's Quilt

Finished Quilt: 20 × 22½ inches

Materials and Cutting

Using a rotary cutter, see-through ruler, and cutting mat, prepare the strips as described in the first column in the chart below. Then from those strips, cut the pieces listed in the second column. Some portions of the quilt need to be cut only once, so no additional cutting information will appear in the second column. Measurements for all pieces include ¼-inch seam allowances.

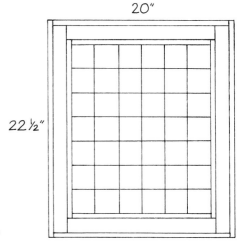

DOLL'S QUILT LAYOUT

	YARDAGE	CUTTING	
		NO. OF PIECES	**DIMENSIONS**
Appliqué Designs and Scrap Top	Several coordinated fabric scraps	**Before You Cut:** Cut 21 tans and 21 blues and reds.	
		42	3-inch squares
Half-Inch Border	¼ yard	2	1 × 15½-inch strips
		2	1 × 19-inch strips
Binding		2	1 × 19½-inch strips
		2	1 × 23-inch strips
One-and-a-Half-Inch Border	¼ yard	2	2 × 16½-inch strips
		2	2 × 22-inch strips
Backing	⅝ yard	1	22 × 25-inch piece
Batting	⅝ yard	1	22 × 25-inch piece
Appliqué film (sewable) Assorted buttons, ranging in size from ½ to 1⅛ inches Black pearl cotton or crochet thread (See page 255 for a mail-order source of bulk buttons.)			

SEW COLORFUL

For the doll's quilt, I used the same color scheme as described in "Sew Colorful" for the Rag Doll Wallhanging on page 204.

Background Squares: For a great "scrappy" look, I used different fabrics to make up all the squares. Just alternate the dark and light squares. The dark is made up of the red and blue fabrics and the light is the tan fabrics.

Appliqué Designs: Have fun and come up with a variety of fabric combinations. Put light hearts on dark squares and dark hearts on light squares. Put a red heart on a blue square or vice versa. I used different browns for the bears and put them all on light squares, but don't be afraid to try different combinations.

Borders and Binding: Dark navy makes a good, strong half-inch border and binding. I chose a red check for the wider border, but you could switch the navy and use it in the wide border with a deep, dark red for the half-inch border. Or try a dark brown for the half-inch border.

Assembly and Appliqué

Step 1. Alternating the tans with the blues and reds, lay out your squares in a pleasing arrangement. Lay out seven rows of six blocks each.

Step 2. Cut the appliqué designs from assorted fabrics using the **Large Heart Appliqué Pattern** on page 210 and the **Teddy Bear Pattern** on page 210. Trace, cut, and fuse eleven hearts and five bears to the squares. It's much easier to hand stitch the appliqué pieces to the squares before assembling the quilt top.

Step 3. Hand stitch the hearts to the background squares using one strand of black quilting thread. Make the stitches ¼ inch apart and approximately ¼ inch in length. See **Diagram 4.** Hand stitch the bears to the background using one strand of black quilting thread. Use a straight running stitch, approximately ⅛ inch in length and ⅛ inch from the edge of the bear. See **Diagram 5.**

DIAGRAM 4

DIAGRAM 5

Step 4. Once the hand sewing is completed, sew together each of the seven rows of six squares. Press all seams in one direction in the first row, and change pressing direction in the second row. Continue to alternate pressing direction with each row. See **Diagram 6.**

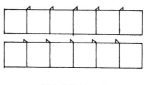

DIAGRAM 6

Step 5. Sew the seven rows together. Press the seams toward the bottom row.

♡ SEW CREATIVE ♡

The placement of appliqué designs and buttons on the squares is random, but try to distribute them evenly so there is a balance. Don't bunch up all the hearts or bears together. Use different sizes and shapes of buttons, and put different amounts of buttons on different squares. You may have a special charm that you'd like to add to your project, too.

Half-Inch Border

Sew the 1 × 15½-inch border strips to the top and bottom of the wallhanging. Press all seams toward the border. Sew the 1 × 19-inch border strips to the sides. Press.

One-and-a-Half-Inch Border

Sew the 2 × 16½-inch border strips to the top and bottom of the wallhanging. Press all seams toward the one-and-a-half-inch border. Sew the 2 × 22-inch border strips to the sides. Press.

Binding

Sew the 1 × 19½-inch binding strips to the top and bottom of the wallhanging. Press all seams toward the binding. Sew the 1 × 23-inch binding strips to the sides. Press.

Finishing

Step 1. Position the top and backing with right sides together. Lay both pieces on top of the batting and pin all three layers together. Trim the batting and backing to the same size as the top. Sew them together, leaving a 3- to 4-inch opening for turning.

Step 2. Turn the quilt right side out and hand stitch the opening.

Step 3. Machine or hand quilt in the ditch around the borders and the binding. Quilt ¼ inch from the seam allowances in the light squares. Quilt diagonal lines from corner to corner through each of the dark squares. (Don't quilt through the appliqué pieces; go behind them through the batting.)

Step 4. Sew assorted buttons to the center of some squares and hearts and to the corners of the borders. Use black pearl cotton or crochet thread to sew the buttons into place. Tie the knot on the top for some of the buttons and on the back of the quilt for other buttons.

LARGE HEART APPLIQUÉ PATTERN

TEDDY BEAR PATTERN

Appliqué Pattern Key

— Tracing Line

- - - - - Tracing Line (will be hidden behind other fabric)

SMALL HEART APPLIQUÉ PATTERN

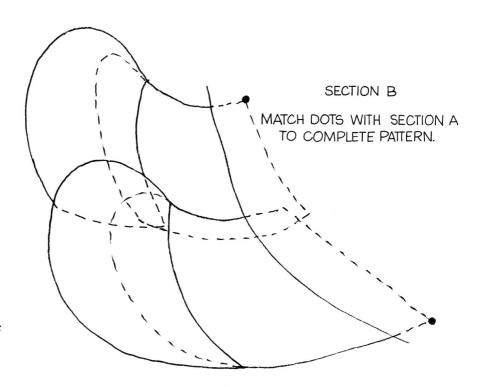

SECTION B

MATCH DOTS WITH SECTION A TO COMPLETE PATTERN.

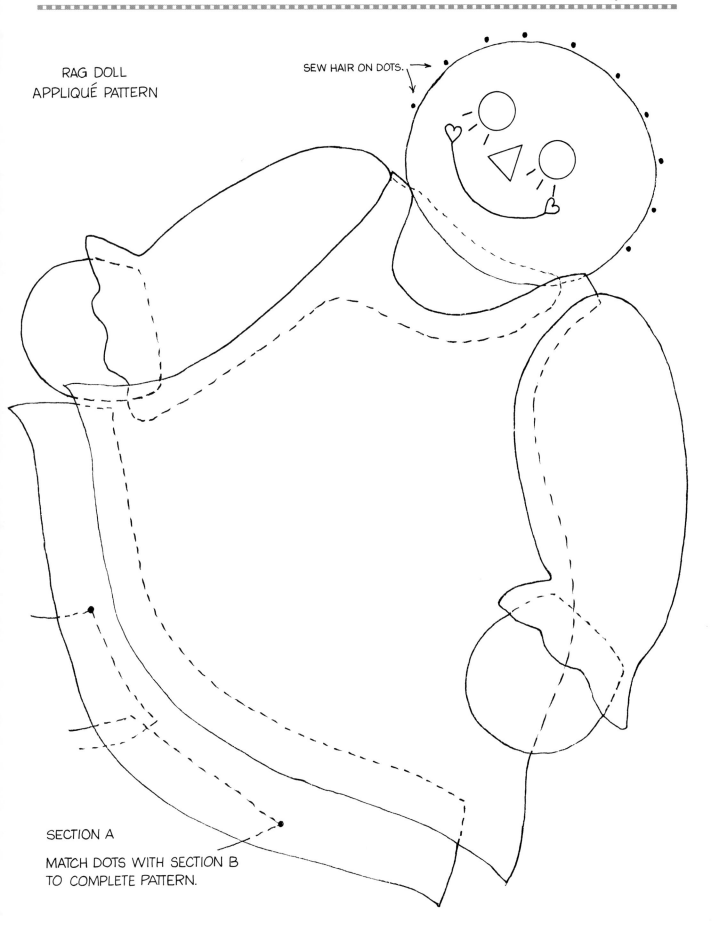

RAG DOLL
APPLIQUÉ PATTERN

SEW HAIR ON DOTS.

SECTION A

MATCH DOTS WITH SECTION B
TO COMPLETE PATTERN.

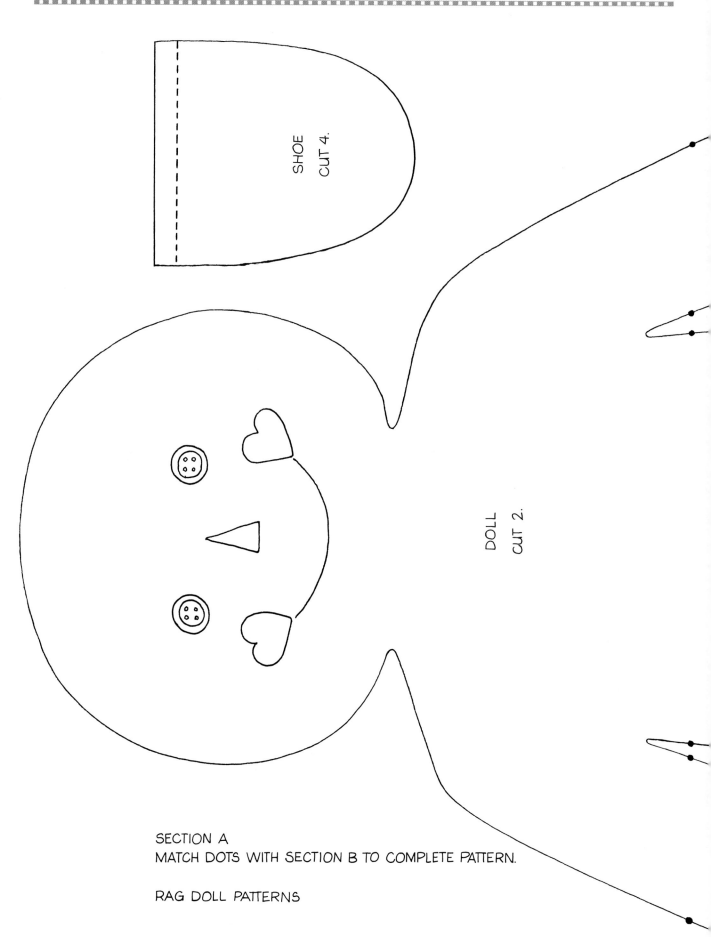

SHOE
CUT 4.

DOLL
CUT 2.

SECTION A
MATCH DOTS WITH SECTION B TO COMPLETE PATTERN.

RAG DOLL PATTERNS

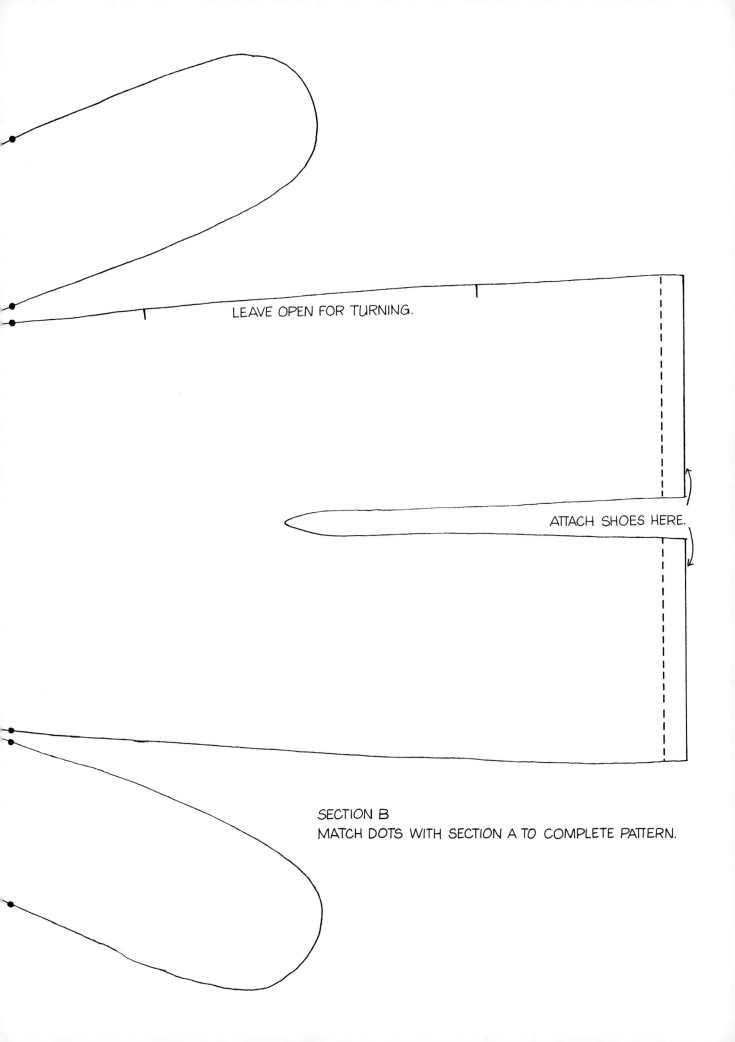

LEAVE OPEN FOR TURNING.

ATTACH SHOES HERE.

SECTION B
MATCH DOTS WITH SECTION A TO COMPLETE PATTERN.

PLACE ON FOLD.

DRESS
CUT 2 ON FOLD.

DRESS PATTERN

Techniques for More Quick Country Quilting

In these chapters you'll find all the details you'll need for making the quilt projects in this book. The "Country Color Guide for Quilters" will help you select fabrics and colors for your quilts. "Timesaving Methods for Cutting and Piecing" highlights the speedy cutting and sewing techniques I incorporate into all of my projects. In "Timesaving Methods for Appliqué," you'll learn my Penstitch appliqué technique, as well as other shortcut methods. "Putting It All Together" takes you from the finished quilt top through the final phase of quilting and binding. Here's a handy checklist of pointers on how to use this section of the book.

♥ Before you make your first project, take the time to read these chapters. They don't take long to read and it's a good way to familiarize yourself with all the techniques that appear in the projects.

♥ Be sure to check "What You'll Need for Cutting and Piecing" on page 227 and "What You'll Need for Appliqué" on page 238. You may want to take this book with you to the quilt shop in case you have any questions about one or more of the items you need to purchase.

♥ Once you are actually working on a project, be sure to flip back to these chapters when you need to refresh your memory about the specific details of a certain technique.

♥ Watch for "Sew Smart" and "Sew Creative" throughout the chapters and project directions. These are handy hints and creative ideas you can use as you make your projects.

Country Color Guide for Quilters

For most of us, color is a mystery. We know what we like and we know what we don't like and that's about the extent of our color expertise. It's quite understandable why many quiltmakers, faced with hundreds, thousands, and very possibly millions of different fabrics and colors to choose from, feel overwhelmed and underequipped to make their selections. My hope is that this section of the book, with its tips, color guidelines, and actual photos of fabric combinations, will help you feel more confident about playing with color and fabric to create pleasing country quilts.

As another color aid for quilters, throughout the book I've included a box called "Sew Colorful" with each project. In these you'll find tips and suggestions on fabrics and color schemes that pertain to that specific design. Since I love the country look, and more specifically the colors associated with folk art, my projects reflect that particular color palette. But remember that there are many other fabric combinations that can work very successfully. Don't be afraid to try something completely different from what I did.

Collecting Fabrics

One of the joys of being a quiltmaker is the opportunity it gives us to explore all the wonderful fabrics that are being made today. We are fortunate to have such a wide array of cottons in solids, prints, stripes, and plaids that come in every color imaginable. It's no wonder there are so many bumper stickers out there proclaiming the existence of another "fabriholic!"

Some quilters have the habit of buying just what they need for a particular project. Other quilters take the point of view that they are building their fabric collection or fabric library, which they go to when they're ready to work on a project. I will admit that I fall into the fabric collector category.

Having a stash of fabric already on hand is a wonderful way to find color inspiration for a project. Fat quarters (half of a half-yard, or pieces 18 × 22 inches) and fat eighths (half of a fat quarter, or 9 × 22 inches)

are relatively inexpensive ways to include a lot of different fabrics in your collection. Because my appliqué projects tend to be small, you really don't need huge amounts of fabric. For my pieced projects, which usually need strips cut the full width, you would be better off sticking to 44-inch-wide fabric.

Once you have a fabric collection started, it's a good idea to group your fabrics by color. That way you'll be able to see exactly what you have and you'll discover whether you have any gaps (maybe you have a towering stack of medium blues, but not a single yellow). Some quilters find that an inventory sheet, made on an index card listing what they already have or what they need, is a handy thing to keep in a purse. That way, when you happen to come across a sale at the fabric store, you'll be able to spend wisely!

How Much Fabric Should I Buy?

I'm often asked by students, "How much should I buy?" "As much as you can!" would be my optimistic answer. Unfortunately, we don't have unlimited funds for fabric (or unlimited storage space), so we need to make choices.

Of course, how much depends on what you plan to use the fabric for and how many projects you make. If you're a fabric collector, it's very likely you may not have a specific project in mind, but you want to add certain pieces to your collection for possible future use. You need to look into the future to imagine what you might use it for.

Another important point to consider is what size project you are likely to make. All of my quilt designs are wall size, so they will obviously take less yardage than a bed-size quilt. Since I'm most experienced with buying fabric for wall-size projects, the guidelines I provide below are oriented toward buying fabric for this size.

Possible Background Fabric: 1½ to 2 yards. If it's a background fabric that I like so much I may use it for several projects, I increase that amount to 3 to 5 yards.

Possible Block Fabric: ⅓ to 1 yard. For a favorite that I may use in blocks for a few projects, 1 to 2 yards. If I like it so much I want leftovers (even after it's been used in a couple of quilts), 2 to 3 yards.

Possible Appliqué Fabrics: ⅛ to ½ yard. Also collect fat quarters and fat eighths. For leftovers of an especially nice appliqué fabric, ½ to 1 yard.

Possible Border Fabrics: ½ to 1 yard. A great border fabric in my favorite color scheme increases the amount to 1 to 2 yards. (Note that border fabrics often need to be coordinated to specific quilt colors, so buying ahead may not always work out.)

Country Quilter's Fabric Motto: Stay well stocked, but always leave room for more! Buying a lot makes you feel secure because you don't have to worry about running out. However, you always want to save some space on your fabric shelves and some extra money in your budget to keep up with the newest fabrics.

Visual Textures

If you are looking for one "golden rule" to help guide your fabric selection, remember this: Variety (meaning a good assortment of visually different fabrics) is the key to an interesting and appealing-looking project. Too many fabrics that look the same make a boring quilt.

How do you ensure good variety? One way is to start to think about "visual texture." Different types of prints create different kinds of textures for your eyes to read. The more variety in visual textures there is, the more there is for your eyes to take in, which translates into a more exciting quilt. It's obvious then that you'll want to collect fabrics with lots of different visual textures. To help you understand what I mean by visual texture, look at the fabric examples on page 218. These are the kinds of visual textures I use in my quilts (there are lots more, but I've decided to focus just on those prints that I've used in this book). As you study the fabric samples, read my hints on how to make the best use of these types of prints.

Quilter's Color and Fabric Checklist

Heading out to the fabric store can be a little overwhelming. There are yards and yards of choices! I've put together a handy list of points to keep in mind as you make your fabric selections.

✄ Visual variety is the spice of life . . . and quiltmaking. Use a lot of different visual textures in every project.

✄ Be conscious of contrast. Be sure there is good contrast between the fabrics you choose for the blocks, background, and borders.

✄ Keep your eye on the scale. Vary the scale of the prints you choose, incorporating small, medium, and large ones.

✄ Examine your values. Look at your project to determine where you want to place light, medium, and dark fabrics.

✄ Start with a multicolor print and use the colors in that print to guide your selection of other fabrics for the quilt.

✄ Follow "directionals" and see where those fabrics lead in your project. Think about how it might look once it's cut out and arranged within your block. Does the print veer off in every direction, or is it subtle enough not to be distracting?

✄ Go rich or bright, but not both. If you're working with deep, rich shades or bright colors, use either one or the other throughout your project. This is not a place where I recommend mixing and matching.

✄ Don't underestimate the value of trial and error. Be open to playing with different fabrics and different colors. Try some you normally wouldn't think about using. You might be pleasantly surprised.

✄ Relax, have fun, and don't worry! There are lots of good choices you can make. There is no one right way to put together a group of colors and fabrics.

Abstract: These prints feature nonrepresentational forms. (In other words, they don't look like anything specific). These are often multicolored prints. These fabrics lend themselves well to contemporary styled quilts. In my own projects, I used abstract prints successfully in High-Flying Kites and Game Quilts.

Geometric: Think of angles or regularly repeating motifs when you think of geometric prints. I love to use prints with squares, rectangles, and triangles in my quilts. Checked prints are among my all-time favorites because they create a wonderful visual contrast to swirly, flowing prints. I find they add a fun, lively aspect to a quilt, and certainly are strongly associated with the country look (although they're equally at home in more contemporary quilts). Look at Bow Tie Bears and the Twelve-Tree Quilt in Whispering Pines to see how I've used geometrics.

Pictorial: Pictorial prints have designs or motifs that represent recognizable objects. Christmas prints with Santas, reindeer, and trees and juvenile prints with animals, crayons, or baby footprints are two popular categories of pictorial prints. If you are trying to make a strong statement about the subject or purpose of your quilt, pictorial prints can enhance this statement. What I caution you to watch for when using this print is to keep the project from looking too cutesy or cliché. With projects for kids, you probably have more leeway before your project risks becoming overly cute. Patriotic Nine-Star Quilt and Rub-a-Dub Ducks are quilts where I've used pictorial prints.

Circular: As you'd expect, circles, ovals, spirals, and other curved shapes make up these prints. I find that circle prints are particularly effective to use for "spotty" animals, like the ones in Noah and Friends and Patchwork Pigs. Circular prints create movement, which can be an exciting element to incorporate into a quilt. A good example of this is the blue curved print used for the water in the All Aboard! quilt in Noah and Friends. You can practically feel those waves!

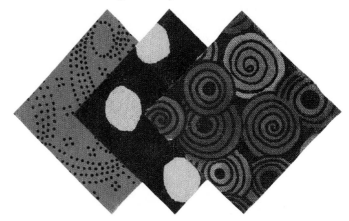

Plaid: There are plaids that combine several colors and those that use just a couple; they also vary in scale—from tiny, subtle plaids to larger, bolder ones. Use these for good visual contrast to circular or other rounded shapes. Although I usually recommend a variety of visual textures, I've seen wonderful quilts made up entirely of plaids. Plaids create a warm, homespun feel and look tremendous in country-style quilts. Crazy for Cats II, Noah and Friends, and Countryside Samplers make good use of plaids.

Floral: These are probably the most abundant and popular type of print on the market. A multicolor floral can be the basis for selecting other fabrics for a project. (Read more about this later under Multicolor Prints on page 224.) A good rule to remember when using more than one floral print in a project is to vary the scales by using both large and small prints. Since florals often have good visual depth and dimension, use them to create movement or a flowing feeling in your quilt. Florals are lovely in traditional and country-style quilts. I found them to be the perfect choice in Basket Bouquets.

Striped: Stripes come in all shapes and sizes. They can be thin or bold; straight or squiggly; bunched together or spaced widely apart. To create a folk-art look, I like to combine stripes with checks and plaids (take a look at Bow Tie Bears for an example of this). High contrast between the colors in the stripes creates a vibrant, energetic feel. See how high contrast works in the border of the Patriotic Nine-Star Quilt. Stripes can be used vertically or horizontally; I prefer to use vertical stripes in a quilt (except when they appear in borders).

Leafy: Leaves are a popular print motif since they have very interesting textures and lines, plus beautiful colors. The basic leaf shape is usually oval, yet there are often angles and points along the edges to create a contrast of textures within the print itself. Calm, subtly colored, small-scale leaf prints can be used effectively as backgrounds, while larger and bolder leafy fabrics make attractive accents (like in corner blocks or borders). You can even use them in blocks, as I did in Whispering Pines.

Combination: Just as the name says, a combination print is made up of two or more types of prints. For instance, if a print combines stripes with circular shapes, those shapes together create a combination print. This contrast of visual textures within one print can really add a lot of interest and energy to your quilts. This type of print isn't quite as common as some but can be fun to use in a variety of quilt projects. I used a combination print for the stegosaurus in the Quilt-O-Saurus Art Holder.

Paisley: There's no mistaking these colorful, curved, abstract shapes. The interesting curving and swirling of a paisley can often add just the right variety of texture to bring your quilt alive. Like florals, paisleys can be counted on to add movement or flow. Since these prints can sometimes be hard to find, when you do spot one that you love, be sure to buy enough to stock your fabric collection. Paisleys work well in traditional, country, or contemporary quilts.

Subtle Texture: I use this phrase to describe a versatile category of fabrics that includes white prints on white or colored backgrounds, black prints on white or colored backgrounds, and colored prints on the same color background (the print being a darker value of that color). Anyplace in your quilt where you would use a solid, consider substituting one of these to give that area more visual interest. These prints make terrific backgrounds, so it's a good idea to buy enough fabric to stock your collection whenever you see one you like. For examples of how I use prints like these, see the white-on-muslin fabric in Best Friends and the blue water fabric in Rub-a-Dub Ducks.

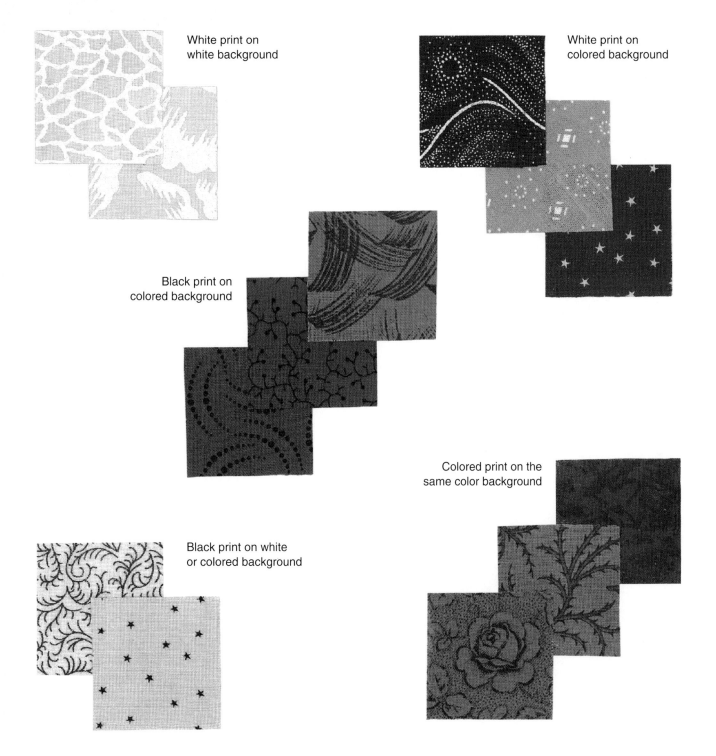

White print on white background

White print on colored background

Black print on colored background

Colored print on the same color background

Black print on white or colored background

Background Fabrics

There are certain things in life that many of us consider "staples," or things we couldn't be without: an extra bag of flour in the pantry, a pair of comfortable shoes, some broken-in jeans. To that list I would add a well-stocked collection of background fabrics.

Think about this: You use a background fabric in nearly every single quilt project. It really does pay to collect a nicely varied selection of background fabrics from which to pull when you're planning your quilt. These are fabrics you'll return to time and again.

I like to use off-white to medium tan for many of my quilt backgrounds. Instead of a solid, I often look for a subtle print to give the background an interesting visual texture. Look at Shooting Stars as an example. In this quilt I chose a gray-to-tan circular background for the blocks. Imagine how plain this quilt would look if I had chosen just a solid tan. Tone-on-tone prints, like white on muslin, are versatile choices for backgrounds, but don't feel limited to those. An overall print that doesn't have a dramatic contrast in the design keeps background spaces interesting but does not detract from the quilt blocks. A small dot, star, or any shape that has a fair amount of space around it in the background can be fun to use.

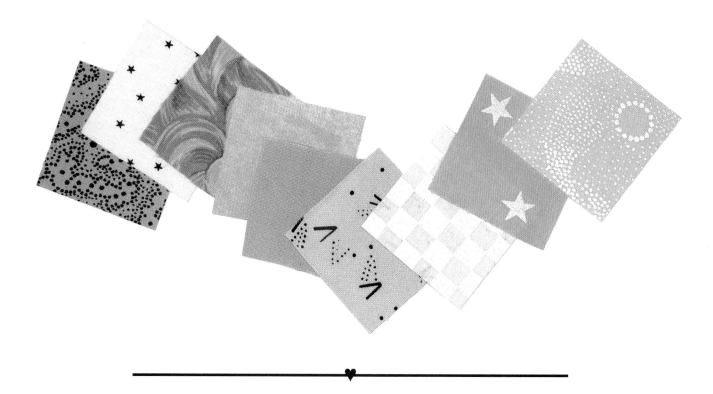

Country Folk-Art Palette

As you look over the projects in this book, you may detect a trend in my color choices. You'll notice lots of turkey reds, deep forest green, soldier blue, tan, and black. I love the country look and am always collecting fabrics that fall into what I call the country folk-art palette. This collection of colors differs from the country look that was popular five or so years ago. Then, country colors were more pastel, with lots of blues, pinks, and mauves. These country pastels had some gray mixed in, which made them work nicely with all the natural wood, baskets, and wicker accents that are well-loved country accents. The country folk-art palette is a step toward deeper, darker colors that are warm and comforting and very often tied to themes in nature. Think of the red of a country barn, the golden yellow of a field of wheat, the blue in the American flag, the rich green of evergreen boughs, and the dark tan of a September field of cornstalks. These are the colors that have inspired me in my recent designs and they also tie in nicely with the current mood of country-style decorating.

Country folk-art colors

Coordinating Fabrics and Colors

Multicolor Print: A nearly foolproof technique for coordinating colors is to use a multicolor print as your fabric selection guide. Look for a print that combines the same colors you want to use for the color scheme of your quilt. This combination of colors is your starting point for coordinating the other fabrics you'll use.

As you walk along the aisles in the fabric store, carry this multicolor print and match fabrics to all the colors it contains. When I coordinate fabrics to a multicolor print, I use them throughout the quilt rather than just within one block. Keep in mind when you're looking for these coordinating colors that you want to use a good mix of visual textures.

Scale: In fabrics, scale refers to the size of the print design, which can range from small to medium to large. Varying the scale of prints within a quilt is a very simple but effective way to create visual interest. If you were to use all small-scale prints in a quilt, no matter how much the visual textures might vary, you would still end up with a rather bland quilt. When you mix different size prints together, you really enliven the mix and create a more visually stimulating quilt. In the fabric swatches, the green-on-green sprigs are small scale; the floral is medium scale; and the leafy print is an example of large scale.

Contrast: In very simple terms, contrast is how much difference you see between two fabrics when they're placed next to each other. The contrast between fabrics is what defines the shapes of your quilt design. If there were no contrast at all between your background fabric and your main block design, you wouldn't be able to tell what was the quilt block and what was the background. Contrast is created by such things as the difference in color, the darkness and lightness of the colors, the visual texture, the scale of the print, and the type of the fabric (print versus solid).

Look at my two sample blocks. In the block on the left, there is not enough contrast, and the bear shape is barely distinguishable from the background. See how much more clearly the bear stands out in the block on the right, with its strongly contrasting fabrics.

When you are selecting fabrics for a project, make sure there is contrast between fabrics that are positioned next to each other. First, look at the contrast of the fabrics within your block. Then, compare your block fabrics to the background fabric to check for appropriate contrast. And last, look for the contrast between the background and borders.

Value: Value has nothing to do with how much your fabric or your quilt is worth! What it really means is the darkness or lightness of a color. As a quiltmaker, it is handy to develop the ability to look at a fabric and determine whether it is a "light," "medium," or "dark." Whether a fabric is light or dark can sometimes depend on what color it is positioned next to. A tan next to a white may look like a medium. However, the same tan next to a green may look like a light. Pull out a pile of different fabrics from your stash and start separating them into light, medium, and dark piles. This exercise will help you recognize the different values of fabrics. In the "Sew Colorful" boxes accompanying each project, I often suggest looking for a light, medium, or dark fabric. See if you can recognize these different values in the different quilts. In the fabric swatches, I've arranged the fabrics from light to dark reading from left to right.

Bright versus Country Folk-Art Colors: Bright, pure colors are intensely saturated with the color. If a color looks strong, pure, and clear, then think of it as a "bright." If a color has black added to it, it becomes a shade of that color. These darker, stronger, richer versions of colors are what I use to create a country folk-art look.

With my country-look quilts, I prefer not to mix bright colors with these folk-art colors in the same project. In the midst of deep, rich shades, a bright, intense color would jump right out of the quilt and end up being distracting. If I had used a few color shades in the Dinosaur Fever quilts, they would have seemed out of place and weakened the overall bright, bold color scheme. A quilt made with all bright colors can be very successful since they will balance each other out with more equal intensity. Brights make fun, cheerful projects, especially ones intended for kids, like the Game Quilts.

For a rich, warm, country look, I stick with the rich shades throughout an entire quilt, never mixing in any brights.

Bright colors   Country folk-art colors

Directional Prints: As the name implies, a directional print is one in which the pattern runs in a definite direction. One-way directional prints run in one direction only; if you turn the fabric any way but up, the print will be upside-down or sideways. In the swatches, this is the floral and scallop fabric on the right. Two-way directional prints have patterns that run in two directions, as seen on the black-and-gold swatch in the middle. If you don't pay attention to how you use these in a quilt, the pattern can end up running in all different directions, creating a chaotic, haphazard look. In all of the projects, I make a point to call out specifically if a directional print is *not* recommended. However, some directional prints are less obvious than others, so sometimes you can get away with using one. If you fall in love with a directional print that is small and subtle, you can probably use it without causing too many problems. I would consider the black-and-white fabric swatch on the right to be in the category of nondirectional prints. I would definitely caution against using *obvious* directional prints, however.

Timesaving Methods for Cutting and Piecing

Timesaving methods for cutting and piecing have opened up the world of quiltmaking to many people who would not otherwise have attempted even a simple beginner's project. It's wonderful to see so much quilting and creativity result from the use of easy-to-master tools and techniques.

In this chapter, I'll list all the tools and supplies you'll need to get started quilting and explain in detail how to use them. Investing in the appropriate tools and learning the techniques will ensure that your projects go together quickly and accurately. I also explain simple sewing techniques that will help you piece your quilt together in no time flat! Be sure to read and understand this chapter before you start any of the projects, and refer back to these pages whenever you need a refresher on any details of the techniques for cutting and piecing.

What You'll Need for Cutting and Piecing

Here's a rundown of items you should have before you begin a project.

Sewing Machine: You'll need a sewing machine that does a good, reliable straight stitch. All the bells, whistles, and stitches of sophisticated machines aren't necessary for basic piecing. Just keep your machine clean, oiled, and in good working condition.

Rotary Cutter: This simple tool has sparked a quiltmaking renaissance. With it, you can cut quilt pieces much more quickly and accurately than with scissors. You can cut four or more layers of fabric at once without marking the fabric or using a template.

Rotary cutters are readily available in quilt shops, fabric stores, and through mail-order catalogs. Select the larger size cutter—its bigger blade will give you more control and will last longer. (By the way, a rotary cutter works comfortably whether you're left- or right-handed.) Be sure to purchase a cutting mat as well. You should never use a rotary cutter without one.

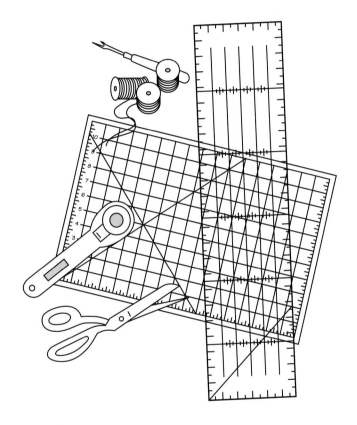

Diagram 1. *Essential quilting tools include: sewing and quilting thread; good, sharp scissors; see-through ruler; self-healing cutting mat; seam ripper; and rotary cutter.*

Cutting Mat: The cutting mat is the surface onto which you lay your fabric before slicing with the cutter. It's essential to use this with your rotary cutter. The mat protects the tabletop on which you are cutting as well as the blade of your cutter. Its surface also helps keep your fabric from slipping. Most mats are "self-healing," meaning you won't see the cutting lines in the surface. Under normal use, these mats will last for many years.

Get the largest size mat you have room for. The 24 × 36-inch mat is an all-around good size. If your mat is small, you will end up moving your fabric all the time while cutting. A cutting mat will warp when exposed to any heat sources, so be sure to store it flat and out of sunlight, and don't set anything hot on it.

See-Through Ruler: The third essential element in your trio of quick-cutting tools is a special, rigid plastic, see-through ruler to use with your rotary cutter and cutting mat. There are lots of shapes and sizes of rulers on the market now, but to start out, I recommend a 6 × 24-inch ruler with ⅛-inch increments and a 45 degree angle line marked on it. If you feel like splurging on an extra accessory, a 6 × 12-inch ruler is also very handy to have, and I find I use this one most often. For cutting smaller pieces, one or two small rulers are great, either a 4 × 4-inch square or a 6 × 6-inch square. For the projects in this book, you don't need any of the specialized rulers that cut different angles or triangles.

Pen: For drawing the Speedy Triangle grids, you will need a fine- or medium-point ballpoint pen or a fine or extra-fine felt-tip pen.

Sewing Thread: Use a good-quality thread for piecing. When you're investing your time and fabrics in a project, you want to make certain that your thread will not compromise your efforts. Use a light, neutral color, such as beige or gray, when piecing light fabrics, and a dark neutral, such as dark gray, when piecing dark fabrics.

Iron, Ironing Board, and Towel: Use your iron on the cotton setting and keep the ironing surface clean. For precise pressing of your pieces, position a thick terry cloth towel on top of your ironing board. Set your ironing board next to your sewing machine and position it at the same height as your sewing machine table. This saves on steps between your machine and ironing board. You can also use the ironing board as a work surface to keep your fabric pieces organized. (See "Precision Pressing" on page 232.)

Seam Ripper: There are times when nothing but a sharp seam ripper will do. The tiny, sharp point can rip out stitches much more effectively and carefully than the tips of scissor blades. When fitting checkerboard and scrap borders to the quilt, a seam ripper is the perfect tool to remove extra border pieces.

Scissors: Most fabric cutting for the projects is done with the rotary cutter, but you still need a good sharp pair of fabric scissors at hand for cutting threads and trimming the backing fabric.

Accuracy Counts!

Accuracy begins with prewashing your fabrics and pressing out all the wrinkles before cutting. When you do start cutting, be certain that you line your ruler up precisely with the edges of your fabric. Do not use the thick lines on your cutting mat for precise cutting. Cut your pieces carefully and they will stitch up beautifully. To achieve precise piecing, take your time, be patient, and make sure to have exact ¼-inch seam allowances. Press as you sew to make sure seams lie flat as you assemble your block. When you add it all up, accurate cutting, piecing, and pressing will bring 100 percent accurate results.

The Basics of Rotary Cutting

If this is the first time you will be using a rotary cutter, cutting mat, and see-through ruler, read through these directions carefully. Then practice on scrap fabrics before you cut into your project fabric.

Precise cutting is the first step in precision sewing. Take your time to measure and cut your strips and pieces accurately. All rotary cutting dimensions include ¼-inch seam allowances.

A work surface that is kitchen-counter height will be easiest on your back and bring you closer to your work. Lay your cutting mat onto your work surface.

Making the Cut

Step 1. Most 44-inch-wide fabric comes off the bolt folded in half with selvage to selvage (finished edge) to measure approximately 22 inches wide. (If you have washed your fabric, refold selvage to selvage.) Make sure the fabric is straight and then fold again, bringing the fold up to the selvages. It will now be approximately 11 inches wide and four layers thick. Refer to **Diagram 2.** Position the folded fabric so that the edge with the selvages is facing away from you and the double folded edge is facing toward you. Again be very careful that the fabric is straight. From this folded length of fabric, you can now start to cut your strips.

In the project directions, the dimension for the first strip cut is often 44 inches long. Don't worry if your fabric is only 42 or 43 inches. This variance has been considered in the yardage and cutting dimensions. If your fabric is *less* than 42 inches, you may occasionally need to cut an extra strip and may need to purchase extra yardage.

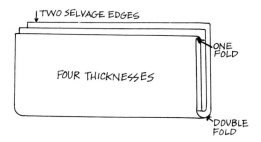

Diagram 2. *Fold the fabric in half, selvage to selvage. Make sure it is straight, then fold it in half again.*

Step 2. Use your see-through ruler for a cutting guide. Align one of the horizontal lines of the ruler with the double-folded edge of the fabric so the ruler is square with the fabric. See **Diagram 3.** Using some pressure, hold the ruler in position and use the rotary cutter to trim off the uneven edges on the right end of the fabric. Make sure you've cut through all four layers. You should now have a perfectly straight edge of fabric.

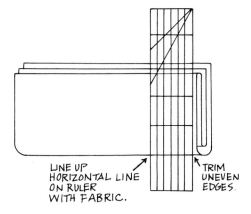

Diagram 3. *Using a see-through ruler and rotary cutter, trim the uneven edge on the right end of the folded fabric.*

Sew-Safe Rotary Cutting

✂ Always retract the blade whenever you set your cutter down, and keep it out of reach of children. The blade is extremely sharp.

✂ For the most control, always stand when cutting. You'll have a straight perspective on your work and can exert more pressure with less effort. A counter-height cutting surface is best.

✂ Always cut away from your body. If you cut toward yourself, your elbow runs into your side, causing the loss of a smooth cutting movement. You also risk slipping and cutting yourself.

✂ Keep fingers from getting too close to the edge of the ruler when cutting.

✂ To prevent your ruler from sliding, hold it with flexed fingers. The ruler will slip more easily if your palm is flat on the ruler.

✂ Cut only on a cutting mat intended for rotary cutting.

✂ Practice on scrap fabric to get the hang of this method of cutting.

✂ If your cutter begins skipping, it's time for a new blade. Don't put off replacing too long or you'll run the risk of mistakes and less-than-accurate cutting.

✂ Wrap cardboard and then tape around blades before you dispose of them. (You can use the packaging from the replacement blade for this.)

✂ Clean and oil your rotary cutter occasionally and after lengthy cutting sessions. Pay close attention when disassembling your cutter so you can reassemble it properly.

✂ Use the rotary cutter only on cotton fabrics (polyester battings and fabrics will dull your blade).

Step 3. Rotate your fabric so that the end you have trimmed is on your left. All of the cutting of strips and pieces for your quilt will be made measuring from this trimmed end of fabric. To move your fabric into the correct position, simply rotate your cutting mat. If you pick up the fabric, you'll risk messing up the four layers.

If you're left-handed, as I am, you will find it more comfortable to measure and make your cuts from the right end of the folded fabric. In that case, simply reverse the directions given in Steps 2 and 3. Trim off uneven edges on the left end of the fabric in Step 2 and rotate the fabric so the trimmed edges are on your right in Step 3. (When you look at the diagrams, keep in mind that they are drawn for right-handers.)

Step 4. Use the horizontal lines on your ruler as your point of reference as you make the next cuts. From the edge of the ruler, going across one of these lines, find the width of the first strip you want to cut. For example, if the strip is 2½ inches wide by 44 inches long, find 2½ inches from the edge of your ruler. Align the 2½-inch line on the ruler with the straight edge of the fabric. See **Diagram 4.** To make sure your ruler is lined up perfectly straight, look for the 2½-inch mark on two or three of the lines that cross the ruler. These marks should also lie directly over the straight edge of the fabric. When the ruler is lined up perfectly with the fabric edge, hold it in position and cut.

SEW SMART

Always double-check your measurements before you cut. There's a lot of wisdom in the old saying, "Measure twice, cut once."

Step 5. After cutting the strips, many of the projects then require you to cut pieces from those strips. If you're cutting several pieces that are the same size, you can leave your strip folded either in quarters or in half so you can cut more than one piece at a time. Lay the ruler on top of the strip. Line up one of the horizontal lines on your ruler with the long edge of your strip. Trim off one end of the strip to square and straighten the edge of the fabric. For fabric folded in quarters, trim the end with one fold and the selvages; for fabric folded in half, trim the end with the selvages. See **Diagrams 5** and **6.** Rotate the fabric so this cut end is on the left, as described in Step 3. Following the cutting procedure explained in Step 4, cut the pieces as specified in the project. See **Diagram 7.** In some cases you may be cutting several different size pieces from one strip. Cut the largest pieces first and then the smaller pieces.

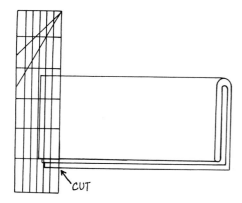

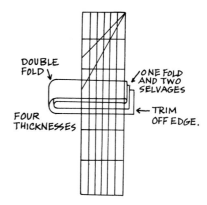

DOUBLE FOLD

ONE FOLD AND TWO SELVAGES

FOUR THICKNESSES

TRIM OFF EDGE.

CUT

Diagram 4. *Rotate the mat so that the trimmed end of the fabric is on the left. Align the ruler with the straight edge of the fabric, hold it in position, and cut the strips.*

Diagram 5. *To cut smaller pieces off a strip, leave the strip folded in quarters so you can cut more than one piece at a time. Align one of the horizontal lines on the ruler with the long edge of the strip and trim off the edge.*

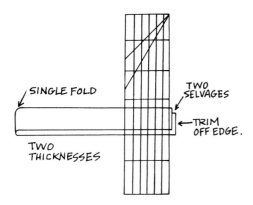

Diagram 6. *Pieces can also be cut with the fabric folded in half rather than quarters. First trim off the edge.*

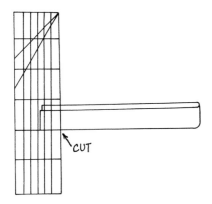

Diagram 7. *Once the edge has been trimmed, rotate the mat so that the cut end of the fabric is on the left, and cut the pieces specified in the pattern.*

SEW SMART

Here are some no-slip tricks to keep your ruler from sliding as you cut:

• Adhere masking tape to the underside of the ruler.

• Fasten sandpaper dots to the underside of the ruler.

• Purchase fabric grips to apply to your ruler.

• Add dabs of rubber cement to the ruler and let them dry.

Speedy Triangles

After all the pieces for your quilt are cut and organized, the next step is to make the triangle sets. A triangle set consists of two triangles sewn together to make a square. The traditional method for preparing these units is to cut two individual triangles, then stitch them together. I use a quick-sew method of constructing several triangle sets at one time. Read through the step-by-step directions below for details on this quick and easy technique. Refer to each specific pattern for fabric color, fabric size, and grid size.

Accuracy is critical in every step of making triangle sets (marking, cutting, sewing, and pressing). If you don't pay close attention, you can alter the size of your triangle set, making piecing the blocks together more difficult.

Marking, Sewing, and Cutting Speedy Triangles

Step 1. Line up and position your selected fabrics with right sides together.

Step 2. To mark the grid, you need a ballpoint pen (or extra-fine felt-tip pen), see-through ruler, and good light. The specific project will list the size of the squares in the grid and how many squares to include in your grid. For an example, let's say our pattern requires a grid of eight 2⅞-inch squares. You should draw the grid on the wrong side of the lightest fabric.

Step 3. Line your ruler approximately ½ to 1 inch from the lengthwise edge of your fabric and draw a line. The size of fabric pieces used for the Speedy Triangles allows a ½- to 1-inch margin of fabric all the way around the grid.

Step 4. Rotate your fabric and line up your ruler to draw a second line exactly 2⅞ inches from the first line. Align your ruler with the second line to draw a third line exactly 2⅞ inches from the second line.

Step 5. To draw perpendicular lines to make the squares, rotate your fabric a quarter turn. Line up one of the horizontal lines on your ruler with one of the lines drawn on your fabric to square your ruler. Draw your first perpendicular line about ½ to 1 inch from the edge of the fabric.

Step 6. Rotate your fabric and line your ruler up to draw a second line exactly 2⅞ inches from the first perpendicular line. Align your ruler with the second line to draw a third line 2⅞ inches away. Repeat two more times to draw a fourth and fifth line. Your grid is now complete.

Step 7. The next step is to draw diagonal lines that will exactly intersect the corners of the squares. Drop the point of your pen exactly on the corners you will intersect and then butt the ruler up to the pen. You will need to shift the pen back and forth between those points until you get your ruler lined up so that the line you draw will precisely intersect the corners. Refer to **Diagram 8.**

Step 8. Now you're ready to sew. Using a ¼-inch seam allowance, stitch along *both* sides of each diagonal line. Use the edge of your presser foot as a ¼-inch guide, or draw a line ¼ inch away from both sides of the pen lines if your presser foot isn't exactly ¼ inch.

To speed up your stitching, start sewing above the grid line marked on the top left square. See **Diagram 9.** (If you've drawn the diagonal lines in the opposite direction from the diagram, start sewing on the lower left square.) Sew a ¼-inch seam along the

diagonal line, and stop sewing when you're a few stitches past the second grid line you cross. Stop stitching and put your needle in the up position. Turn your piece of fabric around and continue sewing the other direction on the opposite side of the diagonal line. (When you turn your fabric, you will pull threads through your machine and bobbin. This thread will hang loose between where you stopped and started sewing.) After you have passed the top grid mark by a few stitches, stop sewing again, pull the threads across, turn the fabric, and start stitching down the second upper left square. Do this continuous sewing until you've stitched along both sides of all the diagonal lines in your grid. When you're done sewing, you should have a piece of fabric that looks like **Diagram 10.**

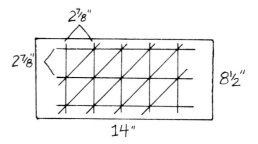

Diagram 8. *To make Speedy Triangles, first mark a grid on your fabric. Then draw diagonal lines that intersect the squares on the grid.*

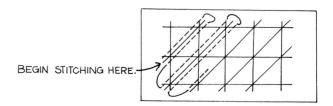

Diagram 9. *Beginning at the top left square, stitch along both sides of the diagonal lines, using a ¼-inch seam allowance.*

Diagram 10. *When you have stitched along all the lines, your triangle sets will look like this. After stitching, cut along all the pen lines to separate the sets.*

Precision Pressing

✂ Always press following each sewing step. Put the tip of your iron right on the seam line on the right side of your fabrics. Come straight down on your fabric and be careful not to stretch your fabric out of shape by moving the iron with too much force across your fabrics. I prefer to use a steam iron on the cotton setting.

✂ Look for the arrows on the piecing diagrams for pressing directions for each step. Following these arrows will ensure that your seams will lie flat.

✂ The surface of your ironing board is very hard. To make a more forgiving surface for pressing, lay a terry cloth towel on your ironing board. It will provide a cushion to absorb the indentations your seam allowances would make on the front of your quilt block and top. The nap of the towel helps prevent distortion of your fabrics when pressing.

Step 9. Use your rotary cutter and ruler to cut along all the pen lines. On many of the points of the triangles, a couple of stitches will remain, as shown in the triangle set in **Diagram 11.** Just open up the triangle set with a gentle tug and the stitches will pull out. Do not tug with force, or you can stretch your triangle set out of shape. Based on our example, you will have made a total of sixteen 2½-inch triangle sets. Each square from the grid you drew makes two triangle sets.

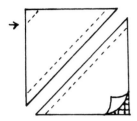

Diagram 11. *A gentle tug will remove any stitches remaining in the corners.*

Step 10. Gently press open the triangle sets. See the individual projects for which direction to press the seam allowances. Triangle sets should be right side up while pressing. Your finished sets should look like the one in **Diagram 12.**

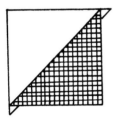

Diagram 12. *Press open the triangle sets.*

Assembly-Line Piecing

For the quickest piecing, you need to apply the principles of an assembly line to your sewing. By repeating the same step over and over, your piecing can go much more quickly and efficiently. You will assemble the blocks one step at a time, repeating the same step for each block at the same time. Instead of finishing the blocks one by one, you will finish the blocks all at the same time.

Let's say you are working on a quilt that has 12 blocks. The first step calls for you to sew together two triangle sets. You repeat this step of sewing the triangle sets *12* times (once for each block). If the next step calls for you to sew a rectangle to the triangle set units, you repeat that step 12 times. As you proceed through the rest of the assembly steps, repeating each step 12 times, all of your blocks will take shape at the same time and will be completed all together.

The Trouble with Triangles

Dilemma: The finished triangle set isn't perfectly square.

✂ Did you mark your grid accurately?

✂ Were the diagonal lines connected exactly across the corners?

✂ Did you tug them out of whack while pressing? Try gently finger-pressing the triangle sets open before using the iron.

Dilemma: The size of the triangle sets varies slightly from set to set.

✂ Did you mark your grid accurately?

✂ Did you sew with an accurate ¼-inch seam?

✂ Did you cut exactly along the pen lines?

✂ Did you fail to open the seams fully when pressing the set open?

Dilemma: Little "tails" of fabric (the seam allowance) stick out on the sides.

✂ If you find these distracting, trim off the seam allowance carefully so it is even with the sides of the square.

Dilemma: Your triangle sets are misshapen.

✂ Try using fewer squares per grid.

✂ Be careful not to pull or tug on your fabrics when sewing and turning your pieces.

Use the **Fabric Key** for each project to identify which fabrics you need for each step of the piecing sequence. In each project, you will find a fabric key at the beginning of the assembly directions.

Besides speeding up your piecing, the assembly-line technique will help keep you organized. You think once, repeat the step for the number of blocks in the quilt, and then move on to the next step.

Continuous-Seam Technique

Assembly-line piecing and the continous-seam technique (also called laundry-line piecing) go hand in hand. Any time you are using the assembly-line method to piece your blocks or sew a series of strips or pieces, you can use the continuous-seam method of sewing them together.

Line up all the same pieces for the first step for each block next to your sewing machine. With right sides together, stitch the first two pieces together. Instead of removing those pieces from under the presser foot and clipping the threads, keep them where they are. Butt the next set of pieces directly behind the set you have just sewn and continue sewing. Add each set without breaking your seam until you have joined all the sets together. (The hardest part about learning this technique is to overcome the natural tendency to want to clip the threads.) Begin and end your stitching with a piece of scrap fabric, and you'll eliminate a mound of thread clippings next to your sewing machine.

You will end up with a long chain of pieces joined together by thread (see **Diagram 13**). Take this chain to your ironing board and press, following the directions for pressing given in the project text. Once you've pressed the seams, you can clip the threads that join all the pieces.

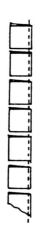

Diagram 13. *Sew the first set of pieces together. Without lifting the presser foot or clipping the threads, butt the second set directly behind the first and continue sewing. Add each set in a continuous seam until you have joined all the sets together.*

Precise Piecing

An exact ¼-inch seam allowance is the foundation for accurate piecing. Check your sewing machine to make sure you can get an accurate ¼-inch seam allowance. Do this test: Cut a double-thickness scrap of fabric with your rotary cutter to get a perfectly straight edge. Line the edge of your scraps with the edge of the presser foot and sew several inches. Use a seam gauge and measure from the edge of the fabric strip to the stitching line. If this is not exactly ¼ inch, start making adjustments until you find just where to align your fabric with the presser foot to achieve a perfect ¼-inch seam allowance.

Mark the throat plate on your sewing machine with masking tape exactly ¼ inch from the center of the needle. Be sure to make a test after your tape is positioned. If you adhere a few layers of tape, the tape

> ### SEW SMART
>
> When you're matching two pieces or rows together, if one is slightly shorter than the other, lay the shorter piece on top. Fit and pin them together and the bottom piece should ease to fit the top piece. The motion of the feed dogs helps to ease in a little extra length.

will create a ridge for your fabric to glide along while you sew.

If you have problems acheiving a perfect ¼-inch seam allowance on your machine, you may want to look for a specialty foot that measures exactly ¼ inch from the needle to the edge of the presser foot. Check with your sewing machine manufacturer to see if such a foot is made for your model. If not, there is a universal foot called the "little foot" that can be adapted to most machines. (See "Quilting by Mail" on page 255 for ordering information.)

When you start a project, try to finish it on the same sewing machine that you started with. If you're using a special foot, such as a walking foot or little foot, be sure to use it for the entire project.

Make sure the needle position on your machine is appropriately set before you start to sew. Many sewing machines have several needle positions. If you have switched your needle position for another sewing purpose, double-check before you start piecing that it is in the correct position for ¼-inch seams.

Speedy Strips

With this basic and very easy technique, you will be able to assemble complex-looking quilt blocks and create two- or three-color checkerboards or multicolored scrap borders in no time flat. For an example, look at Homecoming Wreaths on page 81. Both the wreath blocks and the checkerboard border were created using speedy strips.

The unit assembled using the speedy strip technique is called a strip set. The directions for each project will tell you the number of strips to cut and which fabrics to use to create the required strip sets.

To make a checkerboard or scrap border, sew the strips together along the long edges, alternating the fabrics as directed. As you add each strip, always pause to press the seam. The general rule for pressing is to press seams toward the darkest fabric or all in the same direction. Change sewing direction with each strip. It will help avoid the warping that can occur when sewing several long strips together.

Once you have joined together all the strips, you will have created a large strip set, like the one shown in **Diagram 14.** The directions will then tell you to cut this strip set in half or in thirds and to resew the sections end to end. From this final strip set you will cut

the narrow strips that form the scrap border or checkerboard. (See "Borders" on page 243 for more details on making scrap and checkerboard borders.)

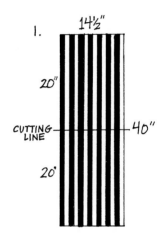

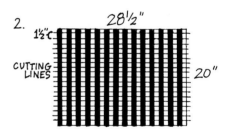

Diagram 14. *To make a checkerboard or scrap border, sew strips together to make a large strip set. Cut the strip set in half and resew the halves together, as shown. From this new strip set, cut narrow strips and either rematch them to form a checkerboard or sew them end to end for a scrap border.*

The same basic principle applies to strip sets you will sew to make quilt blocks. In some of the projects there is a special cutting chart just for cutting these strips. Be sure to read all the directions and cut the strips as described. The step-by-step directions will then tell you how to sew together strips of various widths and different fabric colors to create a number of strip sets (see **Diagram 15**). Once the strip sets are assembled, you will need to slice them into segments with your rotary cutter (see **Diagram 16**) and group them into piles. Each pile of segments will make one block. The directions will very clearly explain in what order you are to assemble these segments. (See **Diagram 17** for an example of how the strips are sewn together to become a block.).

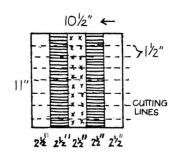

Diagram 16. *The strip sets are then cut into segments.*

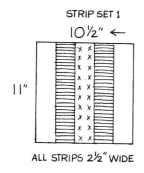

STRIP SET 1

ALL STRIPS 2½" WIDE

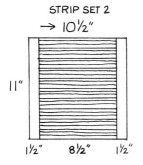

STRIP SET 2

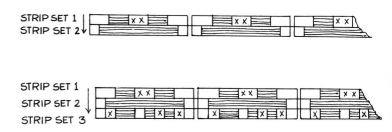

Diagram 17. *The segments are sewn together into blocks using the continuous-seam technique.*

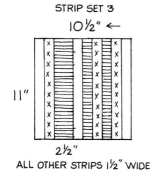

STRIP SET 3

2½"

ALL OTHER STRIPS 1½" WIDE

Diagram 15. *Strip sets are created by sewing together strips of various widths and fabrics.*

SEW SMART

Use colored pencils to color in the squares in the Fabric Key to match the colors you're using in the project. You could also color in the piecing diagrams to make it even easier to follow.

Enlarging a Wall Quilt to Fit a Bed

Nearly all of the quilts in this book are intended to be hung on a wall. However, you may fall in love with one of the designs and decide that you would like to expand it to fit a full-size bed. Here's how I suggest you adapt a smaller quilt to fit a bed.

Step 1. Look up the dimensions of the finished block for the quilt you want to enlarge.

Step 2. Measure the top of your bed. Knowing the finished block size, determine how many blocks it will take to cover the mattress top. Don't forget to include the measurement for the lattice. You could increase the width of the lattice so you wouldn't need to make so many blocks. (When you figure the yardage for the lattice strips, make sure you measure so they're ½ inch wider than the finished size you desire.) Once you have determined how many blocks you will need, refigure the yardage required to make the new number of blocks.

Step 3. Measure from the top of the mattress down the side of the bed (toward the floor). Add two or three borders to the sides of the quilt to acquire that needed length.

Step 4. Draw the bed quilt with borders on graph paper. Use a scale of one square per inch. This important step will help you determine your fabric requirements for the lattice, borders, backing, and batting. (You'll need a calculator, too!) It will also help you visualize your project. When it comes time to translate your drawing into yards of fabric, keep in mind that most cotton fabrics run 42 to 44 inches wide. The width of the fabric is crucial in determining how much you need for the lattice, borders, and backing. If you do your figuring based on a 42-inch width and find out when you get to the fabric store that the fabric you want happens to be narrower or perhaps even wider, you will need to do some refiguring.

Timesaving Methods for Appliqué

Even the most exquisite appliqué started out simply as cut-out shapes of fabric to be applied to a background fabric. In the past, a quilter's only option for fastening these fabric pieces onto the background was to use a needle to turn under the raw edges of the appliquéd pieces and then stitch or embroider them by hand. Many quilts are still made this way, and they are certainly very traditional and beautiful, but they are also very time-consuming.

The techniques and tools have changed over time, and new products have been developed. There are computerized sewing machines to finish the edges with fancy stitches, appliqué film to hold fabric pieces in position while we sew them, tear-away paper to stabilize fabrics to keep them from puckering, and thread made especially for machine embroidery. Plus, I've developed a great technique—Penstitch appliqué— you don't even need to finish the edges with sewing. All of these advances in tools and techniques mean you can create a lovely appliqué project in a mere fraction of the time it takes using traditional methods.

Most of the appliqué projects I've included in this book are designed for the Penstitch technique, but there are some in which I will suggest other possibilities. In this section, I've included complete directions for several appliqué methods, so feel free to choose your technique. Just be aware of the limitations of each method and decide whether it is appropriate for the specific appliqué design you have in mind.

As a general guide, designs with very small pieces should only use the Penstitch appliqué technique. Designs with larger pieces may be done with machine appliqué, buttonhole embroidery, or hand appliqué.

What You'll Need for Appliqué

The supplies you'll need for just about any method of appliqué are included here. Use this checklist when you're planning your project to make certain you'll have everything on hand that you need.

Sewing Machine: Use the best machine you can afford and maintain it in good condition. In addition to straight stitching for piecing backgrounds and borders, your machine should do a nice, even satin stitch for machine appliqué. Some machines have decorative stitches that are fun to use with appliqué.

Sewing Thread: For machine appliqué, use a thread that is specifically meant for machine embroidery or a good-quality, all-purpose thread. For hand appliqué, use a good-quality sewing thread. For either method, make sure the thread color matches the appliqué fabric.

Needles for Appliqué: I prefer quilting needles for hand appliqué, but some people like to use sharps. Sharps are longer needles with a larger eye than the betweens you use for quilting.

Straight Pins: More delicate pins, such as glass-head appliqué pins, are easier to use for appliqué.

Rotary Cutter, Cutting Mat, See-Through Ruler: For appliqué projects, these are used mainly for cutting background pieces, borders, and binding strips. For more details on these tools, see page 227.

Scissors: Use good-quality scissors or a pair of appliqué scissors for cutting designs out of appliqué film. These scissors need to be sharp, but I don't recommend using a really expensive pair of scissors for this.

Iron, Ironing Board, Towel: See page 232 for a discussion of these items. I don't recommend using an automatic shut-off iron when working with Penstitch appliqué. It may drive you crazy!

Appliqué Film: Nearly all of the appliqué projects in this book are perfectly suited for appliqué film. This paper-backed fusible webbing is sold in precut packets or on bolts at most fabric and quilting stores. There are both heavyweight and lightweight types. If you plan to do machine appliqué or buttonhole embroidery, use a lighter weight, *sewable* appliqué film. For Penstitch appliqué and projects with edges that will not be sewn, use a heavier weight, nonsewable appliqué film. Appliqué film replaces laborious hand stitching; a simple stroke of the iron fuses pieces of fabric in place on a background.

Tear-Away Paper: Use tear-away paper (sold with interfacings under names like Stitch-n-Tear) as a stabilizer behind the background fabric when doing machine appliqué. This keeps your fabrics from puckering.

Extra-Fine Point Permanent Felt-Tip Pen: For Penstitch appliqué, use this type of pen to draw your stitches. You can also use it to add details such as eyes, noses, mouths, and buttons to various appliqué designs. If you have trouble finding these pens at your quilt or fabric store, check an art supply store. Bring a fabric swatch along to test the pens.

Embroidery Floss: Embroidery floss is used for adding details such as noses, eyes, and mouths to some of the appliqué designs. Choose a floss color that works well for the details you are adding.

Embroidery floss is also used for the buttonhole embroidery hand appliqué technique. Use black for an old-fashioned look, or coordinate embroidery floss color with your appliqué fabrics.

Light Table: If you do a lot of appliqué, you might want to consider an inexpensive, lightweight, portable light table that is now available and made just for quilters' needs. It is useful for tracing appliqué designs onto appliqué film or tracing quilting designs onto quilt tops. You can also use it for other tracing needs, such as tracing doll faces or making special quilt labels. It's not an essential item, but would make a terrific addition to your stock of quilting aids. (For ordering information, see page 255.)

Using Appliqué Film

For Penstitch, machine, and buttonhole appliqué, you will need to fuse your appliqué pieces onto a background. The quickest and easiest way to do this is to use appliqué film. If you plan to machine or buttonhole appliqué afterward, be sure to use a sewable, lightweight appliqué film. For Penstitch appliqué and other projects that will not be sewn, use a heavier weight, nonsewable film.

Step 1. Trace each of the parts of the selected appliqué design individually onto the paper side of the appliqué film. Since you can see through the film, you can lay it directly over the design in the book and trace it. Remember your design will be the mirror image of what you see on the book page, but it will be in the same position as the finished project in the photo-graph. If you want to reverse this, first trace the design from the book onto a piece of white paper using a dark felt-tip pen. Turn the paper over so the lines you've traced are facing down. Retrace the design onto the side of the paper that is facing up, again using the felt-tip pen. From this second tracing, transfer the design onto the appliqué film. Keep in mind that letters *must* be traced in reverse.

Step 2. Using sharp paper scissors, cut loosely around the traced designs on the appliqué film, as shown in **Diagram 1.** Do not cut along the lines at this point.

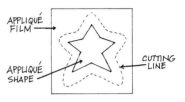

Diagram 1. *Trace the appliqué shape onto the appliqué film and cut it out, loosely following the outline of the design.*

Step 3. Before you fuse, check the manufacturer's instructions for the proper iron setting to use with that brand of appliqué film. Fuse each piece of appliqué film to the *wrong* side of your selected fabrics. Place the appliqué film with the paper side up and the webbing side against your fabric.

Step 4. When all the pieces are fused, cut out the appliqué shapes following the tracing lines (see **Diagram 2**). Remove the paper backing from the appliqué film. A thin fusing film will remain on the wrong side of the fabric.

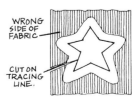

Diagram 2. *Fuse the appliqué film to the wrong side of the fabric. Following the tracing lines, cut out the appliqué.*

Step 5. Arrange and center all the pieces of the appliqué design on the background fabric. Remember to allow ¼ inch for seam allowances on the edges of background fabric if the project directs you to appliqué before piecing. Refer to the appliqué patterns as you position the pieces; the dotted lines will indicate where certain pieces should be placed underneath others. When everything is arranged, fuse the pieces in position with your iron. After the fabric is fused to the background, choose which appliqué technique you prefer: Penstitch, buttonhole embroidery, or machine appliqué.

Penstitch Appliqué

I developed this technique for small projects to give the look of appliqué without having to spend a lot of time. Penstitch is a pseudo-stitch done with an extra-fine point permanent felt-tip pen. After you fuse the appliqué pieces to the background fabric, use the pen to draw in stitches along the edges of the appliqué. Since there is no real stitching, the fusing is what holds the appliqué pieces in place. This technique allows you to use very small pieces of fabric and give much greater detail to the appliqué design. It is simple to do, lots of fun, and very effective. It's great if you want quick results. After all, the pen is much quicker than the needle!

Use this technique in smaller projects that have a lot of detail, but won't have a lot of stress put on them. I wouldn't recommend Penstitch for items like pillows and baby bibs that will be handled a lot or that will need to be laundered frequently. But for other projects like wallhangings or ornaments, Penstitch is perfect.

Once the edges of the appliquéd pieces are held in position with the appliqué film, you can then finish them with Penstitch. Make the stitches along the outer edges of the appliqué shapes. The idea is to have them resemble a running stitch. Working about ¹⁄₁₆ inch from the outer edge of the appliqué pieces, draw lines about ¹⁄₁₆ inch long on the appliqué fabric. See **Diagram 3** for reference.

Diagram 3. *Using your felt-tip pen, make tiny running stitches to outline the appliqué piece.*

For larger appliqué pieces, you can make your running Penstitch "stitches" a little longer, with more space between them. For very small pieces, make your "stitches" shorter, with less space between them.

Machine Appliqué

After fusing your appliqué pieces in place, you can outline the edges with a machine embroidery stitch. This technique may be your best choice for projects you'd like to launder and for those with larger pieces, like the numbers on the Hopscotch and Television Floor Quilt on page 163. This technique takes some practice and a sewing machine in good working order. Spend some time with practice fabrics before starting your project.

Step 1. Fuse all the appliqué pieces in place on the background fabric, following the steps given in "Using Appliqué Film" on page 239.

Step 2. Use tear-away paper as a stabilizer underneath the machine stitches. Cut a piece of paper large enough to cover the area you'll be stitching. Hold or pin the tear-away paper to the *wrong* side of the background fabric in the stitching areas. This keeps your fabrics from puckering when you do your appliqué stitching.

Step 3. Use a neutral color bobbin thread for all of the appliqué. Coordinate several thread colors to match the various appliqué fabric colors. Use these for the top threads, changing them as needed as you work on the appliqué. For best results, use machine embroidery thread.

Step 4. To get a good appliqué stitch, select a satin stitch at about 80 stitches per inch. Be sure to practice on test fabric to adjust your machine settings to exactly where you want them.

Step 5. Stitch along all the edges of each appliqué piece. First appliqué along the edges of the pieces that go underneath other appliqué pieces. Don't stitch along edges that will be hidden under other pieces. (This will help eliminate bulk.) Change top thread color as necessary. When you're all finished, pull away the paper from the back side of the fabric.

Special Tips for Penstitch Appliqué

✄ If you are Penstitch appliquéing onto sweatshirts or other washables, be sure to prewash *all* of your fabrics. Also, prewash sweatshirts two or three times to remove all the sizing and any finish on the fabric. Use one of the heavyweight appliqué films, such as Heat 'N Bond Original, if you won't be stitching them at all. When laundering is necessary for the finished shirt, do so very gently. Hand washing would be best. Expect Penstitched wearables to have a lifetime of a season or two.

✄ Laundering is NOT recommended for Penstitch wallhangings, ornaments, and other projects. Treat them with a stain protector, such as Scotchgard, to help keep them clean.

✄ Use a muffin tin or tray to segregate and organize all the appliqué pieces for the different blocks or designs.

✄ Because your fingers may be a little awkward and clumsy, use a straight pin to move all your pieces into place.

✄ Lay out your appliqué pieces on the ironing board. That way you can avoid moving them once you have them arranged.

✄ With very dark fabrics, skip the Penstitch. Your pen lines won't show.

✄ If the edges of your appliquéd piece ever lift up, don't worry! Just re-press them back in position with your iron.

✄ After fusing, check your iron for residue and use iron cleaner as needed. Keep a towel on your ironing board to protect both the ironing board surface and any clothing that may be ironed afterward!

Buttonhole Embroidery Appliqué

Although this technique does call for hand stitching, it is fairly simple and it gives a very traditional, old-fashioned look to your quilt. The real advantage is that you can take your project along with you in the car, to the doctor's office, or on a plane and continue your stitching. Buttonhole embroidery is best suited to appliqué projects with relatively large, simple pieces. If the appliqué pieces are too small or there are too many small pieces, Penstitch appliqué may be a better choice. Be sure to use a lightweight appliqué film.

After you have fused the appliqué design to the background fabric, outline the edges of the appliqué pieces with the buttonhole stitch done in embroidery floss. Use an assortment of different floss colors to coordinate with the appliqué fabrics, or use one color throughout (black can be quite effective).

Use two to three strands of embroidery floss, and refer to **Diagram 4** for guidance on how to do the stitch. For very small pieces, use one strand of floss.

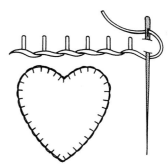

Diagram 4. *Use embroidery floss and the buttonhole stitch to outline appliqué pieces that have been fused in position.*

Hand Appliqué

In some of the appliqué projects in the book, you could choose the option of hand appliqué. Two basic methods are described below.

Quick-and-Easy Hand Appliqué

For larger, relatively simple shapes like hearts, this technique is a quicker alternative to the laborious, needle-turning hand appliqué method that our grandmothers used.

Step 1. For this example, let's assume we're making an appliquéd heart. First, make a heart template. Then, put two pieces of your selected fabric right sides together. With a pen, trace around the heart template onto the wrong side of the fabric.

Step 2. Holding the two pieces of fabric together, cut ¼ inch outside the traced line. Stitch all the way around the heart shape on the pen line. Clip the curves and trim the seam allowance down to ⅛ inch, as shown in **Diagram 5.**

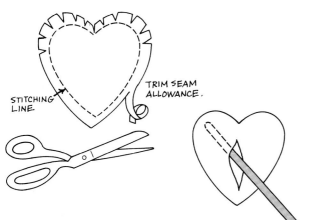

Diagram 5. *After the two pieces are stitched together, trim the seam allowance and clip the curves close to the stitching line. Slit the back, turn the heart right side out, and smooth the seams with a knitting needle or other object.*

Step 3. Slit the back of the heart and turn it right side out. Use a blunt but pointy object (like a knitting needle) to smooth out the seams and create smooth curves. Press flat.

Step 4. Pin the heart in position, baste, and hand stitch in place. You may want to cut out the fabric behind the appliqué to eliminate the extra bulk.

Freezer Paper Appliqué

Like the technique described above, freezer paper appliqué works best with larger, simpler shapes. It is a great way to create nice, smooth curves on appliqué pieces.

Step 1. Trace the appliqué design from the book onto freezer paper and cut out the shape for each piece.

Step 2. Using the freezer paper shape as your pattern, cut out the fabric piece, adding ¼ inch all the way around. See **Diagram 6.**

Step 3. Lay the freezer paper on top of the wrong side of the fabric piece. The waxy side of the freezer paper should be facing up.

Diagram 6. *Cut the appliqué shape out of freezer paper. Using the shape as a pattern, cut out the fabric piece, allowing a ¼-inch seam allowance. Place the freezer paper (waxy side up) on the wrong side of the fabric, fold over the seam allowance, and press it in place with the tip of your iron.*

Step 4. Fold the ¼-inch seam allowance of fabric up and over the edge of the freezer paper shape, referring to **Diagram 6.** Curves and corners will need to be clipped. Use the tip of your iron to press the seam allowances to the waxy side of the freezer paper. The heat will fuse the edges of the fabric in position, creating a perfect appliqué shape.

Step 5. Leaving the freezer paper in place for now, pin the appliqué in position and hand stitch it in place.

Step 6. Cut out the fabric behind the appliqué piece (leaving a ¼-inch seam allowance) and remove the freezer paper, as shown in **Diagram 7.** Press.

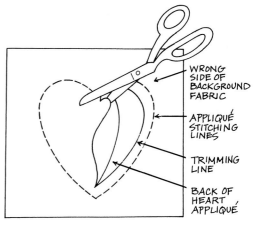

Diagram 7. *After the piece is appliquéd, cut away the fabric from the back side and remove the freezer paper.*

Putting It All Together

Once your blocks are pieced or appliquéd, you are ready to join them together to make the quilt. In this chapter, I'll give you general pointers on everything from attaching the lattice to hanging the quilt to make the process of going from blocks to finished quilt nearly foolproof.

Lattice

Lattice strips are the "glue" that holds the individual quilt blocks together, defining and enhancing the overall quilt design. The lattice includes the strips of fabric that go between and around each of the blocks. (See **Diagram 1.**) In most cases, the lattice fabric I choose is the same as the background of the blocks. If you use a contrasting fabric instead, the lattice will act more like a frame around each block.

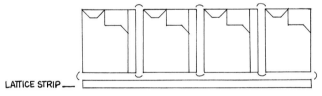

LATTICE STRIP

Diagram 1. *Lattice strips run between blocks and along rows.*

Each project has specific cutting and sewing directions for attaching the lattice to the blocks. For a smooth, flat quilt top, always press as you sew, and press all the seams toward the lattice.

Trimming the Blocks

Before sewing on the lattice strips, compare the size of your blocks. They should all be about the same size (within about ⅛ to ¼ of an inch). If they are not, you may need to do a *little* trimming with your rotary cutter to make them more similar. Do not trim your blocks unless it is really necessary.

Matching the Lattice to the Blocks

Before cutting your strips for the lattice, measure the height of the finished blocks. This measurement should be the same as the length you cut the lattice strips that go between the blocks. If you cut the lattice strips before the blocks were done and find they are too long, trim the excess lattice. If the lattice strips are

less than ¼ inch too short, center the lattice strip along the side of the block. If the lattice strips are *more* than ¼ inch short, cut new strips and match the block dimensions.

Overcoming Uneven Edges

When sewing lattice strips to your blocks, lay the strips on top of the blocks with right sides together. The edge of your block may not have a perfectly straight edge (not uncommon with pieced blocks) but your lattice strip will (since you were able to cut perfectly straight with a rotary cutter). Use the lattice strip as your sewing guide for your ¼-inch seam allowance and adjust the inconsistent edges of your quilt block as needed.

If you have triangles in your blocks, you may want to try sewing with the block on top. You'll be able to see just where the points of the blocks are so you don't cut them off with your sewing or make your stitching too far away from the points in your block.

Borders

The borders are the strips that go around the joined blocks and lattice. Think of a piece of matted and framed artwork: Without the mat between the art and the frame, the total effect could be much less dramatic. The same thing is true for quilts—think of the borders as the mats and the binding as the frame.

In many of the projects, the first border I've used outlines the blocks with a thin strip (frequently about ½ inch wide) using an accent color from the quilt blocks. This border sets off the quilt top.

The second border is usually a wider border that picks up one of the main colors or fabrics of the quilt. A print fabric that incorporates many of the quilt colors often works well. In many of the projects I combine several of the quilt fabrics into a scrap border, or two or three of the colors into a checkerboard border. In these kinds of multifabric borders, I often include the background fabric as one of the fabrics to tie it all together.

Each of the projects will list specific cutting and sewing directions for adding the borders. In this section, I will include some general hints for sewing plain borders, borders with corner squares, scrap borders, and checkerboard borders.

Plain Borders

A plain border, made of strips of just one fabric, is obviously the simplest to sew. However, it can be more difficult to find just the right fabric to tie your quilt project together. (Consider adding corner squares to your border if you feel you need to pull another color into the border.) Basically, you sew strips to the quilt top and bottom and then to the sides (in some projects I will specify to add border strips to the sides first). As you sew, be sure to press all seams toward the border.

Borders with Corner Squares

Corner squares at the ends of the borders can add some "action" to plain borders and have a calming effect on busier borders. Most importantly, they can add that spark of an accent color that helps bring the borders of your quilt alive.

Each of the projects will list specific cutting and sewing requirements for adding the corner squares. Some basic pointers are given here.

Step 1. Fit and sew a plain, scrap, or checkerboard border to the top and bottom of the quilt top (or sides first if specified by the directions).

Step 2. Compare and fit the border to the sides of the quilt. Pay attention so you do not end up with borders that are too short. Measure up to, but do not include, the top and bottom borders you just added. *Then add ¼ inch to each end of the side border strip.* If you do not add this extra ½ inch, the border will be too short. See **Diagram 2.**

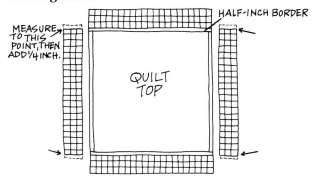

Diagram 2. Before adding corner squares, compare the border strips to the sides of the quilt; then add ¼ inch seam allowances to each end of the strips.

Step 3. Sew a corner square to each end of both side borders. See **Diagram 3.** Press these seams toward the borders. (The corner squares are always the same size as the width of the border.)

Step 4. Pin the side borders, with corner squares in position, to the quilt and stitch. Press the seams toward the border.

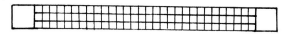

Diagram 3. This checkerboard border strip has corner squares added.

Scrap Borders

I've named this type of border "scrap" because of the finished effect it creates, not because you literally

Hints on Fitting a Scrap Border

✂ Count the scrap strips in the border. There should be the same number in each of the top and bottom border strips. The same should be true for the side border strips; each of those two borders should contain an equal number of strips. (But the side borders don't have to match the top and bottom borders.)

✂ The border will have a fair amount of give and can be stretched to fit an extra ¼ to ⅜ inch if necessary. You can stretch your strip by tugging on it gently while you press it with your iron. Be careful not to overstretch, however.

✂ If your border needs to be adjusted more than ¼ to ⅜ inch, I suggest making your adjustments by taking in or letting out a few of the seam allowances. For example, let's say the border strip is ⅜ inch too long. You can remove one 1-inch strip and stretch the remaining border ¼ inch to perfectly match the side of the quilt. For another example, assume that a border strip is ½ inch too long. You can reasonably expect to take in a seam by ¹⁄₁₆ inch without disrupting the overall look of the scrap border. To "swallow" the excess ½ inch, you would need to take in eight seam allowances by ¹⁄₁₆ inch.

✂ Because the scrap border will stretch, always pin it in position before sewing it to the quilt top. Press all the seams away from the scrap border.

make it out of leftover fabric scraps. As you can see in the photograph of the Whispering Pines quilts on page 70, a scrap border is made up of several or all the fabrics used in the quilt top itself. In each project featuring a scrap border, you will find the fabric yardage listed, as well as specific cutting and sewing requirements. Here are some helpful guidelines.

Step 1. Scrap borders always start with a strip set made using the speedy strip technique described on page 235. Arrange all the strips in a pleasing order and sew them together side by side along the long edges. As you sew, press all the seams in the same direction. The project directions may have you cut this strip set in half (or sometimes in thirds), then resew the halves together before cutting the border strips. In the example shown in **Diagram 4,** this particular strip set is cut and resewn twice before the border strips are finally cut.

Step 2. Fit and sew the border to the quilt top and bottom (or sides first if indicated in the directions), raw edge to raw edge. Use a seam ripper to remove excess strips to make sure there's a perfect fit.

Step 3. Follow Steps 2 through 4 under "Borders with Corner Squares" on the opposite page to finish attaching the scrap border. If the scrap border does not have corner squares, see "Hints on Fitting a Scrap Border" on the opposite page.

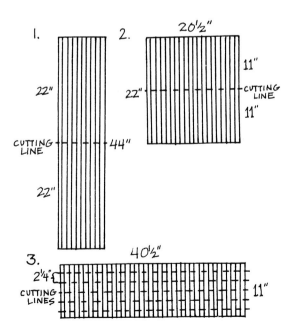

Diagram 4. *Scrap borders are made from strip sets (1) made up of several or all of the fabrics used in the quilt top. The set is cut apart, resewn, and cut and resewn again (2) according to project directions to make the final scrap border strips (3).*

Checkerboard Borders

Checkerboards look so hard and so time-consuming—but looks can be deceiving! Using the speedy strip technique and your rotary cutter, you can put these together in no time at all. And as you can see from projects like Scotties on Parade on page 48, a checker-

Hints on Fitting a Checkerboard Border

✄ Count the squares. There should be the same number in each of the top and bottom borders. Then count the squares in the side borders; the number should be equal for each of those borders. (The side borders don't have to be equal to the top and bottom borders, though.)

✄ The checkerboard will have a fair amount of give and can be stretched to fit an extra ¼ to ⅜ inch if necessary. You can stretch your strip by tugging on it gently while you press it with your iron. Be careful not to overstretch, however.

✄ If your border needs to be adjusted more than ¼ to ⅜ inch, make your adjustments by taking in or letting out a few of the seam allowances. If you do make adjustments, make them in the same place in both strips of the border so they will still match up, as shown below. As with scrap borders, it is best to let out or take in seams by no more than ¹⁄₁₆ inch. For example, if your checkerboard is ½ inch too long, take in eight seam allowances by ¹⁄₁₆ inch to absorb the excess.

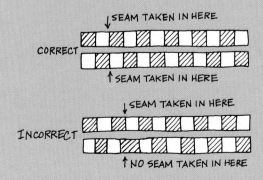

board can really add a delightful finishing touch to the design. Each project with a checkerboard will give you specific dimensions and quantities of strips to cut. Here are some general rules.

Step 1. Checkerboards always start with a strip set made using the speedy strip technique described on page 235. Arrange all the strips in the order given in the directions (alternating the two or three colors) and sew them together side by side along the long edges. As you sew, press all the seams in the same direction.

Step 2. The project directions will have you cut this strip set in half or thirds, then resew the sections together before cutting the strips for the checkerboard. In the example shown in **Diagram 5,** the strip set is first cut into thirds, resewn, then cut in half, resewn, and finally cut into strips to use in the checkerboard.

Step 3. Take two or three of these strips, as directed, and rematch to form the checkerboard pattern.

Step 4. Fit the border strips to the top and bottom of the quilt (or sides first if indicated in the project directions). Use your seam ripper as needed to fit the borders perfectly to the quilt.

Step 5. Follow Steps 2 through 4 under "Borders with Corner Squares" on page 244 to finish attaching your checkerboard border.

Choosing the Best Batting

Once the quilt top is complete, with all the borders sewn on, you are ready to prepare the other two layers, the batting and backing. There are a variety of quilt battings on the market, made of different materials and in different sizes and thicknesses. How can you tell what is the best choice for your project?

I generally use the same type of batting for all my projects. Since most of my quilts are used for wallhangings, I prefer a thin, lightweight, polyester batting. This batting is thinner than standard batting and enhances the country look of the quilts (something a thicker, puffier batting wouldn't do).

Loft

Loft is the term used to describe the thickness of the batting. A thin, lightweight batting with a low loft will give you a flatter quilt. It is also the easiest to slide a quilting needle through. This type of batting would be the best choice for the smaller wallhanging projects in this book. A thicker loft can make a cozy baby or comforter-like quilt. This would be a good choice for the crib bumpers from the Rub-A-Dub-Ducks nursery ensemble on page 170. Machine quilting or tying instead of hand quilting is easier with a very thick loft.

No matter which thickness you choose, a good-quality batting will have an even loft. There shouldn't be thick and thin spots. And it should not pull apart too easily. Always look for good-quality products.

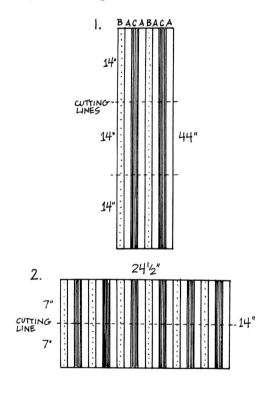

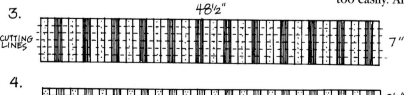

Diagram 5. *Checkerboard borders are easy if you use the speedy strip technique. Simply follow project directions for sewing and cutting strips (1, 2, 3). Rematch the final strips to form the checkerboard pattern (4).*

Content

Batting can be made of cotton, polyester, or a blend of both. With traditional cotton batting, each row of quilting must be no farther than an inch apart, or the cotton fibers will separate and bunch up. That's a lot of quilting! And some people find that cotton is harder to hand quilt than polyester. However, in its favor, cotton batting does give a very flat, traditional look to your quilt. With polyester batting, there is no minimum amount of quilting and the needle slides through the batting easily. One drawback to polyester batting is that the fibers can often work through the grain of the fabric, creating "batting stubble" or "bearding" on the surface of your quilt. The cotton/polyester blend battings promise to give you the best of both worlds—the easy quilting of polyester (without migrating fibers) plus the more traditional appearance of cotton.

Batting comes in white and black. Black batting is perfect when the background or large areas of your quilt are done in very dark colors. If bearding occurs, you won't have fuzzy white "hairs" showing against the dark fabrics.

Marking the Quilt Top

In every project I recommend ways to quilt the design to add some nice finishing details. It's usually easiest to mark the quilting design onto the quilt top before you layer it with the batting and backing fabric.

Choosing Your Marker

First, select a marking tool. New, improved products are always being developed, so get in the habit of checking the displays at your quilt shop or the pages in the quilting supply catalogs. I like to use a sharpened, hard lead pencil for marking. If you have an electric pencil sharpener, you can keep a white chalk pencil sharp enough to mark neat lines on darker fabrics. Whichever marker you use, always test it on a scrap of fabric first to make sure that you can clean away any lines that remain after quilting.

Making a Template

I have suggested quilting patterns for some of the projects, but if you want to quilt a different design, you can make your own template or purchase a ready-made plastic template. To make your own template, buy a sheet of template plastic (available from your favorite quilt-supply shop or through mail-order catalogs). Look for a medium-weight, see-through plastic. If the plastic is too heavy, it will be difficult to cut; if it is too thin, it will buckle and slip, making it hard to trace

the outline onto the fabric. Lay the sheet of plastic over the template pattern you have chosen. With a permanent felt-tip pen, trace the design onto the plastic. Cut it out with a craft knife or paper scissors. Your template is now ready for tracing.

Marking a Grid Pattern

Many of the projects in this book suggest quilting a grid on the background fabric. Your see-through ruler can make this marking quite easy. There should be a 45 degree angle marked on your ruler. Using that as your reference, mark your first line at a 45 degree angle to the horizontal seam lines of the quilt. (See **Diagram 6.**) Then continue to mark lines across your

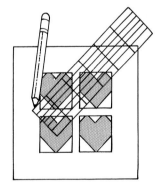
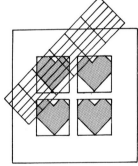
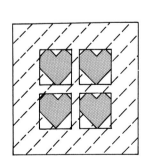
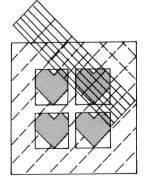

Diagram 6. *To mark a diagonal grid for quilting, align the 45 degree line on your ruler with a horizontal seam line on the quilt and mark your first line. Align your ruler with this first line and mark a second line 1 inch away (or as specified in the project directions). Mark additional lines in regular increments across the quilt. Then, align the 45 degree line on the ruler with a vertical seam line and mark lines in the opposite direction.*

quilt in regular increments, as recommended by the project directions. Next, align the 45 degree angle on your ruler with one of the vertical seam lines of the quilt and mark your grid lines in the other direction. These intersecting lines will form a grid that you can use to quilt in nice, straight lines.

Outline Quilting

For outlining the shapes in your quilt designs, there are two options. You can quilt "in the ditch," which means you add a line of stitches directly next to a seam line, or along the outline of an appliqué shape. This sort of quilting requires no marking. Quilting in the ditch works best when you quilt along the seam line on the side that does not have the seam allowance. If you try to quilt through the seam allowance, you'll be creating extra work for yourself as you push the needle through two extra layers of fabric. Another option is to outline your design ¼ inch from the seam line. If you do this, I recommend using quilter's ¼-inch masking tape. This will save you from having to mark all the quilting lines on your design. Just position strips of tape around the parts of the design you want to outline and use the edge of the tape as your quilting guide. Lift up the tape and reuse it until the stickiness is gone. Do not leave the masking tape on your fabric for long periods of time; some sticky residue may remain on the fabric.

Stitches for Special Touches

Some of the projects call for adding features like eyes, noses, and mouths with embroidery floss. Illustrated below are three embroidery stitches you can use to add these extra details. It's best to add these stitches before layering and quilting.

French Knot: These knots make wonderful eyes! Thread the needle with four to six strands of floss. Knot one end. Bring the needle up through the fabric at the point where you want the knot. Wrap the thread around the needle three times and hold the thread taut with your finger. Insert the needle back into the fabric close to where it came up. Pull the needle through to the back. The knot will remain on top.

Satin Stitch: This stitch is good for filling in solid areas, like animal noses. Thread the needle with three strands of floss and tie a knot in one end. (You may choose to use fewer strands for tiny details or more for a heavier look.) Start at the widest part of the area you want to fill in. Bring the needle up through the fabric on one edge and insert it on the opposite side. Bring the needle up as close to the first stitch as possible, and insert it as close as possible to the second stitch. Continue until the area has been filled in.

Outline or Stem Stitch: Use this stitch to create smiling faces. Thread the needle with three strands of floss and tie a knot in one end. (You may choose to use fewer strands for tiny details or more for a heavier look.) Pull the needle up at A, insert at B, then pull the needle up at C, a point approximately halfway between A and B.

FRENCH KNOT

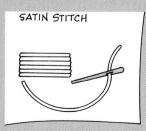

SATIN STITCH

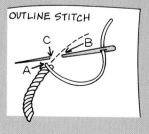

OUTLINE STITCH

Layering the Quilt

Now it's time to turn your quilt top into a quilt. By this point, you should have selected your batting, and your quilting lines should be marked on the quilt top. Purchase the backing fabric if you haven't already done so. Your next task is to layer these and baste them all together. (For all these steps, refer to **Diagram 7.**)

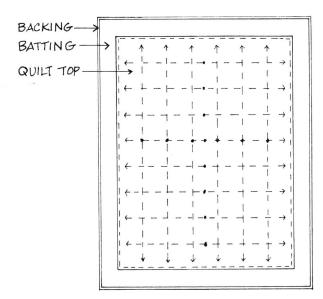

Diagram 7. *Center the quilt top on the backing and batting, making sure all three layers are smooth and flat. Pin the layers together to hold them in place while you baste. Begin basting in the center and work out, forming a 3- to 4-inch grid.*

Step 1. Cut the batting and backing pieces 4 to 6 inches larger than the quilt top.

Step 2. Press the quilt top and backing. Find a large work area, like the dining room table or the floor. Lay the backing piece down first with the right side facing down. Lay the batting on top of the backing and smooth it out. Then place the quilt top (face up) on top. Make sure everything is centered and that the backing, batting, and quilt top are flat.

Step 3. The backing and batting should extend 2 to 3 inches beyond the quilt top on all four sides. Since some shifting will take place during basting, this extra margin of backing and batting will come in handy.

Step 4. To keep the layers in place as you baste, pin them together. Place a pin every 6 inches in vertical and horizontal rows. Begin basting in the center and work out to the outer edges of the quilt. Baste vertical-

ly and horizontally, forming a 3- to 4-inch grid. If you're tempted to skimp on this basting—don't! An adequate amount of basting is critical to keep the layers flat while you are quilting. Last, baste or pin completely around the outer edge of the quilt top.

Basting Hints

Here are some tips for making basting easier.

• Use longer needles than you normally use for hand stitching, such as sharps or darning needles. They are easier to handle for this type of stitching and can make the basting go more quickly.

• Thread several needles with extra-long lengths of thread before you begin and have them handy.

• Take long stitches, about ½ to 1 inch long.

• Divide your quilt into quarters for basting. Work in one quarter at a time, basting from the center to the outer edges. This will save wear and tear on your knees and back since you won't have to shift from one part of the quilt to another.

• Keep one hand underneath while you're basting to make sure your backing remains smooth and flat. Before tying off the thread after doing a row of basting, smooth the top and backing with your hand to make sure you haven't slightly gathered the fabric during your stitching.

• When you're doing your final bit of basting along the outside edges of the quilt, baste inside the ¼ inch seam line. When you sew on the binding, this line of basting won't be visible, saving you from having to rip out the basting threads.

Binding the Quilt

For the wall-size projects in this book that you will be hand quilting, it's okay to add the binding to the quilt before doing the actual quilting. Since the binding finishes the raw edges, it gives your quilt a finished look even before you've done your quilting. If you will be machine quilting or working on larger projects, I suggest you quilt *before* binding.

Step 1. Cut the binding strips as indicated for each project. Press the strips in half with wrong sides together.

Step 2. Trim the batting and backing to within ¼ or ¾ inch of the top, as directed in the individual projects.

Step 3. Align the raw edges of the binding with the front edge of the quilt top and bottom. Pin the binding strips in place. Sew ¼ inch from the quilt edge, being sure to catch all the layers of the quilt. Also, make sure the weight of the quilt is supported by your sewing table. Trim the excess binding and press the seams toward the binding. (Some quilt projects may specify that you sew the bindings to the sides first, then the top and bottom.)

Step 4. Align the raw edges of the binding with the edges of the quilt sides. Repeat the sewing and pressing directions given in Step 3. Your quilt should now look like the one shown in **Diagram 8.**

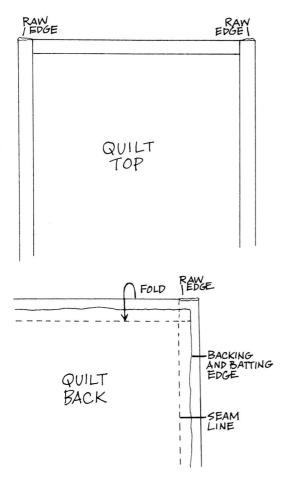

Diagram 8. *Fold the binding strips in half with wrong sides together. Align the raw edges of the binding with the edges of the quilt top; pin in position and sew. Press the seams toward the binding. Your quilt should look like the one shown here.*

Step 5. Bring the top and bottom bindings around to the back. Fold in half so that the outer folded edge of the binding meets the seam line, as shown in **Diagram 9.** Press and pin in position.

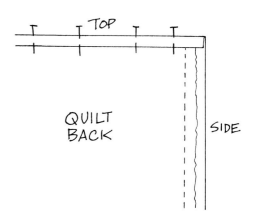

Diagram 9. *Fold the top and bottom bindings in half so that the folded edges meet the seam line on the quilt back. Pin, but do not stitch yet.*

Step 6. Fold the side bindings around to the back so that the outer folded edges meet the seam line. Press. Pin in position and hand stitch all the way around the binding. Stitch closed the little opening at all four corners, as shown in **Diagram 10.**

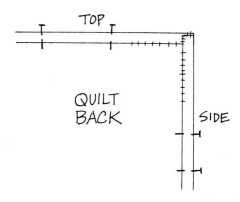

Diagram 10. *Fold the side bindings in half to the seam line in back. Pin in position and hand stitch all the way around the binding.*

Helpful Hints for Attaching Binding

Be careful not to stretch the binding when sewing it onto the quilt. When sewing through several layers, the top layer is pushed forward and that can stretch and warp your binding. To prevent this from happening:

✂ Increase the stitch length on your sewing machine (it should look about average or a little longer than average in length).

✂ Don't skimp on pins when you're attaching the binding to the quilt. Use enough to be sure it is held securely in place while you're stitching.

✂ Sew at a slow pace. If you sew too quickly, it is easy to lose the extra control you need to make sure the binding goes on smoothly.

✂ Use a walking foot or an even feed attachment if you have one for your machine. It feeds all the layers through at the same rate.

Finishing Small Appliqué Projects

Some of the small appliqué projects direct you to use a self-binding method. You layer the top and backing with right sides together on top of the batting, stitch (leaving an opening), turn right side out, and hand stitch the opening closed. For these projects, consider using the same fabric for the backing that you use for the binding. That way, the backing fabric won't stand out if it sneaks around to the front.

Another option for projects with self binding is to sew all the way around the wallhanging edge without leaving an opening for turning. Cut a 2- to 2½-inch slit through the backing and batting and turn right side out. To seal up the slit, make a quilt label and fuse it over the opening using appliqué film. Because you avoid hand stitching the opening in your binding, it will make a nice, smooth edge all the way around your wallhanging. (See "Quilt Labels" on page 254.)

How to Quilt

The quilting I recommend for each project serves the dual function of holding the batting in place between the quilt top and backing and adding decorative stitching. Since my projects are not heavily quilted, hand-stitching is much less time-consuming than you might expect. If you're in a real hurry, however, you can always let your sewing machine do the quilting.

Tools for Hand Quilting

The supplies you need for hand quilting are minimal. Here's a checklist of tools you'll need to have.

Quilting Needles: These are also called betweens. If you are a beginning quilter, I suggest starting with a package of needles that carries an assortment of sizes. For your first couple of quilts, you may want to use a larger needle and then progress to smaller ones after you gain some experience. Size 10 is a commonly used size and is the needle I prefer. The larger the number, the smaller the needle.

Quilting Thread: Always be sure to use extra-strong thread made especially for quilting. The color selection is continually growing, which makes coordinating thread with your project all the more fun. If you want the background to recede, choose a quilting thread color that coordinates with the background fabric color. If you want the background to attract more attention or to make it more active, use a contrasting color of thread. For a special design feature that you want to stand out (like a heart), contrasting thread will show up more.

Thimble: This is another tool that may require some trial and error before you settle on one you like. I really prefer the leather thimbles. Look for one with elastic (it stays on your finger better), a slit for your fingernail, and extra reinforcement at the fingertip. These leather thimbles can be very comfortable to wear and not too cumbersome.

Quilting Hoop or Frame: Hoops or frames hold the three layers taut and smooth while you are quilting. Some people find it easier to make small, evenly spaced stitches when quilting in a hoop. There's also less likelihood that the fabric will pucker or wrinkle under the stitching. Since the projects in the book are relatively small, you don't need a hoop much larger than lap size.

I personally don't use a hoop or frame. I like to use one hand to manipulate my needle and the other to manipulate the fabric (instead of holding the frame). This technique works for smaller projects only (not bed-size quilts).

Quilting by Hand

Hand quilting is similar to playing the piano—the more you do it, the better your fingers get. Good quilting stitches are small and even. At first, you should concentrate on even stitches; as you gain experience, your stitches will naturally become smaller.

Step 1. Cut a length of quilting thread (approximately 18 inches), thread the needle, and knot one end.

Step 2. About 1 inch from the point where you want to begin stitching, insert the needle through the top layer of fabric. See **Diagram 11.** Bring it up right where you want to take the first stitch and pull on the thread until the knot rests against the surface of the fabric. With a gentle tug, pull on the thread to pop the knot through the fabric. The knot will stay securely anchored in the batting beneath the quilt top, hidden out of sight. Whenever you need to start a new piece of thread, repeat this procedure for burying the knot.

Diagram 11. *To hide the knot in the batting, insert the needle through the quilt top and pull the thread until the knot rests on the surface of the fabric. With a gentle tug, pull on the thread to pop the knot through the fabric.*

Step 3. The quilting stitch is a series of running stitches made along the lines of the quilting design you have marked. I would encourage you to practice "stacking" your stitches on the needle right from the start. This technique, once you get the hang of it, allows you to make many small, nicely aligned stitches at a time and makes the quilting go more quickly.

To stack your stitches, push just the tip of the needle down through the three layers, using the finger with the thimble on your top hand, as shown in **Diagram 12.** As soon as your hand on the underside feels the needle come through, rock it up again toward the surface. (Simultaneously press down on the head of the needle with the thimble finger and push up against the needle tip with a finger on the underside.) When the needle tip pokes through the top surface, push it down again, then rock it back through the top. You may start by stacking two stitches, then find as

you get more practice you can stack four or five comfortably. Once you've stacked your stitches on the needle, pull it through the fabric using the thumb and forefinger of your top hand. Pull the thread taut, but don't pull it too tight, or the fabric will pucker. See **Diagram 13.**

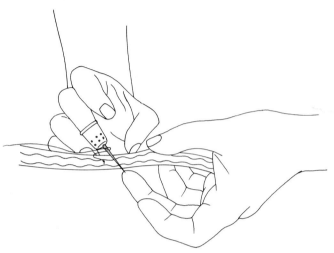

Diagram 12. *Push the tip of the needle down through the three layers. As soon as you feel it come through, rock it up again to the top. When it pokes through the top, push it back down through. When you have several stitches stacked on the needle, pull the needle through the fabric.*

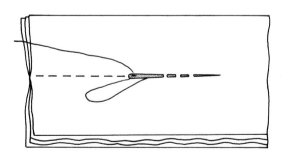

Diagram 13. *Stacking several stitches on the needle before pulling it through allows you to make small, even stitches.*

If you have trouble pulling the needle through the fabric after you've stacked the stitches on it, reach for a needle grabber. These round circles of thin rubber wrap around the needle to give you a good grip. They're inexpensive and available at most sewing and quilting shops. In a pinch, you can also use a deflated rubber balloon.

Step 4. To end a line of stitching, bring the needle up where you want to stop. Wrap the thread around the end of the needle two or three times. Pull the needle through these circles of thread to form a knot. Push the needle back down through the top of the quilt and pull it up about ½ inch away. Tug on the thread to pop the knot through the top of the fabric and bury it in the batting layer, as shown in **Diagram 14.** Pull on the thread slightly and clip it close to the surface of the quilt. The end should disappear back beneath the quilt top.

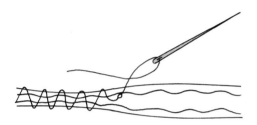

Diagram 14. *To hide the knot at the end of a line of stitching, push the needle down through the quilt top and batting and bring it back up ½ inch away. Gently tug on the thread to pop the knot through the top and into the batting layer.*

Quilting by Machine

Letting your sewing machine do the quilting can be a quick solution (especially if you're in a last-minute rush to get some holiday gifts done), but it is not necessarily easier than hand quilting. Just like hand stitching, machine quilting takes some practice. It can be difficult to control the layers and keep them from bunching up as you feed them through the machine. A walking foot or an even feed attachment is great for machine quilting. It can help avoid the problem of having the three layers bunch up.

Machine quilting works best on smaller projects, like the appliqué wallhangings, where you quilt in the ditch along the borders. These straight quilting lines are a good match for machine stitching. If you are trying machine quilting for the first time, keep in mind that the smaller the project, the easier it will be. For a fun machine quilting technique, see "Machine Stipple Quilting" on page 67.

The layering process is the same as for hand quilting—you sandwich the backing, batting, and quilt top together. However, instead of hand basting the quilt, you can use safety pins to hold the layers together while you stitch. Position the safety pins so they won't get in the way of where you plan to quilt. Do all the quilting *before* you add the binding (unless it has a self binding).

Step 1. Coordinate the thread color with the quilt top or use clear nylon monofilament thread. Coordinate the bobbin thread with the backing fabric. (If you're using clear nylon thread, you must use regular sewing thread in the bobbin.) Never use hand quilting thread for machine quilting.

Step 2. Set your machine for normal straight stitching. You may want to increase the stitch length for stitching through the three layers. Starting in the center of the quilt and working out toward the edges, machine stitch in the ditch (right next to the seam lines) to outline the block designs and borders.

Making Custom-Fit Pillow Forms

A few of the projects in this book have directions for making pillows, while others may leave you with an extra block that you can turn into a pillow. One of the secrets to an attractive finished pillow is a pillow form that fits perfectly inside the pillow top you've stitched together. This isn't always easy to achieve when you rely on the standard-size pillow forms sold in fabric stores. For very little time and money, you can put together a pillow form that will ensure a perfect fit.

The materials list is very short: All you need is some batting or needlepunch and a 1-pound bag of stuffing (the smooth kind, not shredded foam).

Step 1. To determine the measurements for cutting the batting or needlepunch, take the finished size of your pillow and add ½ inch to those dimensions. Cut two pieces of batting or needlepunch to those measurements. For example, if the finished pillow size is listed as 8 inches square, you will cut two pieces of batting, each 8½ inches square.

Step 2. Using a ¼-inch seam allowance, sew the two pieces of batting together, leaving a 3- to 4-inch opening for turning. Turn so the seam allowances are on the inside.

Step 3. Fill the pillow form with stuffing until it reaches the desired firmness. Hand stitch the opening.

Step 4. Slip the custom-made pillow form into the opening of your pillow and hand stitch the opening. The pillow form should be a perfect fit!

Hanging Your Wall Quilts

Using fabric tabs and a wooden dowel is my favorite way to hang wall quilts. But it is not the only way. Here are some possibilities.

Sleeve: Create a sleeve or "tube" of fabric that will run the entire width of your quilt. Cut the strip approximately 5 inches wide by the width of the quilt. With right sides together, fold the strip in half lengthwise and sew the length of the strip. Turn the sleeve right side out and press. Hand stitch the sleeve to the back of your quilt and run a wooden dowel through it. If your quilt is large, this is the preferred technique because it evenly distributes the weight of the quilt.

Hidden Fabric Tabs: For smaller projects, you can use three or four fabric tabs on the back of your wallhanging instead of a sleeve. Cut $1\frac{1}{2} \times 2\frac{1}{2}$-inch pieces of fabric. Fold them in half, right sides together, and stitch. Turn them right side out. Space the tabs evenly across the top of the quilt back, right under the binding. Hand stitch them in place, turning under $\frac{1}{4}$ inch on each end and stitching across the top and bottom of the tabs. Slip a $\frac{1}{2}$-inch-diameter wooden dowel through the tabs. It should be cut $\frac{1}{2}$ inch shorter than the width of the quilt.

Manufactured Wooden Quilt Grippers: Keep an eye open in quilt shops and home decor shops for ready-made hangers especially designed for quilts. These usually come in a variety of widths to accommodate different quilt sizes. They usually grip the top of the quilt and run the entire width of the quilt. Make sure the one you choose is free of wood stain to keep your quilt safe from fiber-damaging chemicals. For a mail-order source, see "Quilting by Mail" on page 256.

Decorative Bars and Rods: Find an attractive towel bar meant for the bathroom and hang it in a spot where you'd like to show off a quilt. Decorative curtain rods with interesting finials can also be used.

Cafe Curtain Rods: Purchase cafe curtain rods, the hanging hardware, and the rings that clip to the curtains. Attach the rod to the wall, put the clips on your quilt, and slide it onto the curtain rod.

Quilt Labels

It's a very special touch to add a label with your name, the name of the quilt, the year you made it, and where you made it. This makes it easier for family historians to identify who made that wonderful quilt! You may also want to consider adding other information, such as what inspired you to make the quilt or what important events were going on in the world when you were stitching it.

Preprinted labels are available for you to fill in the blanks, but you can easily make your own. If you have attractive printing, writing your label may be simple. However, if you do not have confidence in your hand printing, here are a few other surefire options.

✂ Roll a piece of fabric into your typewriter and type your label.

✂ Have your name and sentiment typeset at a quick-print shop and then copied onto fabric. Many of these shops can now print on fabrics.

✂ If you prefer a handwritten look, you can still have your sentiment typeset and then, using a light table, trace the words onto the fabric.

If you're handwriting your label, use an extra-fine point permanent felt-tip pen to do your marking. For an even more personal look, fuse onto the label a simple motif that ties in with your quilt theme. (See "Using Appliqué Film" on page 239.)

To attach the label to the back of your quilt, use your preferred appliqué method.

Quilting by Mail

Clotilde, Inc.
2 Sew Smart Way B8031
Stevens Point, WI 54481-8031
(800) 722-2891

Sewing notions and quilting supplies, including the "little foot" presser foot, Heat 'N Bond appliqué film, thimbles, see-through rulers, rotary cutters, cutting mats, pins, needles, marking pens, and charms for embellishment

Keepsake Quilting
Route 25
P.O. Box 1618
Centre Harbor, NH 03226-1618
(603) 253-8731

Quilting supplies and notions including fabrics, patterns, quilt kits, charms for embellishment, permanent markers, "little foot" presser foot, pins, thimbles, templates, quilting frames and hoops, and cotton, polyester, and wool battings

Me Sew Inc.
24307 Magic Mountain Parkway
Suite 195
Valencia, CA 91355
(800) 846-3739
FAX (805) 255-9104

Three different sizes of light tables

Mumm's the Word
2900 North Nevada
Spokane, WA 99207-2760
(509) 482-0210
FAX (509) 482-2036

$7\frac{3}{4} \times 9\frac{3}{8}$-inch kraft bags with handles; specify brown or white. ½ dozen: $4.50; 1 dozen: $9.00. (Add $3.75 shipping and handling; $4.75 outside United States.)

Country Fabric Line
Designed by Debbie Mumm Six fat-quarter pieces (18×22 inches) $12.50. (Add $3.50 shipping and handling; $5.00 outside United States.)

Write for a brochure of Debbie Mumm's other patterns and stationery products.

The Quilt Basket
1136 Route 376
Wappingers Falls, NY 12590
(914) 227-7606

"Snap It, Hang It" hardwood quilt hangers

Quilts and Other Comforts
741 Corporate Circle
Suite A
Golden, CO 80401
(303) 278-1010

Notions and supplies for quilters, including coordinated fabric packs, patterns, quilt kits, thimbles for collectors, pins, needles, markers, and quilting hoops and frames

Sew Special
9823 Old Winery Place
Suite 20, Department MTH
Sacramento, CA 95827
(916) 361-2086

Bulk buttons, wooden buttons, small wooden spools, wooden thimbles, plastic filler beads, and miniature scissors and sewing machines for embellishment

Credits

Photography Locations

Special thanks to owner Mark Kweller, manager Diane Bieri, and the staff of the Georgetown Manor Ethan Allen in Allentown, Pennsylvania, for their cooperation in allowing photographs to be taken in their store. Thanks to their patience and good-natured ability to step around camera bags, photographs of the following projects were taken: Bow Tie Bears, Crazy for Cats II, Dinosaur Fever, High-Flying Kites, Homecoming Wreaths, Patchwork Pigs, and Whispering Pines.

The balance of the photographs in the book were taken at
The Bucksville House
4501 Durham Road
and Buck Drive
Kintnersville, PA 18930
(215) 847-8948

This bed-and-breakfast inn is also a registered historical landmark in Bucks County, Pennsylvania. Special thanks to owners Barbara and Joe Szollosi for welcoming another photo shoot into their exquisitely restored inn.

The cover was photographed in the home of Tom and Linda Anderson in Neffs, Pennsylvania. The stenciled wall border was designed and painted by Linda. The editors thank them for the gracious way they allowed a crew of nine people to invade their home on a rainy day.

Props Used in the Photographs

The post office desk shown on the cover was made from the *Classic Furniture Projects from Carlyle Lynch* series published by Rodale Press.

The four folk-art Santas shown on page 81 were made by
Pam Dyer
521 West Court
Winterset, IA 50273
(515) 462-4593